The European Community

The European Community
Structure and Process

Clive Archer and Fiona Butler

St. Martin's Press
New York

First published in the United States of America in 1992

Printed in Great Britain

ISBN 0-312-08467-6 (hb)
      0-312-08692-X (pb)

Library of Congress Cataloging-in-Publication Data

Archer, Clive.
    The European Community : structure and process / Clive Archer and
Fiona Butler.
       p.   cm.
    Includes index.
    ISBN 0–312–08467–6
    1. European Economic Community. I. Butler, Fiona. II. Title.
HC241,2.A743   1992
341.24'22—dc20   92–14708
                                                           CIP

Contents

Foreword

The signing of the Treaty on European Union in February 1992 by the twelve governments of the European Communities (EC) represented a further step in the process of post-war integration in Europe. The structures established by that treaty will lead to the drawing together of the institutions of the three European Communities, those of European Political Cooperation, the European Council and intergovernmental co-operation in the spheres of justice and home affairs, into the single institutional framework of the European Union. The Treaty, once ratified, will create a European Union among the twelve members during the year — 1993 — when a single European market would also have been established among the members. At the same time the freedoms of movement of goods, persons, services and capital enjoyed by the EC states is to be extended to the EFTA countries, thereby building the world's largest trade grouping. It is not surprising that other European states — from EFTA, East and Central Europe, and the Mediterranean — are lining up for membership of the new European Union. This book is about that Union and its main component parts in the European Communities and European Political Cooperation.

A note on nomenclature might help at this early stage. The European Communities (EC) are made up of the European Economic Community (EEC), the European Atomic Energy Community (EURATOM) — both created by treaties in 1957 — and the European Coal and Steel Community (ECSC), set up by a 1951 treaty. To the extent that material in this book deals with each of these separately, then the terms EEC, EURATOM and ECSC will be used. However, for the period after the Merger Treaty of 1965 — when the institutions of the three were drawn together — the expression European Communities (EC) will be employed. A further complication is that the Treaty of Maastricht transforms the EEC into simply the European Community.

The authors would like to express their thanks to the following for their assistance in the creation of this volume: Elizabeth Bennett, Bo Fink, Donna Griffin, Roman Hamala, Clive Jones, Doris Mulvad, Dr Ritchie Ovendale, Professor William Paterson, Christopher Smith, Nicola Viinikka. Of course, any mistakes are purely the responsibility of the authors.

Clive Archer
Fiona Butler
February 1992

List of Abbreviations

ACP	African, Caribbean and Pacific states (of the Lome Convention)
ASEAN	Association of South East Asian Nations
Benelux	Belgium, Netherlands and Luxembourg (customs union)
CAP	Common Agricultural Policy
CEMR	Council of European Municipalities and Regions
CET	Common External Tariff
CFE	Conventional Forces in Europe (treaty)
CIS	Commonwealth of Independent States (ex-USSR)
CMEA/ COMECON	Council for Mutual Economic Assistance
COMETT	Community in Education and Training for Technology
COPA	Committee of Professional Agricultural Organizations
COREPER	Committee of Permanent Representatives
CSCE	Conference on Security and Cooperation in Europe
DG	Directorates General
EAEC/ EURATOM	European Atomic Energy Community
EAGGF/FEOGA	European Agricultural Guidance and Guarantee Fund
EBRD	European Bank for Reconstruction and Development
EC	European Communities
ECJ	European Court of Justice
ECSC	European Coal and Steel Community
ECU	European Currency Unit (= £0.70 or $1.25 in 1992)
EDC	European Defence Community
EEA	European Economic Area
EEC	European Economic Community

EFTA	European Free Trade Association
EIB	European Investment Bank
EMS	European Monetary System
EMU	Economic and Monetary Union
EPC	European Political Cooperation
ERASMUS	European Community Action Scheme for the Mobility of University Students
ERDF	European Regional Development Fund
ESC	Economic and Social Committee
ESF	European Social Fund
ESPRIT	European Strategic Programme of Research and Development in Information Technology
EUA	European Unit of Account
GATT	General Agreement on Tariffs and Trade
INF	Intermediate-range Nuclear Forces
IRA	International Ruhr Authority
IULA	International Union of Local Authorities
JET	Joint European Torus
LDCs	Least-Developed Countries
LINGUA	European Community Action Programme to promote foreign language competence
MCA	Monetary Compensatory Amounts
MEP	Member of the European Parliament
NATO	North Atlantic Treaty Organization
OCT	Overseas Countries and Territories
OECD	Organization for Economic Cooperation and Development
OEEC	Organization for European Economic Cooperation
OPEC	Organization of Petroleum Exporting Countries
PHARE	Poland Hungary Aid for Reconstruction (of the EC)
RACE	Research and Development in Advanced Communications Technology for Europe
SEA	Single European Act
SEM	Single European Market
WEU	Western European Union
WTO	Warsaw Treaty Organization

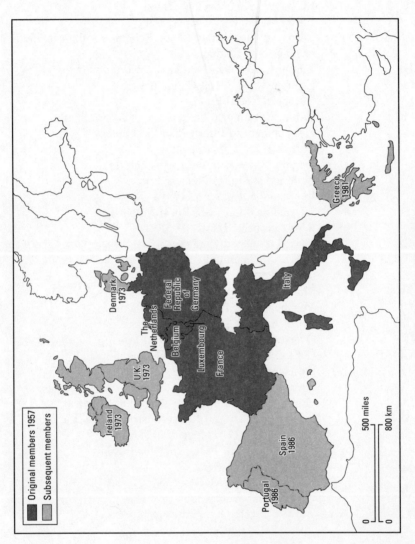

Member states of the EC

Original members 1957
Subsequent members

Denmark 1973

Federal Republic of Germany

The Netherlands

Belgium

Luxembourg

France

Italy

Greece 1981

U.K. 1973

Ireland 1973

Spain 1986

Portugal 1986

500 miles

800 km

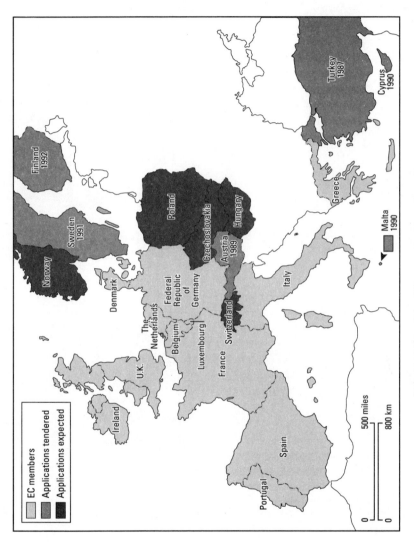

EC membership: The next extensions?

1

A changing Europe

Europe can still surprise. In the three years from early 1989, the continent grabbed the international headlines by a series of rapid and amazing developments. What seemed to be adamantine political and economic structures of some forty years' standing (or longer) were swept away in the hurricane of change in a few months. In the eye of the storm one institution continued to thrive — the European Community (EC). The late 1980s and early 1990s will be remembered for closing the Cold War chapter, for the twilight of communist party rule in Europe and for the end of the Soviet Union, but the period has also seen the transition of the EC from an advanced international organization to a nascent European Union. The consequences of this development will be outlined in terms of institutions, policies and relations throughout this book. First, the reader should glance back in history to understand how Europe has arrived at its present destination.

The rise of the sovereign state

To understand the European Community, one must comprehend the position of the sovereign state in Europe. The sovereign state is, anyhow, a European invention and its genesis can be dated back to the fourteenth century (Strayer 1970, p. 57) with the touchstone of 'constitutional self-containment' (Manning 1962, p. 166) having been well established by a number of states in Europe by the Peace of Westphalia in 1648. If it is true that 'sovereignty . . . consists of being constitutionally apart, of not being contained, however loosely, within a wider constitutional scheme' (James 1986, p. 24), then many of the kingdoms, city states and principalities of Europe failed the test in the late Middle Ages as they were regarded as being under the jurisdiction — the legal authority — of either the Holy Roman Emperor or the Pope.

The Peace of Westphalia, which ended the Thirty Years War, established in agreements between the ruling houses of Europe what was already fact — that there existed sovereign states in Europe that could not be contained within the Holy Roman Empire or within the writ of the Pontiff in Rome. It 'paved the way for a system of states to replace a hierarchical system under the leadership of the Pope and the Habsburg family complex that linked the Holy Roman and Spanish Empires' (Holsti 1991, p. 26).

While this was a triumph for such monarchs as the kings of Sweden and of France, it was also a recognition of the consequence of the Reformation — the splintering of Christendom in Europe. Christian princes had always warred against each other, but, as long as they accepted the subjection to a higher authority on earth, whether an emperor or a pope, there was the chance of disputes being settled within one constitutional framework with its established rules, institutions and sanctions. The Peace of Westphalia, however, represented 'the first successful attempt in European history to establish a continental diplomatic order that was based on the sovereign state' (Holsti 1991, p. 34).

With this advent of the sovereign state system, the nature of the rules to be obeyed by the heads of those states became opaque. The higher moral laws needed to be interpreted and a sovereign ruler could choose his — or her — interpreter. Agreements made with the representatives of other states might last as long as they suited the parties, but there no longer existed an accepted authority — in Vienna or Rome — to interpret such agreements and attempt to enforce them.

From the seventeenth century until the Napoleonic Wars, Europe was fragmented into a patchwork quilt of states, some sovereign, some subject. Warfare was a common form of relationship between these entities, though it was relieved and supplemented by diplomacy between the battles. Every so often there were plans to unite — or re-unite — Christendom, as can be seen in the 'grand designs' of Dante, Dubois and Sully. Later writers — such as Penn, Rousseau and Kant — were more concerned with the search for peace in what had become an anarchic system, that is one without any overall authority (Hinsley 1963, Part I).

Concert and nation

The Napoleonic Wars led to the near — though short-lived — political unification of the continent of Europe under one man. Warfare had also become popularized, in the sense that it was undertaken by the French during the Revolutionary and Napoleonic Wars on behalf of 'the peoples'. The Congress of Vienna (1814–15) reintroduced many of the state entities abolished by Napoleon and the balance of power as a means to maintain stability in Europe. The Great Powers also accepted that there should be occasional meetings of their representatives in order to attempt to manage any change in the European system. This Concert System hid a number of disagreements between the major states in Europe, not least as to what might lead to a joint intervention and what form it might take. On the whole, the British wanted to support only action against a state or groups that threatened the peace of Europe as agreed in the various international conferences of 1814 and 1815, whereas Austria, Russia and France tended to want intervention against any European revolutionary and liberal movement that unsettled their conservative regimes (Holsti 1991, p. 132).

The 1815 system was supplemented by agreements such as the 1856 Congress of Paris which brought in the Ottoman Empire to the system and supplemented it with additions to the law of the sea and the laws of war (Hinsley 1963, pp. 231–7). By the end of the nineteenth century, nationalism had become a significant force in Europe with political consequences. The nation states of Italy and Germany had been created from smaller entities and the aspirations of other national groupings — the Poles, the Slavs, Bulgars and Rumanians — threatened the existence of the large, multinational empires in Europe.

The First World War had the most serious consequences for the organization of the European polity. It led to the destruction of the continental Empires — Imperial Germany, Austro-Hungary, Czarist Russia and the Ottoman Empire — and the creation of a number of nation states such as Estonia, Latvia, Lithuania, Poland and Czechoslovakia. Furthermore the war was won with American assistance and the Versailles settlement was one that the President of the United States, Woodrow Wilson, helped to fashion in general outline and detail. However, Wilson was unable to obtain US Congressional support for his scheme. Versailles, predicated on American involvement in Europe, had to be enforced without US assistance or its membership of the League of Nations. Furthermore, the new states created in Europe were scarcely economically viable and were certainly unable to withstand the economic protectionism of the inter-war period. Many of these states also included national minorities, the international guardianship of which proved less than satisfactory. Uncertain frontiers, discontented national groups, political instability and economic turbulence proved to be a disastrous mixture for an inter-war Europe which had few instruments for managing change or disruption, apart from the diplomatic efforts of the French and United Kingdom governments, cloaked in the garb of the League of Nations.

There was, however, one notable attempt to break through the nationalism and distrust of inter-war European relations. In 1930 the French Prime Minister, Aristide Briand, circulated to the leaders of other European states a proposal for the creation of a confederal Europe. The Briand Memorandum met a good deal of scepticism and was sidelined into a 'Study group on European Union' at the League of Nations (Urwin 1991, p. 7). Nevertheless, an alternative way forward for Europe had been signposted.

The outsiders

The Second World War — like the First — started as a European civil war and spread to other continents. The struggle for the mastery of Europe was again settled by outside powers, the Soviet Union and United States. The Soviet Union, though part European by geography and culture, was still an 'outsider' because its government had been attacked and then isolated by most of the other European states and its leadership had deliberately isolated its population against what it considered to be the corrupting influence of its capitalist neighbours. The United States was separated by an ocean from Europe and, after the First World War, had sunk back into isolationism. However, by the end of the war in May 1945, both countries — the USSR and the USA — had large numbers of troops on the continent of Europe and had been central to the defeat of the Axis Powers of Germany and Italy.

The presence of the USA and the USSR in Europe was to set the mould of European — and world — politics in the post-Second World War era. Much of that time has been typified by the phrase 'Cold War'. These words are used to describe the adversarial relationship between the United States and the Soviet Union. It is different from a 'Hot War' — a shooting war — because neither state has pitched its armed forces against those of the other country. However, each has used other means — espionage, economic warfare, terrorism and surrogates — in their struggle against the adversary. And both have built up nuclear arsenals aimed at the other side. The conflict has been a power one involving control and influence. It has also been ideological with the free enterprise, parliamentary democratic beliefs of the USA and its Western supporters pitched against the central market, communist party-controlled system of the Soviet Union. Despite these differences, the East-West relationship was not entirely conflictual: there were elements of co-operation even at the height of the Cold War. There were also periods when tension lessened, such as in the couple of years after Stalin's death in 1953 or the period of détente in the late 1960s to the late 1970s.

Nevertheless, relations between the USA and the Soviet Union were on the whole hostile from about 1946 to 1989, and Europe was in the middle of these contending superpowers, as they became known. Buzan *et al.* have typified the situation thus:

> With overlay from 1945 to 1989 [by the superpowers], the European security complex virtually ceased to exist as an entity defined by its own interactions. It became instead the nut in the nutcracker of a global rivalry dominated by the two superpowers (1990, p. 31).

A new beginning

With the collapse of communist party rule in Eastern Europe in 1989 and 1990, the tearing down of the Berlin Wall, the withdrawal of Soviet military power from Eastern Europe, the failure of that military nexus to control even its own government and people in the attempted coup in the USSR in August 1991, and with the sudden collapse of Communist institutions in the Soviet Union followed by the implosion of the Union itself, Europe has been faced with a new environment.

This came at a time when the European Community has undergone a revival in its fortunes. Recovering from the 'Eurosclerosis' of the late 1970s and early 1980s, the EC embarked on a programme aimed at creating a single economic market among its member states by the end of 1992. The Single European Act of 1986 gave the EC further policy competence, especially in the important area of the environment, and brought closer together the economic and foreign policies of the EC states. From 1990 to 1991 the EC's governments considered the dual quests of political union and economic and monetary union, culminating in two parallel intergovernmental conferences in Maastricht. By 1992, not only the East and Central European states but also the richer non-EC countries such as Sweden and Austria were in line for either closer links with or full membership of the EC.

It is not unlikely that a future Europe — and one in the not too distant future — will be that of a European Union (see Chapter 13) with many policies — but not those of defence — conducted by 'federal institutions' (Pinder 1991, p. 216). Tied to this core 'European Union' will be a number of poorer states such as Romania, the Baltic states, the Ukraine, with other countries such as Norway and Iceland in an intermediate position. This could mean an end to the system of sovereign states built up in Europe since the Peace of Westphalia. However, the new authority that would end the constitutional self-contained nature of European states would not be one imposed from outside but would be a co-operative effort created by the governments and peoples of the former sovereign states. This would be a landmark in the rise of the European Community. Whether Europe can attain the security-community of a union without first going through a period of warring nation states, remains to be seen. As after the Napoleonic Wars, there is a system emerging to control political change. Its institutions are overlapping and, in some cases, not fully formed. The resulting framework could create a situation whereby European states, as well as having close economic and political relations, will also not even expect the use of force to be used as a method of settling disputes. This framework — or 'European architecture' — will probably consist of a mixture of the North Atlantic Treaty Organization (NATO), the Western European Union (WEU), the Conference on Security and Cooperation in Europe (CSCE) and the EC.

How then did these institutions — especially the EC — establish themselves in the history of post-war Europe?

Europe divided

Europe in 1945 was a defeated and exhausted continent. The Great Powers of inter-war Europe had lost something of their greatness. Germany had been overrun and divided by its conquerers. Italy's African empire had ended. France was burdened with its defeat in 1940 by Germany and its subsequent occupation. Even the United Kingdom, which at one stage during the war had stood alone against Nazi tyranny and domination of Europe, was economically bankrupt.

The new powers in Europe were two outsiders. The United States was geographically separated from the continent of Europe but, as in the First World War, had become embroiled in a European war that turned out to have global consequences. By 1945 American troops were in Germany, France, the Low Countries, Italy and parts of Austria and Czechoslovakia, and US money was backing the United Nations Relief and Rehabilitation Agency (UNRRA), a multilateral organization aimed at bringing succour to the peoples of liberated and occupied Europe.

The Soviet Union was also an 'outsider' for Europe: European powers — as well as the United States and Japan — had tried to strangle the Soviet Republic at birth with military intervention from 1919 to 1921; Stalin had effectively isolated the citizens of the USSR from outside influence; and the country had been outside European economic and political discourse for much of the inter-war period. Even during the war, contact between the Western Allies and the Soviet Union had been precarious. After the war, the Red Army represented Soviet armed power in East and Central Europe. The inter-war states of Estonia, Latvia and Lithuania had been incorporated into the USSR and territory had been taken from Finland, Poland, Czechoslovakia and Romania. Soviet troops had liberated Poland, Romania, Bulgaria, Hungary and parts of Germany, Austria and Czechoslovakia. However, the Soviet Union scarcely had the resources to feed its own people, let alone those of its occupied areas. What they did seem able, and willing, to provide for the newly-liberated peoples of Eastern and Central Europe was an alternative political and social system, that of Soviet socialism.

European political leaders were faced with the reality of two outside powers dominating their continent in 1945. However, at that stage both could be considered to be there 'by invitation', as the Europeans had been unable to throw off the tyranny of Nazi occupation by themselves. The main tasks facing European politicians were those of building a prosperous, peaceful and free Europe. Prosperity seemed a long way off in 1945, and the first economic imperative was to provide basic goods and services for people — UNRRA helped here — and then to attempt to rebuild the economies of Europe. Peace in 1945 meant 'no war' and in particular the prevention of the post-First World War situation whereby German power had risen again to threaten Europe. Freedom in 1945 was an end to the Nazi yoke and the establishment of governments representing those forces that had fought against tyranny during the war.

As the immediate cleaning up of the detritus of war gave way to consideration of long-term goals, so the consensus on the meaning of prosperity, peace and freedom in Europe started to crack. In the end, a rift reflecting politico-economic disagreement appeared in the middle of the European continent and was effectively institutionalized by the actions of the two outside powers — the two superpowers of the United States and the Soviet Union — and by the subsequent Cold War.

It should be noted that this division did not form immediately on the outbreak of peace in 1945, though even then there were signs of disagreement between the Soviet Union and the United States (Feis 1970, Part Three). Indeed, the Four Powers — France, the Soviet Union, the United Kingdom and the United States — jointly ran Germany and Austria, and the United Nations established an Economic Commission for Europe, drawing its membership from all of the continent. Most of the governments of Europe in 1945 — outside those of the USSR, Britain and the two fascist states of Spain and Portugal — were coalitions including communists, socialists, centre and agrarian parties and Christian democrats. This was the case as far apart as France, Norway, Hungary and Bulgaria.

By early 1946 a war of words had started between the former allies, with Stalin, in his February election speech, looking forward to the triumph of Marxism over capitalism, and Churchill — Britain's wartime leader but then Leader of the Opposition — making his Fulton, Missouri, speech in which he warned

> From Stettin in the Baltic to Trieste in the Adriatic, an iron curtain has descended across the Continent. . . . [T]he populations . . . in what I must call the Soviet Sphere . . . are subject in one form or another, not only to Soviet influence but to a very high and, in many cases, increasing measure of control from Moscow . . . (Halle 1967, pp. 103–4).

Although the United States had nuclear weapons (though by then only a few), its troops had been rapidly demobilized from Europe, whereas the Soviet Red Army still seemed to be in Eastern Europe in large numbers.

The Iron Curtain was a political, economic and a military divide. During 1946 and 1947 the communist parties in the East European states and in countries such as France and Italy seemed to be expanding their support and influence. In March 1947 the French and British governments signed the Treaty of Dunkirk which allowed for defence co-operation between the two, ostensibly against German revival but with an eye on the Soviet Union. A few days later, the United States President announced the Truman Doctrine — that the USA would support all free peoples resisting subjugation, with the implication that the main enemy would be communism. In June 1947, US Secretary of State George Marshall proposed massive American aid to assist the rebuilding of Europe and a Committee for European Economic Co-operation met in Paris in July 1947, though the East and Central European governments stayed away from this gathering on the instructions of Moscow. How different the economies of East and Central Europe would now be if they had been allowed to participate in what became known as the Marshall Plan and Marshall Aid. Moscow's response was unimaginative: the Cominform — an organization to co-ordinate action by communist parties throughout the world — was formed in October 1947, and by the end of the year non-communist parties were being dissolved all over Eastern Europe.

The turning-point

Early 1948 proved to be the turning-point. Events in that year clarified what had been already happening almost by stealth: the creation of a communist-run Eastern Europe tied to Moscow opposed by a capitalist-dominated Western Europe eager to enrol the United States in its cause. In the last few days of February 1948, the communists took over control of Czechoslovakia, formerly a democratic state providing a gap in Churchill's descending Iron Curtain. Stalin proposed a 'Treaty of Friendship and Mutual Assistance' to Finland, another democracy which, like Czechoslovakia, had a large communist party and bordered the Soviet Union. Britain and France agreed to expand their defence agreement to include the three Benelux states — Belgium, the Netherlands and Luxembourg — on 29 February 1948. There was the feeling that small countries such as Denmark and Norway might be next on Stalin's list. It seemed that Europe was getting little peace and that freedom had been extinguished in one part of the continent and was being threatened in the other.

Yet the instruments were being forged that were to offer at least the West Europeans the opportunity to re-establish their prosperity, guarantee some form of peace and proclaim their freedom.

By 1948 the Committee for European Economic Co-operation, shorn of East European membership, had reached agreement on the distribution of assistance provided (mostly from the US) by the European Reconstruction Plan and had formed a permanent instrument of economic co-ordination, the Organization for European Economic Co-operation.

In March 1948 France, the United Kingdom and Benelux states signed the Brussels Treaty which, as well as promising common action in the political and economic field, significantly provided a fifty-year defence guarantee to all the members. The Brussels Treaty's real importance, however, lay more in the expression of determination by the five countries to defend themselves and the positive effect this had in encouraging the United States (and Canada) to join talks about a wider collective self-defence treaty. This agreement was less all-embracing than the Brussels Treaty but included states such as Iceland, Norway and Denmark in Northern Europe and Italy and Portugal in the south, as well as the two North American states. The resulting North Atlantic Treaty was signed in April 1949 and came into force in August of that year.

On the political side, a number of groups had been forming associations promoting the closer economic and political unity of Europe, examples being the United Europe Movement in the United Kingdom and the Europa-Bund in Germany. After consolidation of these organizations, they brought together a wide range of opinions and personalities in the Hague Congress of May 1948 which established the influential European Movement (Urwin 1991, p. 27). Although itself a non-governmental organization, the Movement's ideas for European unity were quickly taken up by, especially, the French and Benelux governments. They advanced the proposal for a parliamentary Council of Europe at a ministerial meeting of the Brussels Treaty Powers. The British showed reluctance to have such a body dealing with sensitive political matters which they thought should be within the remit of ministerial consultation. The Statute of the Council of Europe, signed in May 1949, was a compromise with the United Kingdom's wishes dominating: a Committee of Ministers was established but so was a Parliamentary Assembly. However, the latter was to have a consultative status only. The Council's aims, as stated in its Statute, was the achievement of closer unity of those European states that accepted the values of 'individual freedom, political liberty and the rule of law, principles which form the basis of all genuine democracy' (Preamble). This aim was to be achieved by 'discussions of questions of common concern' and agreements and common action in economics, social, cultural, scientific, legal and administrative matters' (Article 1.b).

The OEEC, the Brussels Treaty — and subsequently the North Atlantic Treaty (NAT) — and the Council of Europe represented an institutionalization not only of the division of Europe but also — particularly in the case of the NAT and Marshall Aid — of the underpinning of West Europe's future by the United States. So the reaction to the events of early 1948 was decisive and seemingly effective in reassuring nervous West European governments that they could draw on outside support in facing attacks either from forces within their country or from outside.

However, this institutional response did not solve all the main outstanding political problems in Western Europe, neither did it represent a new approach that would transcend the politics of Europe as the supporters of European federalism had hoped. The OEEC, the Brussels Treaty Organization and the North Atlantic Treaty were all traditional intergovernmental arrangements and even the Council of Europe, with its innovative Parliamentary Assembly, had no real powers at that stage to act without governmental consent. The institutions that were set up in the 1948 to 1949 period were meant to help the existing sovereign states in Western Europe to weather the storms and emerge as strengthened entities.

The Community method

The main problem that was not addressed during this period was the question of an emerging Germany and its relations with the rest of Western Europe, especially France. By April 1949 the three Western Allies — France, the United Kingdom and the United States — had merged the administrations of their zones of occupation in West Germany. In May those Allies had agreed on a Basic Law for a Federal German state in these three zones and in September 1949 the Federal Republic of Germany had come into being with a democratic government headed by Konrad Adenauer.

Yet there were reservations about this reinstatement of Germany. After the Second World War, the French government had expressed concern that an untrammelled economic revival of the German state could lead to that country gaining a political and military dominance, as had happened after the First World War. The French, in particular, wanted a careful control of the industrial areas of Germany — mainly in the Rhineland — that had provided the powerhouse for German rearmament in the 1930s. The British and the Americans were more anxious to bring the Germans back into the comity of nations and recognized that the economic revival of Europe — after all the main aim of Marshall Aid — had to include Germany, at least its Western part.

A compromise was struck in early 1949 with the creation of an International Ruhr Authority (IRA) which, in the words of its Draft Agreement of January 1949, would make sure that 'the resources of the Ruhr shall not in the future be used for the purpose of aggression'. The IRA thus represented a management board for these resources, on which were represented the governments of Britain, France, Germany, the three Benelux states and the US. The IRA seemed to satisfy neither side. The French considered that the British and the Americans were allowing too much coal and steel production in the Ruhr, while the Germans thought it unfair that only their heavy industries should be under such international control. After all, the new democratic Federal Government could not be expected constantly to pay for the sins of its Nazi predecessor.

Other solutions to this dilemma were on offer. The German Minister-President of the federal area (*Land*) of north Rhine-Westphalia — which included the Ruhr — suggested that the IRA system should be extended to include French Lorraine, the Saar (a former German territory then in economic union with France), Belgium and Luxembourg, and this idea was taken up by John McCloy, the powerful American Commissioner in Germany, and a number of other spokesmen, ranging from socialist politicians to businessmen (Diebold 1959, pp. 35–46).

The coal and steel industries of Western Europe straddled the frontiers of France, West Germany, Belgium and Luxembourg and were interdependent. At that time coal and steel also represented the heartbeat of industrial society and the life-blood of any rearmament plans. Furthermore, there was a fear that, as after the First World War, the post-war boom would be followed by a recession which would force the coal and steel industries into cartel agreements and that these would be difficult for national governments to control.

So by 1950 the coal and steel industries of Western Europe offered fertile ground for a political initiative that could help solve the problems of those industries, which would also deal with Franco-German relations and might even touch on the wider question of the future peace, prosperity and freedom of Europe. The seed of a new approach was planted by Jean Monnet who had headed the French post-war planning effort and who was himself a staunch supporter of a federal Europe. He persuaded the French Foreign Minister to advance an ambitious plan in May 1950, that was to have repercussions for the organization of post-war Europe.

The basis of the Schuman Plan was quite simple. Taking up Karl Arnold's point, it was proposed 'to place all Franco-German coal and steel production under a common High Authority, in an organization open to the other countries of Europe' (Willis 1968, p. 80). This Authority would oversee the reduction of coal and steel trade barriers between the participating states, thereby rationalizing those industries on a basis not just decided by narrow national interests or by a cartel of the companies. The proposal — which, after all, came from a French source — also solved the dilemma surrounding the IRA by not picking out West Germany for particular treatment.

Secondly, the proposal bound the fate of Germany and France together. By placing their coal and steel industries under common control, it was felt that neither state would be able to build up the sinews of war against the other. The idea was to create a situation where war between the two states would become 'not merely unthinkable, but materially impossible' (Robert Schuman, 9 May 1950, cited in Hallstein 1962, p. 10).

Thirdly, the Schuman Plan had wider implications for Europe. Not surprisingly, Monnet had imported some federalist sentiments into the proposal, though — for the time being — they were to be exercised in a fairly limited sphere. The High Authority was to be a functional body covering only the coal and steel industries of the member states. But it was also to be 'the first step toward European Federation' and 'a first decisive act in the construction of Europe' (Willis 1968, p. 80). In this sense, the Schuman Plan represented not just a solution to the immediate problems of West European industry but also the beginning of a wider enterprise, one that had a United States of Europe as its end product.

The response to the Schuman Plan from the Federal Republic of Germany, Italy and the Benelux states was positive, and by April 1951 these five countries plus France — the Six — had signed the Treaty of Paris establishing the European Coal and Steel Community (ECSC). This treaty came into force on 25 July 1952.

The Treaty of Paris in its Preamble set as an aim for the signatories 'to substitute for age-old rivalries the merging of their essential interests'. They recognized 'that Europe can be built only through practical achievements'. The Coal and Steel Community would be founded upon 'a common market, common objectives and common institutions' and the attainment of its objectives was to be ensured by a High Authority, a body created to consider the 'general interests of the Community' and independent of the demands of the member states (Article 9). Indeed the signatories of the Treaty undertook to respect the 'supranational character' of the High Authority (Article 9), which suggested that this institution was to be regarded as above the workings of the nation state.

Another problem in Europe left unsolved by 1950 was that of the contribution to their own defence by the states of Western Europe. In signing the North Atlantic Treaty, the United States had agreed to regard an attack on a European signatory of the Treaty in Europe as being an attack on itself, and the US had made available armaments for the hard-pressed West European states. However, no additional American troops were to be stationed in Europe. There was the hope that American dominance in nuclear weapons might deter a Soviet attack on Western Europe, but by September 1949 it was known that the Soviets had exploded their own nuclear device and the US monopoly in this area was over.

At the time, much of the short-term military planning by the West presumed that — if there was a war — the Soviet Red Army would occupy almost all of continental Western Europe. One way to prevent such a disaster was to build up Western armies in Europe so that they could repulse the supposed might of the Soviet armed forces. In the absence of the Americans and with both the French and British stretched by their global colonial commitments, the natural choice seemed to be that of West Germany. Indeed, the US Joint Chiefs of Staff neatly encapsulated the problem in April 1947: 'Without German aid the remaining countries of western Europe could scarcely be expected to withstand the armies of our ideological opponents until the United States could mobilize and place in the field sufficient armed forces to achieve their defeat' (US Department of State 1947; I, p. 741).

However, the idea of placing Germans in uniform so shortly after the bloodbath of the Second World War was not one that attracted European opinion, nor indeed was it popular in Germany. Chancellor Adenauer of the Federal Republic had attempted to address both concerns — the need to defend Western Europe and the fear of revived German militarization — when in 1949 he announced that 'The question of the re-establishment of our Army can only be brought up within the framework of the Western Union [Brussels Treaty]. We are ready to participate in the formation of a European Army' (cited in Greiner 1985, p. 169). It was just this message that was taken up by one of Schuman's colleagues in the French government, Pleven. He adapted the Community idea — as contained in the Schuman Plan — and proposed a European Defence Community (EDC) which would bring the European armed forces of 'the Six' under a common control which would be regulated by a European Political Community (EPC).

While the Schuman Plan was quickly adopted, that advanced by Pleven ran into difficulty. The outbreak of the Korean War in June 1950 was seen by many in the West as a precursor to a Soviet attack on Western Europe. As a result, the American armed forces in Europe *were* bolstered, leading to greater pressure on the Europeans to increase their contribution. This fired the debate on German rearmament and the necessity for this — if it happened — to be controlled by other Western states. The British wanted it to be within a North Atlantic context, whereas the French government preferred a West European solution. In the end, the EDC fell by the wayside and the compromise was an expansion of the 1948 Brussels Treaty to create the Western European Union (WEU), of which West Germany (and Italy) would be members. West Germany also joined NATO and its rearmament was undertaken within the framework of NATO and the WEU. The idea that such a sensitive subject as defence could be placed under a supranational authority proved not to be generally acceptable in the early 1950s.

Relance

By 1955 progress had been made towards the settlement of the two major political problems that Western Europe had been facing in early 1950. France and Germany had started to pool control of their coal and steel industries and had embarked on a qualitatively new relationship. The creation of the WEU had allowed the rearmament of West Germany to go ahead within a wider West European and NATO context and it also saw the commitment of British armed forces to the defence of the European continent. Other advances had been made. A multilateral payment arrangement for trade had been established between the OEEC countries. On the outbreak of the Korean War, the North Atlantic Treaty countries had started to build an organization — NATO — which included a joint military effort. The Nordic states had formed the Nordic Council in 1952 (with Finland joining in 1955) in order to enhance co-operation between those states and societies. The United Kingdom had signed a Treaty of Association with the ECSC in December 1954 that established a practical relationship between the two sides.

However, certain problems endured. Despite plans for the EDC and the eventual creation of the WEU, it was still felt — especially by the Americans —

that the Europeans were not contributing enough to their own defence, and the gap was filled by an increased dependence on nuclear weapons in Europe to deter the expected Soviet attack.

The European Coal and Steel Community started to run into trouble a couple of years after its establishment. By 1954 it was being adversely affected by recession and it seemed that the French and West Germans were increasingly resorting to a bilateral approach to solve their problems (Haas 1968, p. 265). Furthermore, suggestions for the creation of separate agricultural, transport and health communities — based on the ECSC — had not been taken up, and by August 1954 the EDC had also failed. It seemed that the British government — that had scorned the Community idea — was to be proved right.

In November 1954 Jean Monnet, the first president of the ECSC High Authority, resigned from that job in order to supervise the 'relance' — the relaunching of the Community idea. By 1955 Benelux officials had drawn up a memorandum that expanded the Community notion to include a common market in all goods traded between the ECSC members, an idea supported by the powerful non-governmental Action Committee for the United States of Europe, an organization formed by Monnet. The Memorandum was discussed by the ECSC governments at a meeting in Messina in June 1955 and the ground prepared for two further Community organizations — one to cover trade and other economic activity, and the second to embrace the emerging nuclear energy industry.

From July to December 1955 the details of these Communities were worked out in the Spaak Committee, named after the Belgian Foreign Minister who chaired it. The Six wanted the creation of a common market whereby restrictions to trade between them would be abolished and their tariff levels to the rest of the world standardized. Apart from this customs union element, there would also be a harmonization of financial, economic and social policies, as well as aid to the poorer regions, especially southern Italy. The institutions matched those of the ECSC, though were to be less 'supranational' with the governmental representatives having a greater say than in the running of the ECSC.

In April 1956, the Spaak Report was presented to the governments of the ECSC states. It recommended the creation of a European Atomic Energy Community (Euratom) and a European Economic Community (EEC). The latter would be based on a common market between the six members, within which goods, capital, services and labour would eventually be free to move with almost as much facility as within each country. This common market was to be based on the customs union and common economic policies and would be supervised by common institutions fashioning and enforcing common regulations for the entire Community area. A close relationship with other West European states was recommended in the Spaak Report. In May 1956, the Foreign Ministers of the Six adopted the Spaak Report, with the addition of a section on overseas territories and colonies. The plan was that the European Economic Community and Euratom would be established by two treaties to be signed in Rome in March 1957.

Schism

The British government had sent a representative — a civil servant from the Board of Trade rather than a Foreign Office minister — to the Spaak Committee negotiations. However, he had withdrawn once the question of supranational institutions had been raised. The United Kingdom anyhow considered that such institutions had failed in the ECSC and, after the Spaak Committee had continued its work on a customs union, the British government — according to the then Chancellor of the Exchequer (R.A. Butler) — 'just thought it was not going to work' (Charlton 1983, p. 195).

When it became clear that the Six would go ahead with the plans of the Spaak Committee, the United Kingdom came forward with its own suggestion. The British hoped to form an association with the planned Economic Community, just as they had done with the ECSC. They proposed an OEEC Study Group which was to examine, in the words of the British Chancellor of the Exchequer, Harold Macmillan, 'possible forms of association between the proposed customs union and other countries of OEEC' (Hansard, House of Commons, vol. 555, col. 210).

From mid-1956 until early in 1959 (some weeks after the Six had introduced their first tariff cuts among themselves), the British and other OEEC states tried to persuade the Six that their scheme should be carried out in the context of an OEEC-wide free trade area. However, there were basic differences between the Six, led by the French, and the rest of the OEEC, led by the British. The Six did not wish to allow the rest the benefits of access to their markets without them taking on the full responsibility of a customs union rather than the looser free trade area. The United Kingdom was particularly anxious to accept only free trade, which would have allowed it to maintain its own tariffs to Commonwealth countries. Furthermore, the Six insisted that agricultural trade be included in any deal and that social policies should also be considered, both policies that the British rejected. The United Kingdom wanted the institutions managing the proposed free trade area to be fairly loose and intergovernmental, whereas the Six wanted a tighter arrangement with more powerful institutions that could enforce what had been agreed.

Once the EEC had been formed and had begun implementing its programme of tariff cuts and the OEEC negotiations had failed, some of the non-Six OEEC states (mainly the Swiss, the Swedes and the British) decided to form their own trade agreement. Utilizing the work that had been done by OEEC, officials and ministers from the United Kingdom, Denmark, Norway, Sweden, Austria, Switzerland and Portugal met in the summer of 1959 and agreed on a smaller free trade area among their own countries. The Stockholm Convention of January 1960 translated this into a treaty and in May 1960 the European Free Trade Association started work with the above seven countries as members. It had intergovernmental institutions, excluded most agricultural trade from its regulations and aimed at creating free and fair trade — rather than a customs union — among its members. So by the start of the 1960s Western Europe was 'at Sixes and Sevens'.

Further division

By the end of 1960 the OEEC was transformed into the Organization for Economic Co-operation and Development with the USA and Canada as members. This was a recognition that the OEEC had done its job as acting as a consumers' club for European states that were, mostly, recipients of Marshall Aid and, by 1960, were wealthy enough to be aid donors. It was also an acceptance that the OEEC had failed to heal the trade division of Western Europe and indeed had become compromised in the process: a new start was appropriate.

During the 1960s, the process of European integration received setbacks in two main areas. First, there was the continued division between the EEC Six and the EFTA Seven, a divide that was to endure in one form or another until 1991. This was aggravated by the attitude of President de Gaulle of France (who had come to power in 1958) to British attempts to join the European Communities (as the ECSC, the EEC and Euratom became collectively known). By summer 1961, the United Kingdom government, encouraged by the United States, had decided that the EEC was going to survive and it might be best for Britain to be inside. It submitted an application for membership but negotiations were broken off in January 1963 when de Gaulle exercised a French veto, claiming that the British were not ready for EEC membership. In May 1967 the Labour Government in Britain re-submitted a request for membership negotiations but these were once more stopped by a 'non' from de Gaulle in November 1967. Attempts by EFTA to persuade the EC to discuss trade questions on a group-to-group basis were also brushed aside.

Meanwhile division was growing within the European Communities. President de Gaulle's approach to the European Communities was quite different from that of either his predecessors or of most of the other leaders of the Six. While he accepted the reality of the Communities and the necessity of a close Franco-German relationship, he rejected the notion that the EC should have institutions with supranational pretensions. When the Commission of the European Economic Community attempted to use the development of the Common Agricultural Policy — from which French farmers benefited — to increase their own powers, de Gaulle decided to confront 'this machine' in Brussels. He had already come into conflict with other members through his veto of

British membership in 1963 and during discussions about a political union — the Fouchet plan — in 1961 (Urwin 1991, pp. 104–7). In June 1965 French ministers boycotted the EC's Council of Ministers in order to get their way on agriculture without having to pay the price in terms of supranational EC's institutions. Though this crisis was eventually solved by the Luxembourg Compromise of January 1966, it nevertheless circumscribed the development of the Communities' institutions at a time when the economic success of the EC was beginning to slow up after the rapid growth of the 1950s.

Conditions in 1969 led to a change of direction. The Soviet invasion of Czechoslovakia in 1968 and the lack of response from an America embroiled in the Vietnam War had brought reassessments of both the security and economic policies of a number of West European states. France, first under the disillusioned de Gaulle, and then under his successor, President Pompidou, saw that the rapport that they had hoped to open up with the Soviet Union counted for little when the Soviets felt their system was threatened by reform in Czechoslovakia. Furthermore the economic problems of the dollar had exposed the French franc to the rising power of the German currency, the Deutschemark. By December 1969, when the Heads of State and Government of the European Communities met in the Hague, France was ready to see membership of the EC extended, as long as the organization also adopted a programme of 'deepening' co-operation, including the prospect of political co-ordination of foreign policies and of economic and monetary union.

Membership negotiations with the United Kingdom, Denmark, Ireland and Norway were opened by the European Communities in 1970 and a Treaty of Accession for the four — the Treaty of Brussels — was signed in January 1972. The Norwegian people rejected EC membership in a referendum in September 1972 and the other three states joined the EC on 1 January 1973. A major step had been taken to mend the Franco-British rift within Western Europe, and to develop the EC beyond the status of a customs union with a Common Agricultural Policy.

The widening of EC membership and deepening of its policies did not come at an auspicious time. By the end of 1973, Europe was reeling from the effects of the October 1973 Yom Kippur War in the Middle East and the subsequent massive increase in oil prices brought about by the Arab members of the Organization of Petroleum Exporting Countries (OPEC). This had a severe dampening effect on the West European economies, the success of which had partly been built on cheap oil imports in the 1950s and 1960s. The response of the EC countries to shortage of oil and the resulting economic depression in the 1973 to 1974 period was to resort to national instruments both to obtain more oil and to cope with unemployment. The most noticeable international response — that of the creation of the International Energy Agency (Spero 1990, p. 268) — was an American-inspired organization that did not include France as a member.

The development of the European Communities was further impeded by the election of a Labour government in the United Kingdom in 1974, which then proceeded to 'renegotiate' the terms of British membership of the Communities. The results were accepted by the British people in a referendum in the summer of 1975, but the attitude of the Labour Government towards the EC lacked any enthusiasm and did nothing to prevent the re-emergence of a Franco-German axis within the Communities. With the coming to power of the Conservatives under Mrs Thatcher in 1979, the British approach towards the EC grew more aggressive with demands to 'give us our money back' — a reference to the unequal burden of the cost of the CAP that the United Kingdom had to bear — being made at the highest level.

After the flying start that the EC had had in the early 1960s, momentum was squandered in the late 1960s and 1970s by a mixture of internal quarrels — between de Gaulle and rest on the future of the organization and on British membership, then between Britain and most of its partners on terms of membership and the budget question — and external events such as the oil price increase of 1973/74 and the recession of 1979/81.

A second relance

The early 1980s seemed to bear little promise for the regeneration of the European Communities. Indeed, Europe itself lay as divided as ever: between the East and West, between the British and continental EC states, and between federalists and intergovernmentalist.

The Soviet invasion of Afghanistan in December 1979, the election of President Reagan in November 1980, the declaration of martial law by the Communist regime in Poland in December 1981, all signalled the return of a period of chilly relations between the two superpowers, often called 'the New Cold War'. Until 1987, Western Europe was embroiled in an internecine dispute as to whether US intermediate-range nuclear forces (INF) should be placed on their soil in order to strengthen the military links between the United States and Western Europe. A number of NATO European governments had reservations about such a move, and large sections of public opinion also showed an increased 'nuclear allergy'. The response of the ageing (and sometimes dying) Soviet leadership to the move was to send equivalent forces into Czechoslovakia (then still under Soviet domination) and to raise the stakes in international arms control negotiations. It seemed that half of the West Europeans feared the United States deserting them to face a highly armed Soviet Union by themselves, while the other half feared a too close embrace by the US president.

Even within Western Europe, the European Communities seemed to be drifting. True, Greece had joined in 1981 and Spain and Portugal were lining up for membership, but attempts to persuade the member states to consider new strides in political development came to little. One of the most strident opponents of such moves was the British Prime Minister, Margaret Thatcher, who had come to power in May 1979. Mrs Thatcher's Conservative government proved to be as 'Euro-sceptical' as the Labour government it had replaced and EC institutions spent much of the early 1980s responding to British demands for a reconsideration of the budgetary question.

The year of 1985 proved to be a turning-point for Europe. It saw a new leadership in the Kremlin, that of Mr Gorbachev. He reversed Soviet foreign and security policy and initiated reforms at home. His 'new thinking' in external affairs led him to jettison the previous confrontational approach of the Soviet leadership and to place emphasis on achieving 'common security' with the West by a series of arms control and disarmament agreements.

Even during the New Cold War an institution had been kept alive in Europe that proved to be of some value — the Conference on Security and Cooperation in Europe (CSCE). Its genesis lay in the period of détente — in 1972 — when all the European states (including the Soviet Union) plus the United States and Canada (which both had troops in Europe) had met in Helsinki to discuss a more long-term institutionalization of détente. The result had been the Final Act of the CSCE, signed in Helsinki in August 1975 by 33 European states, the United States and Canada. This set down the principles governing security in Europe, allowed for prior notification of major military manoeuvres, outlined a programme of co-operation in economic, scientific and other fields, and introduced human rights as a specific element in European inter-state relations. As superpower relations deteriorated in the late 1970s and early 1980s, the Helsinki Final Act was used as ammunition by both sides against their adversaries. However, the CSCE-offshoot Stockholm Conference in 1983 had allowed a continued discussion of security and disarmament in Europe. With the impetus of the Gorbachev leadership in the Soviet Union, the Stockholm meeting came up — by September 1986 — with a tighter agreement for checking military activities in Europe. The following year the two superpowers agreed a treaty — the INF Treaty — to remove their inter-mediate-range nuclear forces from Europe and destroy them, and by November 1990 the NATO and Warsaw Treaty Organization members had signed the far-reaching Conventional Forces in Europe (CFE) Agreement which limited the size of armed forces across the European continent and introduced an intrusive verification system to make sure that the demobilization went ahead.

Another important event in 1985 was the Milan Summit of the EC leaders, at which a reform of the Treaty of Rome (which had established the European Economic Community) was agreed. The resulting changes were included in the 1986 Single European Act that strengthened the institutions of the EC, gave them greater competence, and increased their involvement in foreign and security matters. These changes were part of a relaunching of the Community idea in the mid–1980s with the intention of creating by the end of 1992 a large home market in the twelve EC states — the Single European Market

('1992'). This was to reflect the internationalization of capital and business within the EC that had been taking place for some time, and would eventually provide industry and commerce with a market larger than that in the United States. These moves gave a new confidence to the EC at a time when the Soviet Union and its East European allies were clearly having problems with their economic and political reforms.

The new Europe

The face of Europe has changed irreversibly since 1989. In that year the strain of imposing political change on the inflexible communist systems of Eastern Europe became too much. First, the anti-communist Solidarity (trade union group) under Lech Walesa was brought into government in Poland without any adverse reaction from the Soviet Union. Indeed, Mr Gorbachev had made it clear to the leaders of the Warsaw Treaty Organization — an organ established by the Soviets to institutionalize their military control of Eastern Europe — that the Soviet Union would not send in tanks to rescue communist leaders from their people. A wave of protest swept Eastern Europe in the late summer and autumn of 1989, culminating in November in the opening of the Berlin Wall, which had been built by the East German communist regime between East and West Berlin. Within two months all the communist governments of the East European states (except Albania) had fallen, with avowedly pro-Western administrations taking their place.

All this drastically changed the security situation in Europe and by 1991 the Warsaw Treaty Organization (WTO) was defunct, the Soviet armies in Eastern Europe were returning home and massive cuts in arms in Europe were being presaged by the CFE agreement. At a CSCE meeting of heads of state in Paris in November 1990, the Cold War was effectively ended and plans were laid for the CSCE to become more active in monitoring human rights and elections and in preventing the outbreak of conflict.

However, this rapid change was not without its casualties. The first was the German Democratic Republic which was swallowed up by the Federal Republic of Germany in October 1990. It was not only the WTO that broke up in 1991: so did Yugoslavia and then the Soviet Union. The latter country jettisoned over seventy years of communism whilst fragmenting into its fifteen component republics. At NATO's Rome Summit in November 1991 the ex-communist states of East and Central Europe and of the decaying Soviet Union were welcomed into a new forum — the North Atlantic Cooperation Council — and a new agenda set for the CSCE that included the possibility of intervention in a state without the consent of its government (NATO review, December 1991, p. 21).

Amid this turmoil in Europe, the EC members were trying to plan their future. Preparation was made for two Intergovernmental Conferences (IGCs), one on political union and the other on economic and monetary union, culminating in a heads of state and government meeting in Maastricht in December 1991. The outcome of Maastricht — recorded in this book — was an agreement to create a European Union, consisting of the three European Communities (with the EEC now renamed the European Community), the institutions of European Political Cooperation (which cover foreign and security matters) and intergovernmental co-operation on justice and home affairs. The institutions are thus not neat and tidy, but there are plans for a further attempt at rationalization in 1996.

The new European Union — like the old European Communities from which it is emerging — offers a beacon of attraction to the rest of Europe. The EFTA countries have negotiated a European Economic Area agreement with the existing EC and a number of the EFTA states had already — by early 1992 — expressed their intention to apply for full membership of the EC-European Union (see Chapter 9). The East and Central European states are eager to have closer relations with the Union and the most advanced have signed association agreements with the EC (see Chapter 10). Furthermore, the members of the EC have provided assistance, particularly humanitarian aid, for the Commonwealth of Independent States (the ex-Soviet Union countries) and, through European Political Cooperation, have become directly involved in brokering peace in Yugoslavia (see Chapters 11 and 12). By the end of the 1990s the European Union could also have a defence identity, taken over from the WEU, and thereby be an even stronger force within both the CSCE and NATO. What sort of entity the European Union might be, is discussed in the final chapter of the book.

References

Buzan, B., Kelstrup, M., Lemaitre, P., Tromer, E. and Wæver, O., 1991, *The European security order recast*, Pinter, London.

Charlton, M., 1983, *The price of victory*, British Broadcasting Corporation, London.

Diebold, W., 1959, *The Schuman plan*, Praeger, New York.

Feis, H., 1970, *From trust to terror*, Anthony Blond, London.

Greiner, C., 1985, 'Rearmament of West Germany 1947–1950', in Riste, O. (ed.), *Western security. The formative years*, Universitetsforlaget, Oslo, 150–77.

Haas, E.B., 1968, *The uniting of Europe. Political, social and economic forces, 1950–1957*, Stanford University Press, Stanford.

Halle, L., 1967, *The Cold War as History*, Chatto and Windus, 103–4.

Hallstein, W., 1962, *United Europe*, OUP, London.

Hinsley, F.H., 1963, *Power and the pursuit of peace*, Cambridge University Press, Cambridge.

Holsti, K.J., 1991, *Peace and war: armed conflicts and international order 1648–1989*, Cambridge University Press, Cambridge.

James, A., 1986, *Sovereign statehood: the basis of international society*, Allen & Unwin, London.

Manning, C.A.W., 1962, *The nature of international society*, Bell, London.

NATO review, 1991, 'The Rome Summit', 39/6, 19–33.

Pinder, J., 1991, *The European Community, The building of a union*, OPUS, Oxford.

Spero, J., 1990, *The politics of international economic relations* (4th ed.), Unwin Hyman, London.

Strayer, J., 1970, *On the medieval origins of the modern state*, Princeton University Press, Princeton NJ.

Urwin, D.W., 1991, *The community of Europe. A history of European integration since 1945*, Longman, London and New York.

US Department of State, 1947, *Foreign relations of the United States 1947: I* (FRUS I), USGPO, Washington DC.

Willis, F.R., 1968, *France, Germany, and new Europe, 1945–1967*, Stanford University Press, Stanford.

2

Institutional framework of the EC

This chapter intends to provide only a brief overview of the major institutions of the EC, their functions and powers, and their roles in the legislative processes.

In a variety of contexts, their political visibility and capacities have altered since the original conceptions of the Treaty of Rome, in parallel with the evolution of the Community itself. However, the reform process begun at Maastricht in December 1991 will undoubtedly mark the start of a new phase in the roles and powers of these institutions. Thus it is important to consider their present position.

The EEC in 1957 was seen by its proponents as following the tactical considerations of Monnet, Schuman and others; in other words a continuation of the sectoral, step by step integration of national activities, bounded by common objectives and institutions to ensure that the integration process was constantly supervised and encouraged.

The institutional framework, equally, was a reflection of the desire of the member states, some perhaps more than others, to retain adequate control and supervision over the application of the Treaty, especially given the fact that the EEC represented a larger step in the direction of integration — that it was not just limited to the integration of and supranational direction over national coal and steel sectors — and that events such as the Suez crisis and colonial troubles had demonstrated to some EEC member states that improved economic strength and any enhanced political stature could only be met effectively by the process of gradual integration.

So, what are the institutions of the European Community? How do they work and what are their functions?

The Commission

There are seventeen Commissioners; two nominated from the 'big five' member states of France, Germany, Italy, Spain and Britain, and one from each remaining member state. Although nominated by national governments — in Britain one representative each from the two established political parties are invariably appointed — the Commissioners are not appointed to act as champions of their national interest.

They are chosen on the basis of their political experience and competence, and essentially their independence and impartiality upon taking office are their major characteristics, although on some occasions national leaders have not approved of 'their' Commissioners' independence — ex-PM Thatcher's refusal to reappoint Lord Cockfield is one example. The Commission, and the individuals comprising it, was expected at the outset in 1957 to act collectively and in the 'European' interest.

Individual Commissioners head a particular subsection of the Commission; these subsections or Directorate-Generals are organized along functional lines, similar to national ministries or civil service departments, for example in external relations, overseas development, agriculture or competition (anti-trust).

Until very recently the members of the Commission were appointed to renewable four-year terms; the new Treaty on European Union signed February 1992 has extended this to a renewable five-year term (Article 158) including the office of President of the Commission in order that the Commission and the EPs term of office runs in tandem. Furthermore, the nominated President and Commission will be subject to a vote of approval by the EP; once approved they will be formally appointed by the governments of the member states.

Article 155 of the Rome Treaty lays down the precise functions of the Commission:

- it shall ensure that the provisions of the Treaty are applied;
- it shall formulate recommendations or deliver opinions on matters dealt with in the Treaties, either if the Treaty provides for such action or if the Commission considers it necessary;
- it shall have its own power of decision and participate in the shaping of legislation by Council and Parliament;
- it shall exercise the powers conferred on it by the Council, for the implementation of the rules laid down by Council.

However, this apparently straightforward description obscures some of the problems that the Commission faces in the execution of its role. In other words, the Commission has been credited with the authority to assume a number of different roles, which can prove problematic.

Firstly, the task of 'ensuring that the provisions of the Treaty are applied': this is generally referred to as the Commission's 'watchdog' role, or the Commission as the 'guardian of the Treaty'.

In this context, the Commission acts in a quasi-bureaucratic/judicial role: it must monitor whether national agencies or actors are complying with Treaty obligations and Community legislation. If the Commission discovers an infringement or breach of such obligations, it may then use its general powers under Article 213 to 'collect any information and carry out any checks required for the performance of the tasks entrusted to it'; and in some specific policy fields, such as the EC's competition policy, the Commission has even greater powers to enable it to investigate more fully any suspected or alleged lack of compliance.

This 'watchdog' role, then, is rather more complicated in practice than the somewhat bland language of Article 155 might suggest; the Commission has to assume a unique blend of administrative, or bureaucratic, and judicial responsibilities in order to ensure that the laws of the Community are being upheld and, if they are not, to take further action by, if necessary, recommending referral of the case to the European Court of Justice. However, in this latter case, the Commission does not necessarily have to resort to legal proceedings instantaneously; Article 169 gives the Commission flexible powers to use its discretion, by engaging the particular member state in dialogue, to ascertain the particular reasons why the member state is being lax in implementing EC law. On the whole, this 'watchdog' role of the Commission relates to Commission-Member state relations, since the vast bulk of EC law is directed at member states. However, in some policy areas, and as a result of a type of legislation called a Decision, EC law can be directly addressed to other actors, such as individuals or businesses.

On the whole, too, this 'watchdog' role is assumed by the Commission, but the Treaty does allow a member state the right to bring another member state before the ECJ if it feels that there has been an infringement of Community law (Article 170). However, the Commission maintains an important role, as the complainant has first to 'bring the matter before the Commission', which can then investigate the matter further, and act as a mediator between the two parties.

The 'watchdog' or 'guardian' function of the Commission is an extremely important one, and can involve the Commission in highly technical and politically-charged arguments; one example being the October 1991 row concerning the Commissioner for Competition Policy's ruling to block a proposed French-Italian (ATR) take-over of the Canadian aircraft firm, De Havilland. The Commission's President, Jacques Delors, threatened to resign after the French Government officially complained that the decision to block the proposed merger would weaken the competitiveness of European industry in the area of commuter aircraft. Delors subsequently stressed the collegiate and independent nature of Commission decisions, as opposed to it being a 'champion' of national interests.

Another equally important set of powers held by the Commission, which is perhaps more directly drawn from the traditional function of government, concerns the original view of the Commission as the 'motor' of European integration, which gives the Commission executive powers.

These executive powers firstly concern the Commission's role as initiator of legislation; primarily these are drawn from Article 155 where the Commission can:

- have its own power of decision and participate in the shaping of measures taken by the Council and the Parliament;
- formulate recommendations or deliver opinions on matters dealt with in this Treaty, or if the Commission considers it necessary.

The Commission's right to act as the sole initiator of legislation has also been strengthened by ECJ rulings, and also by Article 235 where 'if action by the Community should prove necessary to attain . . . one of the objectives of the Community and this Treaty has not provided the necessary powers, the Council shall, acting unanimously on a proposal from the Commission and after consulting the EP, take the appropriate measures', or in other words the Commission may employ subtle interpretation of Article 235 in order to provide the initiative and move the integration process in new policy directions. As far as the 'motor' of integration function is concerned, the Commission was thus endowed with a highly political role.

However, although it was expected that the Commission — given its independence, impartiality from vested political interests, composition and functions — would therefore represent the interests of the Community, and frame legislation in that context, the Commission did not have a monopoly power over the right to initiate legislation.

It was hoped that by giving the Council and the Parliament a right, albeit limited, of input to legislative proposals, a balance of Community-nation and executive-legislative interests could be ensured. So in this sense, the Council in Article 152 may 'request the Commission to undertake any studies the Council considers desirable for the attainment of the common objectives, and to submit to it any appropriate proposals', and the Parliament over the years has developed its Rules of Procedure to enable it to submit 'own initiative' reports to the Commission, in order that the EP may have some limited means to influence the initiation of draft proposals.

Within the Commission's executive function, as well as being endowed with the primary responsibility to initiate legislative proposals, the Commission was also expected to oversee the implementation and management of Community legislation. Returning to Article 155; 'it shall exercise the powers conferred to it by Council, for the implementation of the rules laid down by Council'. The original intention was thus for Council to take the lead in delegating responsibilities and procedures to the Commission which — as guardian of the Treaties and monitor of the implementation of these Treaty responsibilities — could be more coherent and effective.

In the event, the Council did not delegate as much of the responsibility to the Commission as had been intended; instead what tended to happen was the creation and maintenance of committees within the auspices of, and answerable to, the Council — for example the permanent committees covering topics such as energy and education. However, the Council, in delegating its powers as was intended, added to the burden of work for the Commission. In this context, the concern over 'comitology', or the reliance upon a network of committees within the Commission to discuss and monitor legislation, was expressed. The SEA made reference to this situation, in an amended Article 145, where Council confers powers on the Commission for the implementation of Council decisions, but with the proviso that they 'must be consonant with principles and rules to be laid down in advance by the Council, acting unanimously on a proposal from the Commission and after obtaining the opinion of the EP'.

What this has meant in practice is that, depending on the type of committee — management or regulatory — which has to consider whether a draft proposal is acceptable, different types of legislation can be subject to different types of vested interest. For example, although all committees are staffed by national representatives, management committees employ different voting procedures than regulatory committees and, as a result, Council and Commission can clash over legislative proposals.

Finally, also in relation to the Commission's executive powers, the question of budgetary legislation must be briefly examined.

As a result of the 1975 Joint Declaration on the EC's Conciliation Procedure, the 'budgetary authority' of the EC is composed of the Council and the EP. Although it is these institutions which ultimately shape the composition of the Budget (see Chapter 4), or in other words the expenditure levels on EC policies, the Commission also has an important role to play. It is more of a supervisory role in the sense that the Commission is empowered to ensure that the member states' authorities — such as Customs & Excise — do deposit the necessary sums of money with the EC; to ensure, particularly since the 1988 Inter-Institutional Agreement concerning the increase in EC expenditure, that expenditure in various policy areas is not exceeding its maximum rate; and the Commission also has a role, albeit somewhat limited, in the scrutiny of applications for monies from the European Social Fund (ESF) and the European Regional Development Fund (ERDF). Overall, however, the Commission is held to be responsible for the implementation of the EC Budget and thus is required to submit all relevant records to the Council and EP (Article 205).

Finally, after having reviewed the nature of the Commission's powers and functions as regards Article 155, it is also important to remember the other major activity regarding the EC, for which the Commission is responsible. This field of activity comprises the external economic relations of the Community, and also the EC's relationship with other international organizations. Article 228 states that 'where this Treaty provides for the conclusion of agreements between the Community and one or more states or an international organization, such agreements shall be negotiated by the Commission'.

Other Treaty articles go on to mention the Commission's role of representing the EC in specific international organizations, such as the UN and GATT, the Council of Europe and the OECD (229–231).

In addition to Article 228, the Community was also given the right to 'conclude with a third state, Union of States or an international organization agreements establishing an association involving reciprocal rights and obligations' (Article 238), and although the Commission is not specifically mentioned as the prime actor, it invariably does act as a focus for negotiations. Such Association Agreements were signed as long ago in 1962 with Greece, and more recently with individual East European states, in late 1991.

The new Treaty on European Union has revised Article 228 to allow greater influence for Council to assist negotiations; for Council to vote on a qualified majority basis to conclude the agreement; and for the EP's improved power of assent, whereby in certain cases, the EP now has a de facto veto.

Whilst Commission representation, for example during the 1992 Uruguay Round of GATT talks, does not preclude the right for individual EC members also to be present and to take part in negotiations, the presence of the Commission is vital for the common external identity of the EC, and to a certain extent, this role of the Commission refers back to the original intention of the Rome Treaty: where the Commission represented the European interest whereby, and acted consistently in the interests of the process of integration.

This has been a very brief overview of the Commission's composition and functions, which does not do justice to the day-to-day activities and political role of the Commission, such as in the 'brokering' of package deals on important policy issues, maintaining close contact with the other EC institutions and national authorities, or helping to clarify proposals for new legislation.

The Council of the European Communities

This section will look at both the Council of the EC (or the Council of Ministers as it is also called) as well as the European Council, which is an intergovernmental institution undertaking certain activities which remain outside the legal authority of the EC. However, the work and procedures of both these institutions do overlap, and the composition of both is drawn from national governments of the EC member states.

The Council of the European Communities, as it is formally titled, was intended to be and has assumed the role of the legislative institution of the Community. In other words, it is not necessarily the deliberative body of the EC — the original Assembly or European Parliament, as it is now called, assumes this function — but in general the Council is the decision-taking body in the EC. An expression was used in the 1970s; 'the Commission proposes, the Council disposes', summarizing the relationship between the two institutions.

Article 145 of the EEC Treaty states the general functions of the Council whereby it should 'ensure coordination of the general economic policies of the member states', and whereby it has the 'power to take decisions', and it can 'confer on the Commission, in the acts which the Council adopts, powers for the implementation of the rules which the Council lays down'.

The organization of the Council's working methods is equally important as the legal powers conferred on it by the Rome Treaty, especially because the term 'Council' suggests a unified coherent body of individuals who discuss, debate and take decisions, whereas in fact the 'Council' is organized along functional lines. So according to the type of legislation being discussed, different 'Councils' meet to discuss different legislation — for example, if draft proposals concern agricultural policy, then a Council of national ministers representing agricultural ministries will meet, or if a draft proposal concerns monetary and financial policy, then it is a Council of economic and/or finance ministers.

It is important therefore to consider how the Council then organizes its work and provides continuity and coherence, because in addition to the disparate nature of its organization, the Council's work covers other types of activity in addition to its main function of taking decisions on proposed legislation.

When a draft proposal arrives from the Commission, it is not discussed directly by the particular national ministers. Instead, the Council's Committee of Permanent Representatives (COREPER) acts as a 'sieve'. COREPER is itself divided into two sections; COREPER I made up of somewhat more junior civil servants (Deputy level) and COREPER II composed of more senior officials (Ambassador level). Both of these elements are staffed by civil servants on temporary secondment to their national delegations in Brussels.

Usually the draft proposal will first of all be dealt with by a working party, of which there are a large number, organized along policy-area lines and which comprise national experts, diplomats from the national Permanent Representations and staff from other EC institutions, such as the Commission. Then the proposal is sent to COREPER, where its content, general significance and national negotiating positions are sifted. According to how sensitive or straightforward the proposal is (and this will have been ascertained in the working party discussions) it will be dealt with by either COREPER I, or usually if the draft proposal concerns economic-monetary matters or foreign-external affairs, amongst several others, it will be forwarded directly to CORE-PER II. (Proposals concerning agriculture are dealt with by the Special Committee on Agriculture.) This process of 'sifting' politically or technically contentious proposals for further discussion at ministerial level can in many cases prove important. Apart from the Council's practice of not publicizing the passage of legislation and the existence of arguments pro and con over a particular proposal, COREPER's function of either tacitly approving draft legislation, or recognizing that, in other cases, ministers will prefer to negotiate the content of a proposal, has led, inevitably, to criticism by those who prefer to see a more open, democratically accountable process of decision-taking rather than having to rely upon the negotiating skills and interests of non-elected civil servants who, meeting 'in camera', have significant power over the eventual outcome for an individual proposal.

On the other hand, defence of the operating procedures of the Council focuses upon the necessary existence of working parties and committees in order to scrutinize, perhaps more effectively than national ministers, the implications of proposed legislation, and to provide some continuity against the constantly-revolving movement of individual ministers at the European level.

Once having passed through the working parties and COREPER mechanism, the draft arrives at the appropriate Council for debate. Although there exist separate legislative procedures for different types of legislation, usually once all other relevant EC institutions have been approached for their opinion the proposal returns to the appropriate Council for a final decision. Once the Council has approved the draft proposal, it is deemed to be in force: all such adopted legislation is published in the Community's Official Journal. According to the legal basis in the Treaties providing for the particular type of proposal, there are a number of different voting procedures used in Council — these may well affect the likelihood of adoption. (The Treaty on European Union has created a new Article 189a, which specifies that if Council wishes to amend a draft proposal from the Commission, it will have to use unanimous voting procedures.)

So far it has been the Council of the European Communities which has been discussed; it is important to be aware that the Council is headed by a Presidency. The Presidency is a pivotal office, not least because the President co-ordinates the work of both the Council of the European Communities as well as the European Council and the process of foreign policy co-ordination, European Political Cooperation (EPC). The Presidency is not filled by any one directly-elected individual, but is instead assumed, every six months, by a member state of the EC. The order of rotation is designated by the alphabetical ordering of each country defined by its own language, e.g. Greece becomes Hellas, Spain Espagne.

The particular member state not only assumes the Presidency of the Council of the EC; it also presides at other levels of Council business, such as chairing working party and COREPER meetings. The function of the Presidency is primarily to co-ordinate Council activities — in addition to ensuring that the work of the Council runs smoothly, the Presidency can also contribute to agenda-setting, act as an impartial referee between opposing national positions, and of course provide an important focus for attention for the other EC institutions, particularly the Commission which observes the work of the Council by being present at working party and COREPER meetings. In addition to being the President of the Council of the EC, the particular member state holding the Presidency also hosts at least one meeting of the European Council. The European Council — legitimized in the SEA — grew out of the informal practice of 'summitry' between EC Heads of Government in the late 1960s. Unlike the Council of the European Communities, the European Council is a purely intergovernmental institution. Decisions taken by the European Council on matters inside the Treaty competency of the EC can thus be translated into Community legislation and policy. However, as with decisions taken within the process of EPC, any decisions taken by the European Council outside the scope of the treaties, are not legally binding upon the EC itself. The intricate political and legal relationship of these bodies and groups may well appear confusing to the uninitiated, given that within both the EC institution of the Council, and the legally distinct intergovernmental institutions of the European Council and EPC, the same actors — member states of the EC — are present.

The rather more clear distinction, made in the 1970s and early 1980s, between the European Council's development and the function of the Council of the EC — in terms of the European Council being solely a forum for 'fireside chats' and enabling top political leaders to initiate policy recommendations — has over the years been eroded. This is particularly apparent in recent years, where the vast majority of European Council resolutions have concerned the EC's position within a rapidly changing European environment, particularly over German reunification, the 1991 Gulf conflict and the later disintegration of Yugoslavia.

The European Council does remain an important focus for political activity and integration dynamics, for example the 1985 Milan Council regarding the Inter-Governmental Conference which created the SEA, the 1989 Madrid Council for the issues raised by the EC's Social Charter and the 1991 Maastricht Council for the new Treaty on European Union. The other intergovernmental activity which can be loosely grouped under the Council of the EC, is the process of foreign policy co-ordination and consultation known as European Political Cooperation. It can be politically identified with the Council of the EC in that, prior to the Union Treaty, the Rome Treaty or any subsequent amendment did not call for the creation of a common EC foreign policy, although over time member states preferred to co-ordinate and consult each other on matters of foreign policy and external relations. Hence EPC as a process is controlled primarily by member states, acting through their foreign ministers, and over the years has developed administrative backup through a permanent EPC Secretariat, and political co-ordination through the Presidency of the Council of the EC.

As with the European Council, EPC was not formally or legally recognized until the SEA of 1986, but decisions and joint positions continue to exist outside the ambit of the Treaties — or in other words, the European Court of Justice has no legal right to adjudicate over EPC business. Nevertheless, the notion of 'European Union' or 'political Union' expressed by a number of individuals and MEPs since the late 1970s has included the call for bringing EPC, and thus a legally binding European Communities foreign policy, under the EC Treaties structure. Most recently in the Inter-Governmental Conferences covering economic, monetary and political union, the suggestion that majority voting be extended to EPC, to allow for a particular policy or stance to be more easily reached, has not been welcomed by the British Government. The interplay, then, between acceptable areas of intergovernmental co-operation and supranational competence continues to be a major political issue, in relation to any future federal reform of the EC structure. (The eventual incorporation of a common foreign and security policy in the Union Treaty is covered in Chapter 12, although the most important element of this new policy to affect the EC's institutions is the Council's ability to take joint action on the basis of qualified majority voting, if it so decides — Article J.3, Title V.)

The European Parliament (EP)

As mentioned earlier, the Rome Treaty created an Assembly. Article 137 originally stated that 'the Assembly, which shall consist of representatives of the peoples of the states brought together in the Community, shall exercise the advisory and supervisory powers which are conferred upon it by this Treaty'.

The Assembly began calling itself the Parliament in the early 1960s and this official term was formally recognized in the SEA. A point often stressed is that although it is a parliament in name, it is not a parliament in the sense that it possesses functions and powers similar to national parliaments. However, since its creation in 1957 the Parliament of the EC has sought to increase its authority and legitimacy. Perhaps the most fundamental characteristic of parliament in liberal pluralistic democracies is that the representatives of the people are directly elected by the people. This condition did not until relatively recently apply to the EP — Article 138 originally specified that a uniform procedure be employed across the Community to elect MEPs by direct universal suffrage. Direct elections were not introduced until 1979, and prior to that a system of national parliamentary delegations were seconded to the Assembly.

So, although the EP's membership now more accurately reflects democratic practice, the requirement mentioned above, that of a common or uniform voting procedure to be used Community-wide for the election of MEPs, has still not been introduced. Hence MEPs in Britain are returned to the EP via the 'first past the post' or plurality system, and MEPs in mainland Europe and Northern Ireland according to the variety of plurality and proportional representation systems in use.

As well as comprising individual MEPs who are organized into transnational party groupings, the EP's working structure also comprises committees of MEPs. The standing Committees are organized along similar functional lines as the Directorate-General in the Commission and exist to scrutinize, debate and amend draft legislative proposals.

The Committees themselves are a vital component of the EP's effectiveness in debating Community legislation; the chairperson or 'rapporteur' of a particular committee is in a highly influential position, liaising between transnational party group leaders who will have canvassed members of that party for their opinions on draft legislation, between the various DGs of the Commission, and between lobby groups and experts. Politically, too, both the transnational party organizations and the EP's Committee system are based in Brussels, whereas the plenary sessions of the EP along with other EP organizations are based in Strasbourg and Luxembourg. The financial costs, physical burden and symbolic importance of a single seat for the Parliament have led to long-standing dissatisfaction with the presently scattered workings of the EP.

The competence of the EP, as laid down in Article 137, has concerned 'advisory' and 'supervisory' powers for much of its history.

'Advisory' powers generally relate to the EP's involvement in the legislative process (encompassing the consultation, conciliation and co-operation procedures) and also concerning other policy-oriented matters. For example, in relation to Community Acts of Association under Article 238, the EP's assent to any Association agreement with an external party is required before the agreement can be concluded, and in practice the EP is now informed of the step by step negotiation.

Another ad hoc development since the mid-1980s has been the presentation of the incoming Commission's agenda and priorities to the EP: this practice was begun by the President of the Commission, Jacques Delors, and has been subsequently the pattern of a new Commission attempting to emphasize its accountability to the Parliament.

'Supervisory' powers cover a number of significant points. Perhaps the clearest is the EP's right to censure the Commission en masse (Article 144). However, in practice this power has never been used and there is a strong argument to suggest that the EP would not necessarily use this power, since individual Commissioners cannot be singled out if it is they who are incompetent, and furthermore the EP has no ability to appoint a new Commission and hence no leverage over the integrity of any new appointments.

Another significant power of supervision concerns budgetary legislation; the EP under Article 203 has the right to reject the entire draft budget, and the EP also has the ultimate power of deciding, albeit within certain constraints, the level of non-compulsory expenditure (NCE) which is the element of the EC budget covering policy expenditure not legally covered by the treaties, such as the various structural Funds. As regards this power of budget rejection, Marquand has suggested that 'the right to reject the Community Budget in toto would be of great value if Community spending accounted for a grossly excessive proportion of Community GDP . . . in fact, the Community Budget is pathetically small . . . in these circumstances, its right to reject the Budget looks suspiciously like a right to cut off its nose to spite its face' (Marquand 1979, p. 96). More generally, these 'supervisory' powers over the budget have led to criticism of the EP in the sense that it enjoys the power to increase certain types of expenditure, but does not have equal responsibility for making decisions on how the Community should raise monies for budgetary expenditure.

Finally, other 'supervisory' functions of the EP concern its right to instigate proceedings in the ECJ against the Commission or Council if they have failed to act in areas where the treaties require them to act (Article 175).

The most recent acquisition of 'supervisory' powers for the EP are contained in the new Treaty on European Union, signed at Maastricht in February 1992. A new Article 137b enables the Parliament to set up a Temporary Committee of Enquiry to investigate 'alleged contraventions or maladministration in the implementation of Community law, except where the alleged facts are being examined before a court and while the case is still subject to legal proceedings'. Also, a new Article 137d gives the EP the right to appoint an ombudsman who would receive complaints from citizens or residents of the Community over 'instances of maladministration in the activities of the Community institutions or bodies, with the exception of the Court of Justice and the Court of First Instance acting in their judicial role' (CONF-UP-UEM 2017/91, Brussels 18.12.91, pp. 89–90).

On the whole, however, one cannot fully assess the EP's powers and functions merely by assessing the contents of the treaties; the ways in which the Parliament has sought to extend its role in the Community decision-making process, its stature among the other EC institutions, and its authority to speak on a wide range of increasing EC policy competencies, are perhaps more politically significant than the language of the treaties.

Whether the EP has stimulated changes from within — for example by amending its Rule of Procedure to allow it a right of legislative initiative, or 'own initiative' reports, and by developing close working relationships amongst MEPs and Commission staff — or whether its strategy has involved concerted collective pressure upon the EC institutions and member states to reform the Community system, for example through its Draft Treaty on European Union

(1984) which led to the pressures for institutional reform culminating in the SEA, the impact of these moves by the EP has proved highly significant.

It is significant in the sense that the EP has challenged many of the assumptions and expections, particularly of the EC's member states, surrounding the nature of the integration process, for as Lodge states, 'the EP has become very much the EC's conscience and the guardian of European Union and democratic ideals' (Lodge 1989, p. 68).

The Economic and Social Committee (ESC or ECOSOC)

Article 193 of the Rome Treaty brought the ESC into being, although it was very much a reflection of the earlier consultative Committee of the ECSC; the ESC comprised national representatives of 'economic and social activity' or in other words, employers, workers and particular interests such as agriculture, transport, local government and consumer groups. Article 194 stressed that the members of the ESC would be 'appointed in their personal capacity and may not be bound by any mandatory instructions'.

Each EC member state has a national quota for ESC membership; lists are compiled by each member state which are forwarded to the Council of the EC, who then appoint members from the total number on the national lists.

Although the ESC members are put forward on the basis of their national affiliation and representation, as Article 194 makes clear, they should be independent from both national governments and the agencies they are drawn from: the role of ESC members is to function more as a mechanism representing the general viewpoint of such groups, and to act as a link between national and supranational forums.

Article 197 suggested that the Committee could organize itself internally into subsections or specialized groups, the Treaty mentioning in particular a specialized section for agriculture and transport. This internal organization was to be important, for the function of the ESC was initially given more credence and weight in the decision-making process than the Assembly. Article 193 describes the ESC as having 'advisory status', and Article 198 stipulates that the ESC must be consulted for its opinion 'where this Treaty so provides'.

As the EC's policy competency has expanded, hence so has the ESC's role in consultation. Since the mid-1970s the ESC has also had a right of 'own initiative' enabling it to produce reports and suggestions for the other EC institutions to reflect upon, although its 'own initiative' reports are similar to those of the EP, in that they may only be translated into an official draft by the Commission.

Opinion tends to divide over the question of whether the ESC is an important EC institution: although the ESC can be a useful source of opinion, particularly through its subcommittees who incorporate much expert and technical knowledge, on the whole it is not seen as a powerful institution and has not sought the extension and legitimacy of its role in the same way that the EP has.

The European Court of Justice (ECJ) and the Court of Auditors

The ECJ and the more recently created Court of First Instance, are the legal institutions of the EC. Both the institutions and the general role of legal interpretations of the integration process — linked to the ECJ's 'teleological' or policy-oriented jurisprudence — have become significant in the study of the integration process in Western Europe.

However, in the present context, a brief summary of the powers and functions of the Court is of more utility, especially because the nature of EC legislation and policy-making (law) is open to political, economic and legal interpretations, and because Community law is superior to domestic law. The Rome Treaty gave the ECJ the sole right, amongst other EC institutions, to 'ensure that in the interpretation and application of this Treaty the law is observed' (Article 164). Since the most recent expansion of the EC — the accession of Spain and Portugal in 1986 — the ECJ is composed of thirteen Judges and six Advocates-General, whose independence and impartiality is of the highest calibre, and who usually are drawn from the senior ranks of national legal systems.

As mentioned earlier, the Commission's role of 'guardian of the Treaties' enables it, if necessary, to bring any cases of inaction or illegality to the Court (Article 169). Under Article 170 member states may also instigate legal proceedings against another member state by referring their complaint to the Court. Article 173 gives the ECJ a significant power to 'review the legality of acts of the Council and the Commission', and may also rule on the Council and Commission's failure to act (Article 175). However the new Treaty on European Union has extended Article 173 and 175 to allow for the Court to rule on the EP also.

However, when assessing the state and nature of the EC integration process, it soon becomes apparent that the role of judicial interpretation is as significant and central to the development of integration as are political interpretations and dynamics. In this context, it is important to be aware of not only what functions and powers the ECJ possesses, but also the methods and contexts by which the Court has applied its powers.

The Court has not only ruled on the nature and supremacy of EC law — for example on the 'direct effect' of Community law in order that individuals may rely upon it in any legal actions (van Gend en Loos case 26/62); that in situations of conflict between national and Community law, then Community law must be adhered to (Costa case 6/64); or that as a result of the 'Isoglucose' rulings, the ECJ strengthened the requirement upon the Council to wait for the opinion of the Parliament before taking a decision on draft legislation (cases 138/79 and 139/79) — but it has also ruled on the specific application of Community law and the responsibilities incumbent upon member states correctly to implement and apply EC policy, for example, over the 'lamb wars' between Britain and France.

Most recently the ECJ's caseload and organization of work has benefited from the creation of the Court of First Instance in October 1988. The SEA acknowledged the burden of increasing work for the ECJ and so the function of this new court is to hear and give judgment on a number of specific types of legal action, particularly on complaints or disputes arising from the EC's competition policy (see OJC 215/1, 1989). Hence other cases and hearings can pass directly to the ECJ itself.

Finally, another institution of the Community worth noting is the Court of Auditors. It was created as a result of the amended budgetary procedure (1975), which led to the EP and Council being designated as the EC's 'Budgetary Authority'. The Court of Auditors was therefore created with the sole responsibility to carry out an annual audit of the Community's financial affairs, including of course the role of the EC's institutions in managing and disbursing finances. The Court's annual report is published toward the end of the EC's financial year (December) in the Official Journal; such reports, despite their length, make for interesting reading, particularly as the Court introduces its report with a summary of its assessment on the adoption and monitoring procedures for budgetary matters.

In some cases the Court has not hesitated to criticize aspects of EC financial affairs or practices; for example in its report on the 1989 budget, the Court stressed that 'the first cases of implementation of the new rules on budgetary discipline are still a long way from management with "due and proper care" and from the "spirit of rigour" described when the Delors package was introduced' (OJC 313, vol. 33, 12.12.90, p. 15), which is an important point to consider given that the 1988 'Delors Package' on budgetary and CAP reform was designed to avoid excessive EC budget deficits as a result of agricultural price support guarantees.

There are also a number of related institutional mechanisms of the EC — such as the European Investment Bank and the European Development Fund — which are essentially financial and credit institutions administered by the EC institutions.

Legislative processes in the EC

First of all, it is useful to note the four types of 'legislation' which exist in the EC:

- a 'regulation' has general application, and is binding and applicable to all EC member states, for example when Council has set agricultural prices for individual products, these prices are published as regulations;
- a 'directive' is binding in terms of the result to be achieved (for example the reduction of certain emissions from automobile exhausts), but delegates to national authorities or agencies the choice of method by which the result is to be achieved;
- a 'decision' is binding upon whoever it is to be addressed; for example not necessarily just a member state but an individual company;
- 'recommendations' and 'opinions' have no binding force but can be used to clarify views or issues.

Having briefly assessed the powers and functions of the EC's institutions, it is important to understand their respective roles in the processes of Community decision-making, or in other words, how they take part in the legislative process. Having said this, there are in reality a number of different methods by which the EC creates, debates and passes legislation, this being the result of partial reform of the Community's methods since the original Treaty of Rome. In essence there are now four methods by which draft legislation is considered by the EC institutions:

(1) The traditional 'consultation' or 'business as usual' method, which is the result of the formal roles and functions accredited to the different institutions in the Rome Treaty.

The Commission, having the sole right to initiate legislation (Article 155), begins the process. A working draft usually begins life in one of the Commission's Directorates-General, as a result of either treaty or otherwise common decisions, or as a result of pressure from other EC institutions or lobby groups. The draft proceeds through its Directorate-General to the College of Commissioners (the Commission). The Commission will in almost all cases have assessed the likely reception of the proposals via meetings, and barring any government representatives' intuitive feelings that the proposal will be quickly rejected by a majority of opinion, the draft is then passed to the Council.

The proposal will only be briefly considered by the various working parties and COREPER at this stage, in order to gain an approximation of the general viewpoint of national governments. The Council then passes the draft to either the EP or the ESC, or sometimes both. Although as stated previously, the Council under the Rome Treaty was only obliged to consult the ESC, in practice seeking the EP's opinion on draft legislation has developed, especially since the ECJ's rulings on the 'Isoglucose' cases, where it was held that Council could not take decisions on legislation unless the EP had been consulted.

Once the EP or ESC has given its opinion, the draft is passed back to Council. Again, COREPER's work can be highly significant, because these national representatives will discuss among themselves their governments' respective positions on the draft, before any national ministers meet to finalize any decision. If agreement on the draft can be reached within COREPER, the draft is placed in section A of the particular Council's agenda; if there is disagreement, it is placed on section B. The agenda for the meeting of the particular Council is thus itself classified into two groups: section A denoting those draft proposals where there is consensus on acceptance or rejection, and section B signifying drafts where agreement has yet to be reached so that ministers may take a final decision.

Throughout this entire process the Commission has the right to intervene and amend the draft proposal, for example after the opinion(s) of either the EP or the ESC have been given, or if the draft itself is unable to be agreed upon during the later Council sessions.

Once the Council has voted on the draft and it has received a sufficient majority (or unanimity, according to the precise type of legislation), it is deemed to have passed into law, and is subsequently published in the Official Journal.

This process has, for much of the Community's existence, provided the major method of decision-making. Although the Rome Treaty envisaged Council acting on a qualified or simple majority voting procedure and also on unanimity, this expectation was undermined by the French Government's boycott of EC institutions in 1965 and the resulting Luxembourg Accords — or compromise — of 1966. The French Government was displeased at plans to extend the powers of the EP in relation to the proposed increase in the EC Budget for the operation of the CAP. After the 'boycott', the Luxembourg Accords introduced a de facto power of veto for member states if they perceived that 'vital national interests' were threatened by draft legislative proposals.

Hence, the process described above occasionally broke down, as member states claimed a vital national interest to be at stake, and legislation was thus either 'frozen' in Council or withdrawn by the Commission.

This shift in emphasis from a balance of national and Community interests, to a clearer assertion of the ultimate sanctioning power of national governments has been described in depth elsewhere (see Taylor, 1983). The log-jam problems of the legislative process which resulted, was one of the major factors in the pressure for institutional reform by the early 1980s. A partial response to this perceived problem of national governments remaining fundamentally in control of the speed and direction of EC integration was the introduction of a new legislative procedure in the SEA.

(2) So, the second major legislative procedure in the EC is the 'co-operation' procedure. This is essentially a system where draft proposals have two

readings, unlike the above method of consultation. Hence this procedure is designed to bring the EC institutions closer and emphasize the need for each institution to not only clearly define its collective 'position' on a proposal, but 'co-operate' and acknowledge that each institution's 'position' is legitimate, and therefore that they should attempt to reach agreement on a draft proposal wherever possible, together.

The procedure itself begins in the same way as above: the Commission proposes, and the Council begins its internal 'sifting' and negotiation.

However, under the co-operation procedure, the Council must then meet to produce a 'common position'; whether this is by informal consensus among ministers or whether by a majority vote, the Council must in any case make its general feelings clear. The Commission's 'position' and justification for the draft, along with the Council's common position is then forwarded to the EP. The EP has a three-month period in which to discuss the draft in committee and then to take a majority vote in plenary session — i.e. a sitting of the entire Parliament — in order to amend, accept or reject the proposal. If, within this three-month period, the EP approves the legislation or if it fails to take any decision, the Council may then pass the legislation, since the EP has not essentially changed the Council's 'common position'.

If however, the EP rejects the proposal by an absolute majority vote the Council, if it still wishes to accept the proposal, must take a unanimous vote in order for the legislation to be passed.

So far the co-operation procedure has been based on the assumption of a single reading by the EP. As mentioned earlier, though, the co-operation procedure does allow for a second Parliamentary reading.

A second reading, then, will occur if the EP wishes to amend the proposal — the EP again requires an absolute majority to amend any proposals, and if this is the case, the EP's amendments and voting position will be sent to the Commission. The Commission has a great deal of political flexibility as to whether it then includes the EP's amendments to the final proposal and sends it to Council, or whether it decides to send the unaltered proposal back to Council. This can be an intensely important point in the co-operation procedure, with the Commission generally acting as an 'honest broker' between often opposing 'governmental' and 'parliamentary' interests.

The final stage of the co-operation procedure concerns the return of the proposal to the Council, which may or may not be accompanied by the Commission's endorsement of the EP's amendments. If the proposal has been amended by the Commission, the Council can take a final decision by qualified majority voting, but if the Commission has forwarded the draft proposal without having supported the EP's amendments, the Council must use unanimous voting procedures if it wishes to pass the legislation.

On a more general point the co-operation procedure — although created by the SEA which intended to provide the EP with stronger influence over the shaping of EC legislation — does only apply to certain types of legislation. The procedure only relates to legislation enacted under the auspices of the 1992 programme, or in other words, legislative measures necessary for the completion of the single market. In theory this was the intention; in practice member states have interpreted some aspects of 1992 legislation as being too 'sensitive' for the method of second reading and qualified majority.

So legislation relating to certain fiscal 'barriers' to a single market — notably the approximation of VAT rates — and also relating to social and environmental standards of a single economic market remain subject to unanimous voting. The question of extending the co-operation procedure to these and other policy areas of the EC has become an increasingly contentious issue between the EC institutions, the EP generally arguing that ultimate decision-taking power is still concentrated in the hands of national governments — the Council — whilst effective and open participation of other EC institutions — the EP and Commission — remains limited.

(3) Prior to the Union Treaty there was one other method of enacting legislation. This is the conciliation procedure, which operates between the Council, EP and Commission when budgetary or other legislation having 'serious financial consequences' is being considered.

This method, then, does not apply to legislation other than 'financial' legislation; indeed the entire process of drafting, debating and finalizing the EC Budget is a distinct process, differing from both the consultation and co-operation procedures summarized above. The Commission has overall responsibility for collecting estimates of expenditure from the other institutions and will start the process of creating the EC Budget, but the Budget itself, as a result of the 1975 Treaty amending certain financial provisions, is determined by its twin arms of Council and Parliament. Each of these institutions has powers to determine final levels of expenditure; the Council over 'compulsory' expenditure (CE) arising from Treaty obligations, and the Parliament over 'non-compulsory' expenditure (NCE), deriving from policies or commitments not expressly created by the original EEC Treaty. Invariably the EP has sought to restrain Council decisions on CE, primarily the Common Agricultural Policy, in order to strengthen levels of funding incurred in the NCE field, such as the structural Funds and R&D projects. Council has in turn occasionally refused to accept Parliamentary amendments to proposed expenditure levels, and as a result of this potentially conflict-prone situation, the conciliation procedure was set up in 1975. It is a procedure whereby the Commission again acting in its 'honest broker' role, can attempt to bring representatives of the Budgetary

Authority together in order to avoid lengthy wrangles and delays whilst the preliminary budget is being debated.

(4) The most recent revision made to the legislative procedures of Community decision-making is the new Article 189b, contained in the Treaty on European Union (Maastricht, 1992). The Commission will submit a draft proposal to the EP and Council. The EP sends its opinion to Council, which must take a qualified majority vote to produce its common position.

The proposal, with Council's common position and a full explanation of it together with the Commission's views, will be returned to the EP.

During the following three months,

- if the EP approves Council's common position, Council will definitely adopt the draft;
- if the EP was not yet taken a position on the draft, Council may adopt it in accordance with its own common position;
- if the EP acting by an absolute majority wishes to reject the Council's common position, it must inform Council.

'The Council may convene a meeting of the Conciliation Committee . . . to explain further its position', which would comprise members, or their representatives, of Council and equal numbers of EP representatives.

After this Committee has met to discuss the Parliament's reservations, the EP must either confirm, again by absolute majority, its rejection of the common position, in which case the draft proposal will not be adopted, or, the EP may propose amendments to the draft by absolute majority.

If, after this three-month period, the council approves the EPs amendments by qualified majority voting, the draft proposal is adopted. But, if the Commission has delivered a negative opinion on any of those EP amendments, Council will have to employ unanimous voting methods to adopt the draft proposal. If Council cannot bring itself to approve EP amendments, the President of the Council with the EP President's agreement must convene the Conciliation Committee again.

The new Article 189b is clearly laying down a stringent procedure where there is serious dispute between Council and Parliament over a draft proposal: in essence this new Article has introduced the earlier conciliation procedure (see (3) above) to legislation not previously subject to such perusal, or in other words, power of co-decision between the EP and Council. This is an important development in the inter-institutional relations of the Community; the fact is Article 189b indicates that after using the Conciliation Committee to overcome fundamental disagreement, if the EP continues to have reservations over the draft and rejects the Council's position, the draft proposal is thus not adopted. This marks a fundamental reform of Community decision-making procedures — given that in previous years, a draft proposal accompanied by serious Parliamentary reservations could none the less continue to be adopted by Council, and was thus seen as a function of the 'democratic deficit'. The Parliament therefore is endowed with a power of veto. This new procedure may be widened in scope as a result of the expected reform of the Treaty on European Union due by 1996; after such reform this procedure could apply to social policy (new Title VIII); trans-European networks for transport, tele-communications and energy infrastructures; R&D programmes; environmental programmes; free movement of persons, services capital and payments; and the internal market.

The new Article 189c in the Union Treaty replaces Article 149 under which the co-operation procedure was laid out; the procedure remains the same, and has been extended to cover for example the implementation of the European Social Fund (ESF); environmental policy objectives; and development co-operation.

The institutional framework of the Community has benefited a great deal form the eventual Union Treaty — despite many compromises made by a number of member states for a variety of domestic political purposes. Institutional actors, particularly the EP but also the Council of Ministers, have found themselves with improved and increased influence over a greater number of policy competencies — the Council acting by qualified majority if it so decides, in relation to foreign policy activities, and the EP's de facto veto and co-decision-making power arising from the new Article 189b conciliation procedure. For the Parliament, the review of the EC's constitution in 1996 will offer another opportunity to build on the incremental nature of change in the Community.

References and further reading

Bulmer, S. and Wessels, W. 1987, *The European Council*, Macmillan, Basing-stoke.

Ehrlermann, C.D., 1990, 'The institutional development of the EC under the SEA', *Aussenpontik*, 41 (2), 135–46.

Hayes-Renshaw, F. *et al.*, 1989, 'The permanent representation of member states to the EC', *Journal of Common Market Studies*, 28 (2), 119–37.

Keohane, R.D. and Hoffman, S. (eds), 1991, *The new European Community: decisionmaking and institutional change*, Westview Press, Oxford.

Lodge, J. (ed.), 1989, *The EC and the challenge of the future*, Pinter, London.

Marquand, D., 1979, *Parliament for Europe*, Jonathan Cape, London.

Nugent, N., 1991, *The government and politics of the EC* (2nd ed.), Macmillan, Basingstoke.

Pinder, J., 1991, 'The EC, the rule of law and representative government: the significance of the IGCs', *Government and Opposition*, 26 (2), 199–214.

Taylor, P., 1983, *The limits of European integration*, Croom Helm, London.

Weber, S. and Wiesmeth, H., 1991, 'Issue linkage in the EC', *Journal of Common Market Studies*, 29 (3), 255–67.

3
From common market to single market

The purpose of this chapter is primarily to examine the Single Market programme with its technical, economic and political implications for future Community development. However, given that the bulk of the '1992' legislation is
intended to bring economic integration into line with the original intentions
of the 1957 Rome Treaty establishing the EEC, a brief overview of the Treaty's
commitment to a common market and customs union is necessary.

Although a distinct chapter on the Single Market programme may appear
to be a ubiquitous acknowledgement of recent Community history, the 1992
vision of 'L'Europe sans frontières' is firstly a visible and powerful image of
EC integration, interpreted and presented differently by the various member
states — and is thus an important symbol of what the present integration
process means to European politics. Secondly, the political and constitutional
implications of realizing a single market have led to interpretations of '1992'
being fed into political expectations concerning the future direction of European integration, with some seeing the internal market as the destination of
the integration process, and others seeing it merely as an antechamber, leading
to qualitatively new directions. For those reasons, it was felt that a chapter
should be set aside for the examination of both the content of, and political
expectations surrounding, the 1992 programme.

The Treaty of Rome and the Common Market

The signing of the Treaty of Rome in 1957, creating the European Economic
Community (EEC), came less than three years after the collapse of the draft
Treaty for the European Defence Community (EDC). Given that both original
and contemporary analysis saw the plans for the EDC leading to the eventual
highpoint of political union, how was it that such hopes were translated into

further and deeper forms of economic integration, and what explicitly did the Treaty of Rome attempt to achieve? Urwin points out that within Western Europe, it was primarily the Benelux states who continued to stress the desirability of total economic integration, as opposed to merely multilateral cooperation through the OEEC and sectoral integration via the ECSC (Urwin 1991, p. 73). As a result of such viewpoints and particularly through the direction of Paul-Henri Spaak (Belgium's Foreign Minister), the process of integration was again set on course and negotiations for the creation of a European Economic Community soon got under way. The Spaak Report constituted the basis for negotiations, and was careful not to overemphasize the political aim of any further integration. Instead the creation of a common market was seen to be a positive contribution to the strengthening of Europe and of its ability to take part, economically and politically, in world affairs.

The Treaty of Rome's primary emphasis was thus upon creating a common market and customs union between its members. The customs union entailed the removal of tariff barriers and other obstacles to trade, and the creation of a common trade policy to non-members which was expressed through the Common External Tariff (CET) and the variable levy imposed on agricultural imports by the Common Agricultural Policy (CAP). The common market took the concept and practice of a customs union further by setting joint rules allowing the free movement of the factors of production — labour and capital, as well as goods and services already covered by the customs union.

The Treaty of Rome entered into force on 1 January 1958; the rules and procedures setting up the customs union and common market were essentially those of the free market — a fact not lost on UK Prime Minister Thatcher's Government in endorsing the 1992 programme — with the functioning of the customs union expected to take place without obstacles to trade such as tariff and non-tariff barriers. This supplemented free trade by the operation of a competition policy including rules to ensure fair and independent competition between traders, such as the elimination or at least severe curtailment of state aids or subsidies to national economic sectors. The customs union existed within the wider framework of a common market and its basic premises — removal of internal tariffs and quotas and the application of the CET — were realized prior to the end of the transitional period, as laid down in the Rome Treaty with 1970 being the final completion date.

As for the functioning of the common market, the Treaty laid down its essential elements:

- A common competition policy whereby 'distorting' measures such as state aids or subsidies to domestic industries, were to be minimized if not abolished; cartel or monopoly power would be investigated and prevented; preferential treatment, such as public or governmental purchasing of domestic tenders for contracts, should be encouraged to widen its tendering and competition procedures; and where competition may be undermined by different national practices, such as health and safety requirements and technical standards (Articles 85–94).

• The coordination of member states' economic policies, rather than a common economic policy, was emphasized, with the Treaty suggesting that each member state attempt to maintain stable and productive economic performance, through the co-ordination of national economic policies (Article 102a).

Because of political differences, a common economic policy could not be supported by all Six original EEC members, so this emphasis on co-ordination suggested that any eventual supranational control and direction of economic policy would result from political agreement to do so, by the EC member states. This area remains one of political dissent, even for those pro-integrationist member states.

• Other elements of the common market were designed to create supra-national direction of, and responsibility for, certain essential structural and policy areas.

The Common Agricultural Policy (CAP) had been identified during the EEC negotiations as a substantive activity for any common market: agri-culture's leading political and economic role in West European economies in the post-war period meant that if agricultural trade was excluded from common market rules, it could jeopardize the operation of the common market and the unity of the EC in terms of its external economic interests.

In addition to the CAP, the Treaty envisaged a common transport policy (Articles 74–84); although the onus upon member states and the institutions of the Community to realize such a common policy was not as great as a common agricultural policy. The EC has not developed this original inten-tion — leading to the EP arguing that the Council of Ministers had failed to live up to its obligations in implementing a common transport policy. It is only in recent years that the Commission has begun to forward draft proposals concerning transport.

• Finally, there are the until recently largely marginalized remaining elements of the Treaty — where progress since 1958 has been discreet and largely peripheral, and where only in comparatively recent years have these policies been elucidated comprehensively.

They include social matters, with specific legislation having evolved over time to cover topics such as equal pay for equal work, social security and certain rights of residence for migrant workers, and rights established by cases involving the free movement of workers. The European Social Fund (ESF) created by the EEC Treaty has also evolved from being purely a method of funding employment schemes in member states, to a more proactive (and financially more robust) mechanism to encourage and improve vocational training and retraining schemes across the EC (Title III).

The Treaty included the basis for a regional policy (Article 130a–e), although the political impetus for a directly supranational policy on regional problems was not to become a reality until British negotiations for accession and the subsequent creation of the European Regional Development Fund (ERDF) in 1975.

As far as the pillars of the customs union and common market are concerned, the above policies and procedures are the essential constitutent items to note, and it is these which will be dealt with more fully in the following section on 1992.

It is useful to examine the factors leading to the Commission's 1985 White Paper on completing the Single Market, in order to understand why and how the 1992 programme should complete and extend the 1957 vision.

The economic expectations of the 1957 Treaty were only partially realized; although the operation of the CAP with its price and support mechanisms as well as protective shields (variable import levies) did constitute a truly common policy by 1967, even the CAP began to be eroded by national political interests in maintaining stable prices, and certainly as far as other prospective common and co-ordinated policies were concerned — particularly transport — the Common Market simply did not exist.

Regarding the more technical requirements of a customs union and common market, although tariff barriers were removed and the CET applied ahead of schedule in 1969, quotas and quantitative restrictions proved somewhat less amenable, and the wider problem of non-tariff barriers to free trade became increasingly apparent by the early 1980s. It was recognized that national protectionism had become an undesirable feature of the economically troubled decade of the 1970s. The commitment to the free movement of the factors of production, enshrined in the Treaty, was not practised; with Court of Justice rulings required to overcome discriminatory national barriers to the free movement of persons, and fiscal barriers such as differing rates of indirect taxation — VAT — and excise duties: such cases include Defrenne v. SABENA, Reyners v. Belgian State and Van Gend en Loos (Freestone and Davidson 1988, pp. 33–41).

From a political point of view, two important trends during the early 1980s were influential in shaping the eventual White Paper. Domestically, the rise of right-of-centre and neo-liberal parties led to the increasing political weight of monetarist economics and governmental preferences for deregulation, and the 'new' commitment of these parties to anti-inflationary policies was evident both in the successes of the EMS and the standard British policy interest in the Community until the mid-1980s: the desire for budgetary discipline.

The other major trend, at Community level, was supranational dissatisfaction with the image of the EC in the 1970s as being one of 'Eurosclerosis', stagnation and national retreat from the integration process. Hence the buildup of supranational wishes to see Europe free from the economic instability of the previous decade, to bring about meaningful institutional reform, and to enable the EC to promote a stronger economic and political profile in world politics, were partially incorporated into the White Paper, whilst the Single European Act (SEA) of 1987 formalized political and institutional change within the EC in a direct response to the perceived impact of the single market.

The 1985 White Paper on Completing the Single Internal Market

The incoming Commission headed by Jacques Delors — the former French Finance Minister — took office in early 1985, and at the Milan Council in June of that year, the White Paper was unveiled.

The White Paper was a recommendation by the Commission for the adoption of specific legislative acts (originally 300, subsequently 289) to remove barriers, visible and invisible, to the free workings of the common market as created by the Rome Treaty. As the collective name for this legislation is identical to the method by which the British Government introduces legislative proposals to the House of Commons, it thus owes recognition to its British architect Lord Cockfield, and it is important to recognize that unlike British White and Green Papers, the Commission's White Paper required further legal and institutional elaboration.

In essence, the Paper sought to identify and prioritize specific legislative proposals covering the major problem areas of the 'uncommon' market, and was clearly aimed at those European sectoral and governmental interests keen to relaunch the free market spirit of the Rome Treaty and thereby stimulate economic growth in the Community. The Commission subsequently sponsored an investigation into the 'costs of non-Europe', or in other words, an enquiry into the problems which would continue to plague European economic activity if the single market was not completed, known as the Cecchini Report.

The SEA covered aspects of economic integration by declaring the timetable for completion of the internal market to expire by 31 December 1992, and by stressing the need for closer national economic convergence, and also addressed itself to the political and social aspects of the future integration process, in direct response to the calls for directional change in institutional and policy matters — as expressed in the Tindemans Report (1975), the report of the Three Wise Men (1979), the EP's Draft Treaty on European Union (1984) and the Stuttgart Solemn Declaration on European Union (1983).

Thus the SEA, as a single reform of the EC's Treaties introduced important changes such as the strengthening of majority voting in Council (qualified majority voting for all internal market legislation); a 'co-operation procedure' designed to increase the Parliament's role in EC decision-making (although this fell far short of the EP's expectations); the linking of the EC to the existing intergovernmental process of foreign policy co-ordination (EPC); and particularly stressed that the economic and social cohesion of the EC should be promoted more directly through all policy activities. The SEA contained important references to the development of other emerging policy frameworks, notably R&D programmes and environmental co-operation.

Having briefly outlined the relationship between the White Paper and the SEA, it is important to clarify in more depth the contents of the 1992 programme and the ways in which wider political and economic aspects of the integration process have dovetailed during the late 1980s.

The contents of the White Paper

It has been suggested that 'at the heart of the economic case for the single market is the assumption that the improvements in output, competitiveness and inflation will create space for more vigorous government action to boost growth' (Palmer 1989, p. 27). The Commission focused upon these 'improvements' in three broad areas: the removal of physical, technical and fiscal barriers to the operation of a common/single market.

Physical barriers, not surprisingly, comprise those customs controls at borders — roads, sea, air — and related costs such as delays incurring increased operating costs, and administrative necessities (passport, luggage and export documentation checks).

The Cecchini Report (produced for the Commission, which attempted to quantify in financial terms, the costs of doing business in the EC if the 'uncommon' market remained unreformed) argued that the overall cost to European business of these physical barriers was approximately 8bn ECU 'or getting on for 2%' of the total value of intra-EC trade, whilst 'the turnover companies forego as a result is at least ECU 4.5bn' (Cecchini 1988, pp. 8–9).

Although in general terms the 1992 programme was supported enthusiastically by the British Government, and governmental information on 1992 for the business sector was adequate, the message received by the general public was that total abolition of physical barriers to trade — notably customs posts and controls — was irreconcilable with public safety requirements to control illegal trafficking and terrorist movements. The EC enthusiastically endorsed the introduction of the Single Administrative Document in early 1988 — although it had been negotiated earlier in the 1980s — to be used for all imports, exports and movement of goods across EC borders. This marked a welcome reduction in the burden of administration and paperwork involved at border controls, and was later adopted for use by EFTA states, given that the EC is their largest export destination.

The issue of physical barriers to a single market necessarily poses an immediate question mark over the provision and functioning of transport. Legislation concerning the deregulation initially of the road haulage sector, and more recently of air transport, and the liberalization of road transport national permit quotas may in the long term benefit the Community transport sector. It could be argued, however, that transport infrastructures and mass investment in European public transport networks is a necessary corollary of any deregulatory activity, yet which itself may pose environmental and aesthetic costs.

In addition to such measures involving changes to goods documentation and transport deregulation, the area of physical barriers in the 1992 programme has included a large number of proposals concerning plant and animal health controls and the abandonment of internal Community frontier checks on animal products, although the progress on this legislation has been slow (see Featherstone 1990; Commission of the EC 1990).

Technical barriers to a single market, as identified by the White Paper and the Cecchini Report, include the harmonization of technical standards, liberalization of public procurement and of provision of services (notably concerning banking/financial services and information technologies), the problem of conflicting business laws and practices (company law, taxation and patent/trademark law), and obstacles to the free movement of workers/persons (educational qualifications and employment status).

Before looking in more detail at the specifics, one important point requires mention. The Cockfield White Paper at the outset recognized that in this particular area, the traditional and time-honoured practice of 'harmonization' would seriously jeopardize the prospects of a speedy adoption of the legislation. Given that 'harmonization' is the process of decision-making reliant upon centralizing national practices and interests in order to provide a rough aggregate of Community policy, it was seen as too time-consuming and cumbersome, with the real possibility of proposals languishing for months if not years in Council.

Thus the White Paper suggested that the EC and its members adopt a 'new approach' known as '*mutual recognition and equivalence*' — applying to much, but not all, of the original 300 proposals (subsequently reduced to 289). It would therefore result in a draft framework Directive being forwarded to Council, which would only have to agree in principle to the framework, leaving the minutiae to be decided upon at the national level, according to national preference. For example, if one member state had higher safety requirements concerning domestic electrical appliances, the 'new approach' would mean that the draft framework Directive would merely affirm the principle of reasonable safety requirements, and differing levels of safety requirements would be legally and politically acceptable. It was no wonder then that over 80 per cent of technical barriers legislation had been adopted or approved by Council by 1990 (COM (90) 90 final: 11).

However, this 'new approach' is not without its drawbacks; the onus now rests, more than ever, on national and local authorities involved in the monitoring of technical standards, and Commission involvement in general monitoring and investigation of national compliance will thus require strengthening.

Concerning the specific details of the White Paper's emphasis upon the removal of technical barriers to trade, first came the actual technical standards and requirements covering goods and services. Already covered are items like toys, boilers and other pressure vessels, emissions from motor cars — which was strenuously fought by the EP to lower the permissible emission rates of poisonous gases — artificial additives and preservatives in food, the listing of nutritional information on processed foods and the labelling of alcohol content. Apart from this group, other aspects include the mutual recognition of higher education qualifications for most professions and the creation of the COMETT programme to facilitate academic-industrial co-operation in the field of information technologies (barriers to the free movement of persons). The Cecchini Report highlighted another area, that of public procurement or purchasing; that is, the tenders and contracts offered by central and local governments and their agencies in the EC which Cecchini argued was a lucrative yet highly protected sector of EC trade, 'in 1986 total purchasing controlled by the public sector . . . amounts to 15% of the Community's gross domestic product' and although a large proportion of this could not necessarily be liberalized, Cecchini argued that there was still a considerable proportion of public purchasing which should be subject to greater competition (Cecchini 1988, p. 16), which if forthcoming could lead to

- greater efficiency — public agencies purchasing from the cheapest tenderer which may not necessarily be a domestic firm;
- reduced prices — as a result of open competition for lucrative contracts;
- a long-term benefit from the rationalization of such industries (ibid., pp. 17–18).

The White Paper recommended in the first instance the liberalization of closed markets such as energy supply, telecommunications, water supply and services, and transport. The fact that deregulation of these types of public contracts has been carried out according to domestic political goals, particularly in the UK, emphasizes the importance of other EC legislation to ensure the fair treatment of advertising contracts and to provide businesses with review procedures if they feel that their tender has not been properly considered. However, highly sensitive although equally lucrative areas of public purchasing, notably defence procurement, have yet to be placed on the single market agenda, despite intra-European forums for wider defence collaboration such as the WEU and the EC's European Economic Interest Grouping (EEIG) mechanism.

Another fundamental plank within the technical barriers legislation concerns the provision of services. For banking and other financial services, the 1992 programme has resulted in a wider and freer environment. Banking Directives have allowed banks free operation and establishment throughout the EC and generally speaking, insurance companies, building societies and credit institutions have found themselves covered by legislation enabling them the free movement and provision of their services — a fact well publicized in the UK press for some time, given the strength and status of the City of London. The Commission has also forwarded draft proposals to tighten up rules on insider trading and the publication of mergers/take-overs.

It is this specific area of a free market in financial services with the corollary of the free movement of capital through the abolition of exchange controls which has acted as a catalyst, both for economic and monetary union — in that national central banks can no longer effectively control nor guarantee the stability of domestic monetary policy in a completely free market — and for the progressive tightening of budgetary expenditure, in order to help correct any regional imbalances as wealth flows to the richer and stronger areas within the free financial market (Pinder 1989, p. 105; Grahl and Teague 1990, Chapter 3). The White Paper, moreover, highlighted the provision of banking and financial services within a wider framework of impediments to a single market in services; the importance of this desire to create a common market in services cannot be overstated, given the present economic position of the service sector in Western economies. So the elucidation over time of common rules and the 'new approach' of mutual recognition to cover such services as advertising, information and computer services, satellite broadcasting and transport will be an important element of the 1992 strategy to stimulate growth and investment, whilst ensuring fair and open competition within the Community.

One final element of the White Paper's proposals on technical barriers concerns national legal and administrative obstacles to the operation of businesses, such as differences in company law, taxation and accounting procedures. One of the more novel legislative frameworks relevant here is the European Economic Interest Grouping (EEIG). However, other White Paper proposals — including earlier proposals which had languished in Council for some time — regarding EC company law, are proving harder to adopt. The Commission has tended to emphasize the proposals for a European Company Statute and the Thirteenth Directive on take-over bids, rather than the draft Fifth Directive on company structure, due to its emphasis on worker participation in the running of industry and which has met vocal opposition particularly from the UK Government (on the social and industrial relations aspects of such legislation, see Chapter 6). Also, the White Paper's original intent to provide legislation for common fiscal policies toward businesses (taxation on companies, mergers and assets) has not progressed as speedily as it was hoped, and by late 1991, this legislation remained in Council.

The final notion of barriers to a single market concerns *fiscal* matters. As Palmer points out, 'the wide difference in indirect tax rates — fiscal frontiers — combined with the conseqential need to de-tax intra-Community trade when it is exported, and tax it when it is imported "in effect divide the Community into 12 self-contained fiscal compartments" ' (Palmer 1989, p. 34).

The primary thrust of legislation concerning fiscal barriers revolves around different national levels of indirect taxation (VAT) although excise duties concerning a range of goods are also involved. The inclusion of fiscal barriers as elements of the 1992 strategy was prompted by various criteria.

Firstly, as made clear in the above quote, there is the argument that if all, or at least most, of the physical and technical barriers to trade are removed, and if the various different levels of indirect taxation remain unreformed businesses and consumers will continue to be unnecessarily penalized by exporting and consuming goods in a high indirect-taxation state, and in any case, the genuine efficiency of distribution in an uncommon market — whilst considerable differentials in indirect taxes continue to exist — is impaired.

Secondly, that for the White Paper's legislative programme to be adopted is a large enough task given often divergent national interests, but that the conclusions drawn from acceptance of the White Paper is that the completion of a single market is itself dependent on wider factors such as closer co-operation over and convergence of national economic policy, and thus the ability of the single market to withstand inflationary pressures.

From this viewpoint, the White Paper's emphasis upon approximating rates of VAT amongst member states not only has immediate effects upon the mobility of goods and business confidence in intra-EC trade. It also can contribute an initial step towards bringing the previously artificial divide between the EMS and the expectations of the single market's completion to an end, in order to make explicit in policy terms the link between greater macroeconomic co-ordination and existing expectations regarding the benefits of the single market (microeconomic considerations).

Put simply, the precise proposals to deal with differing national rates of VAT do not involve harmonization necessarily, but aim at the approximation of those rates — the Commission proposed that VAT could fall into two broad bands, one of 14–20 per cent and the other of 4–9 per cent, with member states being free to determine the exact point within each of those bands for the application of VAT to their luxury and essential items.

However, one only has to examine the annual reports from the Commission concerning the White Paper's implementation to realize that many of these approximating measures have been stalled in Council for some time. Constant British objections to approximation concern not only the political rhetoric over taxation and sovereignty, but also the intended application of the lower rate

(4–9 per cent) to presently zero-rated items such as books, domestic energy consumption and foodstuffs. Equally, other members — particularly the Irish — are concerned with the probable fall in revenue gained from VAT collection, as a result of approximating their currently high levels of indirect taxation, and other members — such as France and Italy — will face fundamental restructuring of their taxation systems if approximation were to be achieved.

Not surprisingly, then, the White Paper's fiscal approximation legislation is not subject to the 'new approach' but to unanimous voting in Council and as the EC moves quickly to Stage II of EMU, such issues as approximation of VAT become even more pressing — 1991 was the date set by Council to decide upon a rate band for normal or standard VAT rates, as well as the application of the reduced band to goods and services. Although there is a considerable level of academic agreement upon the desirability of VAT approximation, it has been pointed out that political considerations may well outweigh economic ones. As Pelkmans and Winters illustrate, 'interim solutions, derogations and temporary exceptions would lead to second best measures. It seems advisable, however, to proceed on the principle that the best (economically) may be the enemy of the good (politically)' (Pelkmans and Winters 1988, p. 98).

The previous section has attempted to outline the major elements contained within the White Paper: measures, which both collectively and conceptually, do mark an important milestone in EC integration. Thus it is appropriate to conclude this chapter by reviewing the implications of the 1992 programme.

The EC after 1992

It is true that in relation to the question of extending EC membership to East and Central Europe 'in the new mood of urgency, the very danger of enlargement, that it weakens the ability to make decisions, has also had the effect of reinforcing rules for taking them' (Duchene 1990, p. 19). Indeed events outside the EC such as the Gulf crisis, the changes in the Republic of South Africa, the Yugoslavian crisis and the failed Soviet coup add to Duchene's appreciation of events in Eastern Europe.

The above means that a 'sense of urgency' has produced a paradox in that existing institutional and political procedures within the EC are not yet strong enough to deal with outside events and yet they are sufficiently capable of embarking upon radical reform. This to a certain extent encapsulates the nature of EC integration in that the EC has often reacted to external events with a sense of crisis and thus brought about change from within. Although undue exaggerations of the global importance of 1992 should be avoided, equally the perceptions of this programme by third countries has been an important factor.

Internally, the White Paper can be interpreted according to its explicit or economic, and implicit or political, objectives. It is hoped that the previous section clarified that the Paper was aimed in the first instance at legislative measures to correct or invigorate the Rome Treaty's creation of a customs union and common market. So, these economic objectives were concerned with removing or severely constraining the variety of 'barriers' to a truly single market. The less obvious and more political objectives were concerned with the effects of completing the internal market — notably via economic and social cohesion — upon the institutional stature and effectiveness of the EC.

These are SEA treatment of majority voting, the co-operation procedure with the EP, the relationship between new policy competencies (the EC-environmental policy particularly) and the future ability of the EC to manage and co-ordinate its external political identity as a result of greater economic presence in world affairs.

In a general sense one can view the development of policy and the response of political and economic actors in an 'internal' context. As a result of the direct economic implications of the White Paper, there has been considerable restructuring and rationalization within European industry — with a flurry of mergers and take-overs in various sectors, and the correspondingly more visible intervention of EC competition policy, for example in relation to the Commission's decision to block the proposed take-over of Canada's De Havilland by the Franco-Italian bid of ATR in late 1991 — as well as industrial co-operation between EC and non-EC firms. Governmental intervention in the economic sphere has increasingly become measured against White Paper aims.

The mobilization of the private sector and the growth of lobby groups, as well as the strength of the UNICE and ETUC, has occurred directly as a result of enhanced business strategies for '1992', as well as from the increased dialogue between the 'social partners' via the Val Duchesse or social policy framework. Equally, the attainment and non-attainment of White Paper legislation has prompted in part a political response which has sought to strengthen and extend the nature of the integration process — and this is precisely the reason underpinning the impetus given to the EC (both through the efforts of Jacques Delors and the national Presidencies of the Council) to develop support for the extension of EC competency initially over social and regional policies, but latterly through the concepts of EMU and political Union.

Irrespective of whether one adopts a pro-integration ('federalist' or 'supra-nationalist') or a status quo perspective ('intergovernmentalist' or 'confederalist'), the fact remains that both these competing views recognize the impact of the White Paper and the reinforcing effect of the SEA upon the integration process.

Externally, the immediate impact of the White Paper gave rise to fears of a protectionist, introverted 'Fortress Europe' in an economic sense. Politically, however, the perceptions of the EC post-1992 together with the rapid changes in the European security framework, have culminated in enlargement pressure upon the Community. The Treaty on European Union signed at Maastricht in February 1992 has demonstrated the desire of the existing EC members to 'deepen' the integration process prior to 'widening' it — this prospect looks increasingly likely by 1996.

However, the mood of optimism and liberation still surrounding the EC's relationship with fellow European states does not necessarily extend to other states — persistent divergences of economic and political interests have characterized the EC's external economic relations, especially with the USA and Japan, but recently within the GATT's Uruguay Round there have been notable differences of opinion between the EC and Southern exporting states.

The EC's emphasis, since the White Paper, concerning GATT rules on reciprocity has come under attack from third countries who rightly point out that whilst the EC has chosen to remove all internal barriers to trade and thus allow greater market penetration by non-EC business, by the same token such reciprocity cannot necessarily be extended to EC companies wishing for similar liberalization abroad. However, it is clear that the EC does not pursue reciprocity to the letter, as the EFTA states have discovered, since the EC will not permit complete economic freedom to trade as de facto members without a minimal political commitment to decision-making responsibility, as the 1991 European Economic Area (EEA) agreement has demonstrated.

Again, while the Commission has sought to remove some national restrictions on non-EC imports — such as the national import quotas on Japanese cars, under Article 115 EEC — in order to liberalize the EC's external commercial policy, there remain problem areas for the EC's trading partners. After all, one of the primary aims of the 1992 programme was to improve European competitiveness in world markets; this has been seen by some as possibly resulting in the displacement of non-EC goods by the new and improved availability and quality of domestically produced goods, for example, 'several well-known European industrialists . . . who believe that they can use the Single Market to keep others out and have their own protected playground' (Dahrendorf et al. 1989, p. 4).

Whilst this may be a legitimate fear of non-EC exporters, there are a number of other problems they may face:

- As to whether national barriers will be replaced by Community barriers, the record is mixed. Despite the August 1991 EC-Japan agreement to limit Japanese car imports which removes the existing national import quotas, there are still other sectors facing restrictions, such as textiles, clothing and agriculture.
- Some technical barriers, whilst removed from national control, are being set at a European level and particularly the LDCs have feared the introduction of stricter standards, such as health, safety and environmental which they fear may discriminate against their products.

• Changes in fiscal policies (particularly excise duties) may benefit some non-EC producers and disadvantage others: 'increases in the value of exports of tropical beverages are estimated to be more than $650 million, of which about $200 million are from ACP countries, as a result of higher import demand and prices' (Koekkoek *et al.* 1990, p. 119). Hence EC-ACP relations within the Lome Conventions may become strained as some ACP members may benefit, as the above quote suggests, from the revised fiscal regulations.

In general though, there is a point of view which argues that whatever the outcome of the 1992 programme — regardless of whether it is actually completed on time — the extent to which Europe will become an economic 'fortress' is dependent upon other actors in world politics. Some actors are strong, some are weak, and some have inverse weight in world affairs comparative to others. From that viewpoint, it may be suggested that, at the very least, the EC is unlikely to become any more protectionist than at present given the realities of economic interdependence; that its interactions with other equally protectionist states despite rhetoric to the contrary will again be a function of compromise and bargaining; and that the weaker actors will continue to seek leverage in specific areas of interest.

All that can be predicted, with a modicum of certainty, is that the White Paper and the eventual completion of the single market, having emphasized the role of *supranational* policy formation thus restricts, both politically and financially, the ability of the EC to intervene for the protection of one particular sector — given that under free market conditions both the latitude for intervention and the competing demands upon the EC framework will be heightened — and thus the traditional role of some European policies of aiming to please all national interests may well be unsustainable.

References and further reading

Bieber, R. *et al.* (eds), 1988, *1992: One European market? A critical analysis of the Commission's internal market strategy*, Nomos, Baden-Baden.
Cecchini, P. 1988, *The European challenge; 1992 the benefits of a single market*, Gower/Commission of the EC, Aldershot.
Commission of the EC, 1990, *Fifth report to the Council and the EP on the implementation of the White Paper*, COM (90) 90 final.
Dahrendorf, R. *et al.*, 1989, *Whose Europe? Competing visions for 1992*, Institute for Economic Affairs, London.
Duchene, F., 1990 'Less or more than Europe? European integration in retrospect', in Crouch, C. and Marquand, D. (eds), 1990, *The politics of 1992*, Basil Blackwell/Political Quarterly, Oxford.

El-Agraa, A.M. (ed.), 1990, *The economics of the European Community* (3rd ed.), Philip Allan, London.

Featherstone, K., 1990, *European internal market policy*, Routledge, London.

Freestone, D.A.C. and Davidson, J.S., 1988, *The Institutional Framework of the EC*, Croom Helm, Beckenham.

Grahl, J. and Teague, P., 1990, *1992 — the big market*, Lawrence and Wishart, London.

Harrop, J., 1989, *The political economy of integration in the European Community*, Edward Elgar, Aldershot.

Koekkoek, A. *et al.*, 1990, 'Europe 1992 and the developing countries, *Journal of Common Market Studies*, Special Issue, 24 (2).

Palmer, J., 1989, *1992 and beyond*, Commission of the EC, Brussels.

Pelkmans, J. and Winters, A., 1988, *Europe's domestic market*, Routledge/RIIA, Chatham House Papers 43, London.

Pinder, J., 1989, 'The single market: a step toward European Union', in Lodge, J. (ed.), *The European Community and the challenge of the future*, Pinter, London.

Urwin, D.W., 1991, *The Community of Europe: a history of European Integration since 1945*, Longman, London.

von der Groeben, H., 1985, *The European Community, the formative years: the struggle to establish the Common Market and the Political Union 1958–66*, Commission of the EC, European Perspectives series, Brussels.

Wistrich, E., 1991, *After 1992: the United States of Europe* (rev. ed.), Routledge, London.

Woolcock, S., Hodges, M. and Schrieber, K., 1991, *Britain, Germany and 1992: the limits of deregulation*, Pinter/RIIA, London.

4
The Common Agricultural Policy and the EC budget

The Common Agricultural Policy (CAP)

Policy analysis of the CAP can be extremely complicated at a *technical* level, and can also suffer from a variety of levels of analysis. The CAP is unique and continues to occupy a pivotal role in European integration not merely as a result of its scope, content and direction as an agricultural policy, but as a 'barometer' of national expectations and interests regarding the process of integration, and as a political issue area defining the EC's external identity and relations at the global level.

The CAP has been in existence since the early 1960s, and is a compromise or aggregate policy reflecting the differing national practices and problems of the founding Six; for example, some of the original problems faced included the comparatively poor earnings from agriculture, occasional and persistent surpluses, differing national support policies for the agricultural sector, and the role of agricultural exports in national terms of trade and balance of payments.

If there were significant differences between the founding EC states in these terms, how did the CAP overcome these problems? What were the aims of and expectations underlying the operation of a common policy, and how were opposing interests thus reconciled?

First of all, let us consider a summary of the basic principles of the CAP, as laid down in the 1957 Treaty of Rome;

- that the CAP should encourage increased productivity via the use of technological progress and efficient human capital;
- that the CAP should promote a fair standard of living for those employed in the agricultural sector;
- that the CAP should act as a stabilizing influence upon markets;

- that under the CAP availability and security of supplies should be promoted;
- that the CAP should work to ensure that reasonable prices prevailed (Article 39).

The CAP's principles have been translated into three pillars of legislative activity: *market unity*, *Community preference* and *financial solidarity*. These 'pillars' or cornerstones of the CAP, originally developed in the early 1960s during the Council 'marathons' to establish common prices, were intended to give substance to the aims of the supranational agriculture policy.

In addition to the explicit aims of Article 39, the *implicit* expectations and government strategies concerning the integration process should be remembered:

- that a *common* (i.e. supranational) policy on agriculture would provide a firm basis for further integration thereby not only developing the Common Market but also providing a stepping stone to further political integration;
- that an overtly federalist policy could demonstrate to member states that the importance of increased production, self-sufficiency, and exportability could be managed effectively at a supranational level, thus releasing national governments and elites to pursue other political and economic goals;
- from the viewpont of the founding states, that the CAP could serve to facilitate a range of domestic political and economic tactics — such as France's desire to expand her agricultural exports in the Federal Republic's direction in return for FRG industrial goods, and other members' desires to maintain high prices for their domestic producers, as in Belgium, Italy and the FRG.

Bearing in mind these explicit and implicit interests in creating a CAP, how were these pillars subsequently developed through the European Agricultural Guidance and Guarantee Fund (EAGGF)?

The EAGGF spans two financial objectives: firstly, the Guidance section, which is concerned with structural improvement — such as upgrading the marketing and processing facilities for agricultural produce; improving farm buildings; providing equipment and aiding the application of technology for farmers; and developing social structures to aid those employed in the agricultural sector such as pensions and illness benefits. The Guidance section of the EAGGF is expected to operate in tandem with national governments in the area of structural reform.

Secondly, the EAGGF's Guarantee section is that which deals with the various price and market supports, and which has over the years provided the focus for both criticism of the CAP, and its rigorous defence by organized groups and governments. As it is a central aspect of the CAP, it is important to assess in detail the application of the Guarantee funds, the problems that have been incurred, and the resulting calls for reform.

The pillars of market unity and Community preference have been directly expressed through the Guarantee section — theoretically, so has the pillar of financial solidarity, although in practice, common financing has not been achieved. Market unity is expressed in terms of a minimum and maximum level of internal price support, via target prices, intervention prices, threshold prices and deficiency payments for some products (see Fennell 1979; OECD 1987, pp. 65–92).

Community preference takes the form of variable levies and customs duties imposed on imported agricultural produce, part of the wider Common External Tariff (CET), and this pillar also extends to the granting of export refunds or subsidies for EC producers wishing to export agricultural produce.

The final pillar, financial solidarity, was expected to evolve into a system of common financing for the CAP; it is this pillar of the CAP which was intended to dovetail with the wider EC budget, as the intention here was to construct a system of resource and national budgetary transfers in order that the EC could have control over its nominal 'own resources'. In other words, it was intended that the EC institutions themselves would be in receipt of monies gathered from member states and the CET, and hence would have some degree of financial autonomy. Discussion of how and why truly common financing in the EC has been so difficult to achieve will be covered in the next section of this chapter.

The CAP since 1957

Some principles of the CAP have certainly been achieved — 'increased productivity', 'stabilizing influence on markets', and 'security of supplies' have been particularly well served over the years. However, of the remaining principles, some require examination.

The principle that the CAP should work to ensure that 'reasonable prices' prevail is a flexible and subjective concept open to some interpretation; for political reasons, the CAP has evolved in favour of high prices, the stabilization of these prices relative to both the particular product and to intra-EC agricultural trade, and the almost total reliance upon price-setting as the determinant of market conditions. The support of consistently high prices shows that it is a function of obvious domestic political criteria, as well as the supranational intent to promote a uniform regime and harness the support of national lobbies and groups in favour of the maintenance of such a regime.

From the outset, there was general consensus that because Europe in the post-war period required large and stable food supplies, and because the economies of the Six generally reflected small farming holdings with considerably lower wages than in other economic sectors of activity, the CAP was thus set up to maintain the belief that higher prices would directly increase farmers' incomes. This represented a different view from the British who in the 1947 Agriculture Act maintained a free market for agricultural goods but supplemented farmers' incomes with deficiency payments, rather than encourage the artificial manipulation of market conditions.

The problem with maintaining these high prices soon became apparent to some observers — such as Commissioner Mansholt, who by 1968 was advocating a more prudent price policy and improved structural reforms to avoid problems of surpluses and rising expenditure — although it was not until the late 1970s and early 1980s that the excesses of the CAP became clear. Because support prices — intervention, target and threshold — were maintained at a high level, farmers were encouraged to improve their incomes via increasing production and productivity, rationalizing their use of land, by using chemicals and fertilizers, by improving their farm machinery and so on.

As this price policy was perceived by producers as offering the sole method of increasing their incomes and relative economic position, overproduction and surpluses in key products soon became the visible manifestation of the CAP's shortcomings; particularly for dairy products and cereals, although beef and sugar production was also in excess at times (Commission of the EC 1990).

Connected to this problem of price support and overproduction was the exponential growth of the EAGGF within the EC budget; during the 1970s and well in the 1980s the EC budget regularly devoted two-thirds of its total resources to funding the EAGGF, primarily the result of increased spending under the Guarantee section. The Guarantee section consumed these financial resources as a result of increased intervention buying, the storage of the surpluses, and the disposal of the surpluses in world markets through the granting of export refunds.

Hence one can see that the high price support regime was particularly flawed when the EC became a net exporter of key products, although overall it remains the largest food importer in the world.

Over the years problems have been created by the pillars of market unity and common prices evolving to the extent where high prices, high levels of production and increasing self-sufficiency led to the position of agricultural exports being regarded as useful, if not primary, trade and export sectors.

During the late 1960s and early 1970s when the post-war Bretton Woods system of fixed exchange rates began to collapse, the Six were keen to adopt a method whereby agriculture could be cushioned from any wild swings in the value of official currencies.

The common prices which had been set in the early 1960s were denominated in terms of the European Unit of Account (UA) which was fixed to the value of the US dollar. However, the collapse of the international monetary system, especially the effects of the French franc's devaluation and the Deutschmark's revaluation in 1969, led to the EC states reinforcing this system of green currencies with Monetary Compensatory Amounts (MCAs). MCAs were intended to iron out the difference between the pre-1969 and the post-1969 agricultural prices; for the FRG, MCAs acted as a positive subsidy for German agricultural exports — because the FRG's green currency had not been revalued to correspond with the higher value of the mark — and for France, MCAs acted as a negative levy on agricultural imports. Therefore, MCAs acted as short-term fiscal tools to preserve the uniformity of CAP prices, and to allow breathing-space for agriculture if national currencies suffered from large fluctuations in value.

MCAs were, however, acknowledged as expensive to maintain and in the long term detrimental to the functioning of the national economies and competitiveness. Politically they were perceived as essential, and the Franco-German dispute over MCAs prior to the introduction of the EMS in 1979 eventually led to a compromise: any new MCAs were to be eliminated within two years of the introduction of the EMS, and by 1986 the EC had agreed automatically to remove the use of MCAs by 31 December 1992.

Finally, another trickle-down effect of the CAP which is as important as the internal issues, is that the system of high guaranteed support prices have external repercussions. Community preference has in practice ensured that Community agricultural produce has absolute priority for sale within the EC, carried out through application of the CET and the CAP's variable levies, as well as through export refunds (subsidies). On the whole, these tools act to provide either a disincentive for imports of products for which the Community has surplus, or if the EC is in short supply of particular goods or cannot produce a substitute then the CET and CAP mechanisms act to raise the entry price of these goods. High internal minimum prices thus require a commensurate level of protection when EC producers export — the OECD calculated that in the period 1979–81, beef and cereals prices were protected by as much as 70 per cent, whilst for dairy products (especially butter) protection was as high as 267 per cent and for skimmed milk powder the figure was around 247 per cent (OECD 1987, p. 86).

Although the EC is one of the world's largest agricultural importers — of products which cannot be readily produced or substituted in the EC such as tea, coffee, vegetable oils, and animal feedstuffs — it has come to dominate world trade as an agricultural exporter, particularly regarding cereals, sugar and dairy products, and as a result the disperson of funds within the Guarantee section has tended to divide the bulk of EAGGF funds between export refunds and intervention buying of surplus production.

Not only has this state of affairs create large deficits for the EC budget, with expenditure outstripping revenue, but the ability of the EC to use its export refunds to sell EC produce at lower prices in world markets (dumping) led to serious and divergent international political and economic strains. Apart from the various 'trade wars' with the USA, this situation was graphically illustrated in the hostile collapse of the GATT's Uruguay Round in Brussels in December 1990.

So, the international implications of the CAP and the EC's external identity defined in terms of a protectionist 'fortress' are a key factor in the Commission's persistent attempts during 1991 to advance reform of the CAP. The reality of the CAP's development has given rise to several problems:

- the system of price and market support being maintained at an artificially high level, encouraging farmers to sustain their incomes by ever-increasing production levels;
- the associated problem of surplus production and the disposal of these surpluses which endanger patterns and expectations of international trade;
- the problem of reconciling such 'compulsory expenditure' with other competing claims in the integration process, illustrated by the frequent clashes between the Council of Ministers and the EP over maximum levels of 'non-compulsory expenditure' during the 1980s.

Reform of the CAP

First of all, it is important to recognize that the essential principles and pillars of the CAP have not been questioned; market unity, Community preference and financial solidarity remain the fundamentals of the CAP.

Reform has instead been directed at the ways in which political and commercial interests have shaped the evolution of the CAP: it has thus been directed at the *price and market support mechanisms* of the Guarantee section. In general, the EC has sought to remove and constrain the production of surplus produce, which would also relieve the burden of the CAP upon the EC budget. It was felt initially that the price policy should be reformed, rather than introduce outright penalties to farmers for overproduction although quotas were used to limit milk production by the mid-1970s. Subsequent co-responsibility levies for EC cereals producers were intended to limit the total output of cereal production, and not necessarily penalize individual farmers.

Reform of the price and market regimes became a formal EC objective by 1985. Price support reductions and procedures for intervention buying were tightened, although these reforms were lessened in their impact, due to the serious budgetary crisis of the mid to late 1980s, where EC export subsidies were the primary cause of a 40 per cent increase in Guarantee expenditure.

Price support, then, was reduced for several successive years during the 1980s, although in real terms prices received by the individual farmer were even lower, due to non-CAP factors of recession and high inflation rates. The level of reduction in the CAP price support system was not sufficient to bring the problem of surpluses under control, so further reforms during the 1980s have included the 'budget stabilizers' agreed at the 1988 Brussels summit.

Maximum guaranteed quantities (MGQs) have been set for individual products, so if total production exceeds the MGQ set by Council, price support and intervention is automatically reduced. Other reforms aimed at involving the producer directly include the extension of co-responsibility levies where producers pay a levy to aid the disposal or storage of surplus products — although these have not been particularly effective since high levies have been resisted by Council — and since the early 1980s guarantee thresholds for products in which the EC was already self-sufficient or likely to become so were set, so that when production exceeded the threshold an automatic reduction in market support prices ensued.

These reforms are rather bureaucratic and long-winded attempts to mimic free market conditions; any overproduction swamping the market for a product causes a drop in prices and therefore returns, for the producer. However, as cereal production has continued to rise, the efficacy of guarantee thresholds without accompanying large price reductions should be questioned (for a good overview of these reforms, see Commission of the EC 1990).

Guaranteed support has been curtailed in recent years; the 1988 budgetary reforms have resulted in the EC seeking greater political and financial discipline over the workings of the CAP, which perhaps for too long has been geared toward national and competing interests, and yet which has signally failed to provide an acceptable standard of living for all those employed in the sector. The most recent reforms directed at the CAPs Guarantee funds were put forward in late 1990 as the GATT Uruguay Round was hoping for completion.

The Commission sought overall cuts in price support of 30 per cent. By mid-1991 Commissioner MacSharry proposed cuts of 35 per cent in price support for cereal production, 15 per cent cuts in milk and beef price support, the setting of lower production quotas, and full compensation for smaller farmers although only 15 per cent compensation was suggested for set-aside schemes for larger farmers. Despite the seemingly overwhelming pressures for reform of the Guarantee mechanisms — notably from external agricultural producers within the GATT forum, and from wide-ranging allocation of budgetary resources for new aid packages — there seemed little prospect for national acceptance of these proposals, with many national agriculture ministers hostile to reform.

By July 1991 the Commission had still not reached agreement with Council, because of the repercussions of the proposed reforms, including the future of income support and the apparent Commission desire to maintain smaller units. However, the negotiating positions of some member states previously opposed to the MacSharry reforms — such as Germany — appear to be softening, given the political and tactical considerations of EC-East European relations. The public row between France and Poland over allegedly restrictive entry requirements for Polish beef demonstrates the dilemma for the CAP given the imminent pressures of EC enlargement. In this context it may well be that EC member states must accept that the price of tying these fledgling partners to the integration process is a radical overhaul of the established mechanisms and budgetary costs of the CAP.

Originally, the Guidance section was designed to play an important role within the common policy. The structural impact of a common market for agricultural products would clearly entail a loss of competitiveness in some sectors or geographical areas. By having a supranational agricultural policy with firm structural implications, common objectives and financing, it was felt that national policies towards improving the structural position and strength of agriculture could be supplemented. Hence the Guidance section of the EAGGF was intended to provide funds for the CAP's structural aims; such as helping to increase agricultural productivity, to maintain the rural fabric of society, and to acknowledge the link between agriculture and the wider domestic economy. By the late 1970s the Guidance section was generally concerned with the realization of certain aims: the removal of regional disparities in the agricultural sector, assistance to both farmers and their farms and attempts to improve the marketing and processing of agricultural produce.

One point should be made clear — whereas the CAP's Guarantee section provides for total Community financing of the price and market support systems, the Guidance section instead operates in tandem, as far as funding is concerned, with national authorities. Hence any modernization of equipment, creation of marketing boards or producers associations, or legislation setting up training for agricultural workers, is not wholly funded or identified at the supranational level; structural policies are co-financed by the Guidance section and the EC member states — and depending upon the particular project in question, Guidance funding may exceed 50 per cent of the total cost of a project. This tends to occur more frequently in the less-developed regions of the EC.

However, as has become apparent in the preceding discussion, expenditure under the CAP has consistently risen — as production and the range of goods produced increased, the legal requirement for the EC to intervene to purchase surplus stocks, to store these surpluses and to aid EC exporters to sell produce overseas resulted in the familiar sight of Guarantee expenditure taking up the bulk of the EAGGF funds, and hence the expansion of EAGGF budgetary requirements within the wider budget.

This 'agri-monetary' dilemma is covered in the following section of this chapter, but it is important to note here because of its relationship to the total size of EAGGF funds — the Guidance section as a result, receiving on average 5 per cent of total EAGGF funds. Thus, it is clear that apart from any other factors, the EC's desire to implement effective structural reform of European agriculture is sharply constrained by inadequate funds.

By the mid-1980s the EC had faced successive budgetary crises, well-publicized political wrangles over national contributions to the EC budget, and equally well-publicized media images of groaning storage depots juxtaposed with Ethiopian famine victims — these and other factors, notably the supranational political intent to relaunch the integration process, led to a number of coalescing events — the 1985 White Paper on Completing the Single Internal Market, and the 1986 Single European Act giving greater political impetus to the need for reform.

This impetus gave rise to the Brussels summit of early 1988, where reform of the CAP in relation to the EC budget was negotiated. The new procedures resulting from the Brussels agreement were intended to tackle seemingly intractable and conflicting problems — persistent surpluses, the protection and advancement of agriculture in less-developed regions, and the conservation of the natural environment. The legislation concerning set-aside schemes, extensification, production conversion measures and early retirement of farmers is intended to bring about these aims. Another point to note here is that these activities stemming from the Brussels decisions are funded under the Guarantee section of the EAGGF, not the Guidance section which is the obvious focus for structural reform.

On the whole, EC structural policies for agricultural development have worked well for northern EC members — the high productivity, rationalization and efficiency of particularly British and Dutch farmers are good examples here — although accession in the early and mid-1980s of Greece, Spain and Portugal has led to the creation of distinct regional aid schemes, such as the Integrated Mediterranean Programmes (IMPs) and specific industrial development projects.

Hence the moves made at Brussels towards reducing the level of Guarantee expenditure and reinvigorating the wider concern for regional economic and social development, have been seen by many as long overdue and politically justifiable, although clearly much remains to be done in terms of strengthening agricultural development in poorly developed areas, whilst balancing the needs and interests of northern agriculture.

To sum up, although the development and operation of the CAP has given rise to fundamental issues both within and between member states as well as between member states and the EC's supranational institutions, and which have caused sporadic divergences of international opinion, the EC has attempted since the mid-1980s some semblance of reform within the CAP, and between the CAP and the budget.

No one, least of all the Commission, pretends that these reforms are adequate in themselves; given the difficulties of arriving at consensus both within and outside the Community, these reforms cannot be meaningfully considered as anything other than an initial modest step in the direction of reform, since 'both Community demand and supply remain to a large extent isolated from world market signals' (OECD 1991, p. 161).

This point is particularly true in relation to the Commission's projected view of the 1991–92 annual price review; the 1988 Brussels package included a general commitment to double the EC's Structural Funds by 1993, which would be funded by a decrease in resources allocated to the EAGGF's Guarantee section. However, the economic and budgetary outlook was not as positive in 1991 — the Commission has expressed its concern over 'persistent structural imbalances' on world markets and the effects of the world recession upon prices and thus surplus production: 'we have again entered an era of oversupply putting considerable pressure not only on the Community Budget but also on the markets . . . producer prices and farm incomes' (Commission of the EC, 1991, p. 5).

In this context, the Commission's emphasis since its Reflections paper — *The development and future of the CAP* (COM (91) 100 final) — leading to Commissioner MacSharry's attempts to cut producer prices on surplus-prone products, illustrates the extent to which both domestic and international political expectations have impinged upon the nature of the integration process, and therefore the extent to which the CAP, though facing a considerably large constituency calling for its overhaul, has so far remained immune to substantial and radical change.

The European Communities' budget

The subject of the EC's budget and the CAP are entwined because of the CAP's function as an expenditure item in the budget.

Moreover, the methods by which the EC has sought to restrain expenditure on the CAP, and the often seemingly intractable disputes not just over the CAP but over the wider question of extending the policy competency of the EC — and which thus requires a commensurate level of funding for new policies and commitments — illustrates the increasing dichotomy within the present EC. In other words, the political and economic momentum which has caused the EC to move more rapidly towards a truly single market and a political union has in the meantime highlighted the serious need for structural reform of traditional foci of integration, the financing of the EC being just one of these needs.

Thus it is necessary to understand how the budget is drawn up, the role of the EC institutions and member states, and the different 'pressure-points' during the budgetary process whereby often opposing interests can influence the final outcome. References to the budget here means the General Budget of the EEC and Euratom, as the ECSC budget is still legally separate.

As with other policies or commitments undertaken by the EC, the first stage in the process of setting the draft budget is controlled by the Commission, which puts forward a draft outlining its own estimates for the likely level of expenditure and revenue for the forthcoming budgetary year — which in the EC runs from January to December. Since the 1975 EEC Treaty revision where the EP was given greater powers to take part in and influence the budgetary process — the conciliation process — the draft budget is passed to the 'budgetary authority' comprising the Council of Ministers and the EP. By law, the draft must reach the Council before 1 September in the year preceding the beginning of the new financial year. The Council then becomes responsible for debating the draft within a fairly flexible timeframe, although on the whole the Council passes the draft to the EP for its discussion by October; the EP then may amend or reject elements, or the entire draft, within a 45-day period.

This marks the end of the 'first reading' stage: the draft budget is then returned to Council for the start of the 'second reading' stage. This is perhaps the single most important stage in the budget deliberations; partly because the deadline for adoption is not far away (December), and partly because the negotiating positions of the three institutions has become clearer — hence the second reading stage can be extremely contentious, given that they are attempting to reach consensus, invariably based on a conflict of interest, within a short timeframe. The Council thus has fifteen days to examine the EP's first reading amendments and proposals, as does the EP which subsequently debates Council's second reading position. If agreement can be reached, the signature of the President of the EP on the draft gives de facto recognition that the draft is now the official budget of the EC coming into force by the next January.

Revenue and expenditure issues within the budget

Budgetary revenue, as with expenditure, has not remained static in terms of its sources; the methods and processes by which the EC has gained receipts in order to fulfil its expenditure commitments have been adapted over time, primarily in response to the EEC Treaty obligation that the yearly budget of the EC must balance — that is, that the EC cannot run persistent deficits, and that commitments to compulsory expenditure must be met with a requisite ability to fund them — and partly in response to political criteria favouring the EC's control of more substantial 'own resources'.

So, where does the EC get its money from? Until the late 1960s the budget relied solely upon national contributions from the founding Six, based on relative wealth and domestic economic needs. However, it soon became apparent that monies collected from the application of the CET and the CAP's variable levies were of sufficient weight for them to be used as sources of revenue for the Community as a whole, and the fact that the ECSC controlled a direct source of revenue from levies on domestic coal and steel production, combined with other factors such as the increasing instability of world financial markets and the prospect of further enlargement, led the Community to prefer a somewhat more autonomous form of financing its budget.

So by 1970 the notion of EC 'own resources' was established. This replaced the earlier national contributions system and comprised three sources of revenue-customs: duties, variable levies on agricultural imports, and a common proportion of national VAT receipts — equivalent to 1 per cent of total EC VAT collection and not 1 per cent of nationally collected VAT.

This system itself survived until the 1984 Fontainebleau Council when the issue of budgetary revenue and expenditure was of paramount importance to the UK's Thatcher government. The introduction of a certain proportion of VAT collected by national authorities and given over to the EC was an attempt to override the earlier system of differentiation between national wealth and economic growth as expressed through GNP. Instead a more harmonized system was preferred in that all EC states would pay the common proportion of nationally-collected VAT irrespective of their wealth or consumption patterns. In that sense, the system was seen as equitable — the same rules for all club members — but in practice and especially over time, it became clear that the VAT 'own resource' was unfairly felt by poorer import-dependent members. This entire issue dominated the Thatcher Government's European agenda, and as Paul Taylor points out, 'determined the pace of integration' until the mid-1980s (Taylor 1989, p. 3).

Moreover, as the years progressed the original 1 per cent VAT ceiling was outstripped by the exponential growth of EC expenditure (the result of increased Guarantee support under the EAGGF) and so political dissatisfaction voiced by one particular member state acting in tandem with persistent financial difficulties during the early 1980s brought crisis-like pressure upon the EC seriously to upgrade its ability to provide adequate revenue for its activities.

The eventual outcome was the Fontainebleau Council agreement of June 1984 to increase the EC's own resources by raising the VAT ceiling to 1.4 per cent by 1986. The British rebate issue was also finally settled, the UK receiving a 66 per cent refund per year from 1985. However, as was noted at the time, 'all that the agreement will achieve . . . will be a limited increase in revenues of about 25%, which will barely suffice over the years between now and 1987 to meet the immediate requirements of UK refunds, enlargement, and the needs of the CAP' (Denton 1984, p. 139).

In the event, the VAT increase was insufficient: further European Councils took emergency decisions to finance the deficits occurring by the mid-1980s, and the Fontainebleau ceiling of 1.4 per cent was patently inadequate, even to allow the EC budget to keep pace with expenditure — as Shackleton suggests, 'the compensation scheme agreed at Fontainebleau to remedy the British problem had the perverse effect of reducing the effective VAT call-up rate ceiling after 1986 from 1.4% to 1.25%' (Shackleton 1990, p. 11).

After 'muddling through' for some time, and after having consulted member states as to the best possible methods of reforming sources of budget revenue, the Community at the Brussels Council of February 1988 undertook perhaps one of the most fundamental steps on the road to reform in the history of the EC:

(1) Since 1984 the Commission had consistently suggested that the budget be more directly linked to the economic fortunes of the Community as a

whole, a radical departure from the 'intergovernmental' style of financing the EC. Although this had raised the spectre of fully autonomous supranational funding — not completely acceptable even to pro-integrationist member states — the eventual agreement took the somewhat diluted form of increasing total budget resources; in other words, this decision laid down that the overall ceiling on the EC's own resources (revenue or payments) should be set at 1.2 per cent of total EC GNP — EC of the 12 — and that in terms of expenditure (commitments) a ceiling of 1.3 per cent of total EC GNP should be created.

The importance of this decision was recognized 'at a time of significant efforts to limit national budgets, it represented a commitment to allow the Community budget to expand over 5 years by as much as 14% in payments and 16.5% in commitments' (Shackleton 1990, p. 14).

(2) In addition to increasing the volume of available revenue, the Brussels Council agreed to create a 'fourth resource', given the diminishing returns offered by the earlier three own resources. The 'fourth resource' was based on national GNP: although broadly perceived as a national contribution, the new budgetary resource does take account of differential economic wealth and growth between member states, and thus derives from the differences between the GNP and VAT base of each EC member state.

(3) Another element of the Brussels package intended to bring greater discipline to the EC's expenditure commitments, was effectively a method of 'capping' agricultural spending. The Council agreed to a 'guideline' which placed a ceiling on market support funds, to be effective in the first instance for a five-year period (until 1992). The 'guideline' was fixed at 27,500m ECU for 1988, and for subsequent years was not allowed to rise beyond 74 per cent of the annual growth in EC GNP. As a political gesture intended to underline the importance of this 'capping', the Commission set up an 'Early Warning System' whereby monthly reports on Guarantee spending (related to previous spending levels) were presented to both Council and Parliament. In this context the agricultural 'stabilizers' mentioned in the previous section then come into play, and if expenditure begins to outrun its ceiling, automatic cuts in support prices follow.

(4) Finally, the Brussels Council agreed to double expenditure for the EC's Structural Funds (CAP's Guidance section, the European Social Fund and the European Regional Development Fund) between 1988 and 1993.

In other words, the Community had not only embarked on an upgrading of total resources available to the budget, the introduction of a new resource to realize an increase in total finances available and procedures whereby automatic and fully guaranteed funding would not entirely accompany the EC's traditional compulsory spending commitments, but political recognition had been won on where to direct the EC's new and improved budgetary status. The Commission's stress upon the need to revitalize the economic and social cohesion of the Community in the face of expected benefits flowing from the operation of the SEM seemed to have been finally accepted.

Another widely acknowledged significance of this decision concerned the relationship of the EP both to other EC institutions and to member states; the EP having struggled during the 1980s to limit CAP expenditure in order to free resources for other newer policies.

However, although the EP had fought long and hard with Council over increasing non-compulsory expenditure according to the Commission's 'maximum rate' for any such increase, the Brussels Council did agree to expand the volume of monies allocated to the Structural Funds and, despite the legal position over 'maximum rate' rules being countermanded by the June 1988 Inter-Institutional Agreement ratifying the Council decisions, the EP continues to face a battle of sorts in the immediate period, as the Brussels Council financial perspective only covers the years 1988–92.

However, although the Commission has stressed the utility of these reforms and most observers have recognized their contribution to the beginnings of reform, the picture is not wholly positive; the EC's Court of Auditors on examination of the 1989 budget declared that '. . . of the measures adopted to impose discipline on agricultural expenditure, those it examined have not, as yet, attained the desired level of effectiveness. The apparent control of agricultural expenditure is above all the result of a favourable situation on world markets' (Court of Auditors 1990, p. 5). This comment reflects the reality not only of present recessionary trends but the problem of how to achieve short-term benefits from the overhaul of long-established practices and political choices.

Although budget spending was reasonably contained during 1989 and 1990, the 1991 budget has faced considerable upward pressure given not only the falling world prices for agricultural goods, but the effects of emergency aid packages to Eastern European states and the frontline Gulf states hit by the UN sanctions. In evidence to the House of Commons debate on the 1991 EC budget, Francis Maude suggested that the 1991 budget would be approximately 13 per cent larger in commitments than the 1990 budget, but would retain a 4bn ECU safety net before the ceiling was reached (Hansard 1990, pp. 200–28).

The future for the budget of the EC

The relaunching of the 'European idea', formalized in the White Paper on the SEM and in the Single European Act, has unleashed a number of aspirations and highlighted long-standing difficulties concerning the process of European integration — and, in this sense, speculation over the future structure and content of the EC's budget is no exception. The moves taken to institute EMU have, in this sense, provided the impetus for a wide-ranging discussion on the future direction and form of Community competency, the IGC negotiations over fiscal policy, economic convergence and a single European currency being one example.

Given that one of the White Paper's significant elements concerned the harmonization of national rates of VAT and the resulting political dissension between EC member states which led to a virtual 'freeze' of that proposal, a wider discussion of 'for what purpose should the budget exist' and 'how will the implications of EMU affect its composition and workings', is clearly overdue.

If, as Taylor argues, 'the budgetary discipline agreements were implicitly about the EC's future structure and boosted those who preferred an inter-governmental rather than a more supranational approach' (Taylor 1989, p. 20), then the immediate future of both the goals of the EC budget (expenditure commitments) and the institutional/political control of the budget is now far more intertwined with supranational concerns.

As regards future budgets, the most outstanding issue concerns the cohesion of the Community: although the implications of the 1992 programme — which strongly motivated the argument for doubling the Structural Funds in 1988 — are now more clearly visible, there still remain pressing grounds for strengthening the social and economic cohesion of the EC, not least through environmental programmes but also through urban renewal and employment retraining schemes.

The prospect of imminent progression to Stage II of EMU reinforces this argument even more, given that national fiscal and economic policies are expected to converge more closely, thereby removing some national autonomy in the protection of economic or geographical sectors.

Other future goals for EC budgetary affairs may be concerned with integrating the European Development Fund (EDF) which funds the EC-ACP commitments made under the Lome Conventions; and a more topical example regarding this issue of redistribution and development concerns the EC's financial aid relationship with East and Central European states.

World economic conditions in 1989/90 enabled the EC to distribute loans and emergency aid to these states, but it may not be as straightforward, in a budgetary context, in the near future, given the global recession and the increasing strains upon budget discipline. Indeed, the entire question of future accession to the EC — not just by the Eastern and Central Europeans, but by present EFTA members — poses an immediate dilemma for existing methods of funding the EC, as well as procedures for redistributing wealth.

As mentioned earlier, the General Budget of the EC was not designed to perform redistributive or welfare funtions in the way that national budgets do; the EC budget is more an 'accounting'-type of budget where revenue and expenditure are expected to balance, and as we have seen, whatever 'resource transfers' do take place are generally the result of Treaty commitments, which have over the years been subject to political pressure for reform, such as the creation of the ERDF in 1975, and the institutional wrangles over increases in non-compulsory expenditure (NCE) during the 1980s.

Hence discussion since the early 1970s had focused upon reform of the EC budget in terms of a more federal nature — 'fiscal federalism'. The MacDougall Report of 1977 recommended that the EC budget could be increased in volume, relative to other federal states, so that 2.5 per cent of EC GNP could be made available for redistribution and allocation, notably to strengthen existing national structural policies and to fund more EC-level programmes. If the overall size of the budget were to be increased to such proportions, most commentators are agreed on the necessity of progressive taxation or national contributions, in order that richer EC members contribute more of their wealth to the budget while poorer members contribute less.

In El-Agraa's hypothetical model, he outlines how progressive national income taxes could be applied in order to provide a more equitable revenue-driven budget — '. . . this type of taxation introduces a strong fiscal incentive to reduce disequilibria within the EC . . . the stronger countries take an interest in the growth of per capita income in the weaker member nations insofar as, if convergence ensues, their own burden of income taxation is reduced' (El-Agraa 1990, p. 302). In other words, one way for the rich to end their subsidy of the poor is to encourage the poor to become rich themselves. The question of how to finance the EC budget more equitably is of course linked with equally politically contentious issues of how to reform structurally the direction of EC spending in order to reduce economic disparities, which in turn raises the spectre of increasing supranational competency over economic fiscal and budgetary affairs.

Any reform of the budget thus raises fundamental questions over what 'sovereignity' really means to a nation state. Accordingly any federal reform, or otherwise, of the budget will be conducted through Treaty amendment; such moves will be forthcoming as the EC moves closer to EMU, and traditional reluctance from northern EC members to reform budgetary affairs may well change in the light of German trade deficits and Italy's move toward becoming a net contributor to the EC budget.

The so-called 'Delors II' package, announced by the Commission President in February 1992, marks the start of this phase in budgetary reform. The Commission, in attempting to revise the previous 1988 Delors package, suggested that the EC would require an increase in appropriations for payments of approximately 20bn ECU by 1997 — the bulk of this increase to finance the ECs cohesion programme (11bn ECU), with the remainder split between programmes designed to enhance industrial competitiveness, and 'external action' in the form of increased aid commitments to Eastern Europe and the CIS (Commission of the EC, 1992; p. 12). This increase in available appropriations would be raised by reforming the 'fourth resource'; by raising the maximum ceiling from 1.2 per cent to 1.37 per cent of EC GNP, the Commission hoped to increase the total size of the EC budget from £46bn to £62bn by 1997 (The *Guardian*, 11 February 1992).

This phase in budgetary reform will not be settled until late 1992, and has not faced an auspicious reception: with Germany and Britain hostile to such suggestions in the present recessionary period.

In relation to the institutional and political control of the budget, a number of interrelated points can be made. Because the 1988 Brussels Council (and the later Inter-Institutional Agreement) laid down clear budgetary ceilings for commitments (expenditure) and payments (revenue), and because the twin arms of the 'budgetary authority' agreed to respect both the ceilings and permissible rates of growth in itemized areas, it was felt at the time that political conflict between the EC institutions would be lessened.

However, this has not necessarily been the case — the way in which governments made distinctions within the old non-compulsory expenditure bracket (NCE), between privileged (traditional Structural Funds) and non-privileged expenditure (for example covering R&D and environmental programmes) clearly demonstrates the lack of consensus regarding the form of the budget.

Another institutional problem of control and accountability, often referred to in Court of Auditors Reports, is the particular issue of fraud and the subsequent effectiveness of Community institutions and their links with national authorities in order to reduce and eradicate the problem.

Levy points out that in its discharge to the Commission for the 1986 budget, the EP argued that since 1970 'the Council has still not granted the Commission the powers it requires . . . to obtain accurate information on the practices followed in the member states and to carry out on-the-spot checks . . .' (Levy 1990, p. 198). The problem of fraudulent activity and corruption in relation to the budget is a serious one — estimates range from 10–20 per cent of EAGGF spending — and not least in terms of the European public's perception of the Community.

So the Commission President, Jacques Delors, in highlighting the notion of a People's Europe, with rights, citizenship and democratic accountability, clearly recognizes the value of presenting the integration process with a 'human face'. Apart from any other sound criteria for extending EC institutional control and accountability over budgetary procedures, the issue of combating fraud is an important move in creating a Community widely acceptable to its citizens.

References and further reading

Commission of the EC, 1989, *Community public finance: the European Budget after the 1988 reform*, Commission of the EC, Brussels.

Commission of the EC, 1990, *The agricultural situation in the Community*, Commission of the EC, Brussels.

Commission of the EC, 1991, *The development and future of the CAP*, COM (91) 100 final.

Commission of the EC, 1992, Bulletin of the EC Supplement 1/92.

Court of Auditors of the EC, 1990, *Annual report of the Court of Auditors*, OJ C 313, 12/12/90.

Denton, G., 1984, 'Restructuring the EC Budget: implications of the Fontaine-bleau agreement', *Journal of Common Market Studies*, 23 (2), 119–40.

Duchene, F. *et al.*, 1985, *New limits on European agriculture: politics and the CAP*, Croom Helm, London.

El-Agraa, A.M. (ed.), 1990, *The economics of the EC* (3rd ed.), Philip Allan, London.

Fennell, R., 1979, *The CAP of the European Communities* , Granada, London.

Franklin, M., 1990, *Britain's future in Europe*, Pinter/RIIA, London.

George, S., 1990, *An awkward partner: Britain in the EC*, OUP, Oxford.

Green Europe, Restoring equilibrium on the agricultural markets, 3/90.

Green Europe, Agricultural prices 1991–92; Commission proposals, 1/91.

Levy, R., 1990, 'That obscure object of desire: budgetary control in the EC', *Public Administration*, 68 (2), 191–206.

Neville-Rolfe, E., 1984, *The politics of agriculture in the EC*, Policy Studies Institute, London.

OECD, 1991, *Agricultural policies, markets and trade*, OECD, Paris.

OECD, 1987, *National policies and agricultural trade: study on the EEC*, OECD, Paris.

Parliamentary Debates (Hansard), House of Commons Official Report, Sixth Series, Vol. 182, Session 1990–91, 4th December 1990, pp. 200–226.

Shackleton, M., 1990, *Financing the EC*, Pinter/RIIA, London.

Shackleton, M., 1989, 'The budget of the EC', in Lodge, J. (ed.), *The EC and the challenge of the future*, Pinter, London.

Taylor, P., 1989, 'The new dynamics of EC integration in the 1980's', in Lodge, J. (ed.), *The EC and the challenge of the future*, Pinter, London.

5

Economic and monetary union

First of all, it is important to define our terms and understand what is meant by the terms 'economic' and 'monetary' and 'union'. Precise definitions vary from one to another, but on the whole 'economic union' can be described as a completely unrestricted market between previously independent national markets; this would be governed by a set of rules and institutions — similar to those of national governments — but which are created and maintained at the supranational level. Hence these common rules cover all aspects of a single internal market — free movement of the factors of production, competition and behaviour rules for businesses, a common budgetary authority and resources and common rules on governmental intervention in economic matters.

Monetary union, again in a very general sense, can be seen as the reverse side of the economic union coin, where national currencies and exchange rates are permanently fixed — or where they may be replaced by a single currency — and where all monetary and financial movements or services are liberalized in order that there are no restrictions between them.

These very basic definitions obviously have political and institutional dimensions, which will be discussed in this chapter.

It is generally accepted that whilst the Treaty of Rome was specifically concerned with the creation of the common market, there was no corresponding clear definition of both the desirability of moving towards EMU or the aims and institutions necessary to sustain it — so the goal of EMU was not an immediate one for the EC in 1957.

The Treaty did, however, contain articles relating to the management of European macroeconomic policy: Articles 103–9 emphasized the desirability of co-ordination of national economic policies especially to avoid serious balance of payments deficits. By the 1960s a number of institutional mechanisms were brought into being in order to improve national consultation and co-ordination, such as the Committee of Governors of Central Banks and a short-term Economic Policy Committee.

The Hague Summit (1969) and the Werner Report

The summit did mark an important change in political attitudes toward the EC — French President Pompidou in the immediate post-de Gaulle period, and Germany's Chancellor Brandt pursuing the 'Europeanization' of the FRG within an external framework of prospective EC extension and growing international monetary strains.

The political significance of the Hague Summit's decisions lie in the fact that the Community was facing fundamental changes to its established structure: the major one being the imminent enlargement of the original Six members to include Denmark, Britain, Ireland and Norway, although other internal questions had to be resolved if the Community was not to stagnate or fail to meet the growing economic and political challenges. This is the background to the Hague Summit's decision to create an EMU in the EC.

An expert working group chaired by the Prime Minister of Luxembourg, Pierre Werner, was set up in order to investigate the possibilities and propose recommendations to later Summits. After several intermediate reports, the final version of the Werner Report was adopted by the EC Council of Ministers in March 1971.

The overriding goal of EMU was sanctioned and expected to be in operation by 1980, and of course would be completed in stages. The vision of EMU, as conceived by the Report, would ultimately require the total fixation of exchange rates — no freedom of movement or fluctuation against one another — and the complete freedom of capial movement. Unlike the recent Delors Report (1989), the Werner Report did not explicitly call for the creation of a single European currency. It preferred to identify short- and medium-term objectives, such as the setting up of short- and medium-term credit facilities to aid excessive exchange rate fluctuations and balance of payments problems, and the narrowing of permissible exchange rate fluctuations.

However, the weaknesses of the Bretton Woods international economic system had become increasingly apparent to the Western Europeans by the early 1970s; as the US dollar became more unstable, particularly during 1971, and large speculative capital movements of US dollars affected the functioning of some EC stock exchanges. The Federal Republic and the Netherlands were forced to close their foreign exchange markets and allow their currencies to float.

These events put paid to the first policy recommendation of the Werner Report: the decision taken by the Council of Ministers in early 1971 to narrow the permissible margin of fluctuation aginst the US dollar, from 0.75 per cent to 0.60 per cent. This plan, designed to reduce the freedom of movement of

European currencies against the US dollar in terms of the IMF limits, would have meant greater pressure upon national central banks to intervene if a currency was nearing the reduced limit of 0.60 per cent. This initial step was further affected by the subsequent suspension of the dollar's convertibility into gold, taken by the US in August 1971: this floating of the dollar in effect assured the instability of the international monetary system.

By the end of the year, the Western industrialized states had managed to respond: the Smithsonian agreement of December 1971 involved a devaluation of the US dollar and a widening of the permissible margin for fluctuation to 2.25 per cent above and below the value of the dollar. What then happened in practice was a wider 'tunnel' for the US dollar, and the subsequent tightening of the permissible movement of European currencies *vis-à-vis* the dollar. The Smithsonian agreement essentially widened the scope for currency fluctuations against the US dollar, but the EC decision in early 1972 to limit the freedom of movement of European currencies against each other, resulted in the so-called 'snake in a tunnel' system.

The Smithsonian agreement of a maximum fluctuation limit of plus or minus 2.25 per cent created the 'tunnel' — an area of 'space' bounded by fixed and unmovable limits — and the EC's decision to limit the permissible fluctuation of their currencies against one another, again by only plus or minus a maximum of 2.25 per cent, effectively created the 'snake'. In practice, this meant that the European 'snake' could move about within the Smithsonian 'tunnel': a flexible arrangement which, although providing for structural stability in terms of currency values, could also enable central bank intervention to respond to any problems.

In reality, this 'snake in a tunnel' system required greater collective political and fiscal responsibility and theoretically, could produce positive results for the stability of European currencies, given that they would be intervening in the first instance to adjust their exchange rates in terms of other European currencies — to stabilize monetary affairs within Western Europe or within the snake — and only in the last instance, intervening to maintain the value of European currencies against the dollar, or snake intervention within the tunnel.

Another advantage to this snake in a tunnel system was its membership; first and foremost was the involvement of the EC Six, but snake participation included the four prospective members at that time: UK, Eire, Norway and Denmark. Their participation was of course dominated by political factors pertaining to their accession, but was also a result of the general economic and monetary climate of the time.

However, the plan for a snake in a tunnel was itself to be overtaken by more fundamental structural weaknesses in the international economy: no sooner had the system officially been created when speculation against the UK sterling in 1972 resulted in sterling being floated and British withdrawal from the snake. Other participating members soon followed suit, and despite strict exchange controls being imposed by EC members such as France and Italy, the snake system collapsed, eventually leading to the situation whereby collective action over exchange rates was replaced by a confusing and detrimental mixture of unilateral floating exchange rates — France, UK, Italy and Eire — and a partial co-operation of some Western European states remaining within the snake.

Given that both the Werner Report recommendations for EMU, and the crisis management measure of the 'snake in a tunnel' had failed, why did the Community maintain its search for monetary integration?

Not only was there a certain degree of stability injected into some Western European economies — notably the remaining snake participants — but lessons learned from the failure to progress any further towards EMU were equally important. Some of the experiences of the snake system and the partial application of the Werner Report were useful and, to a greater or lesser extent, were built upon in the later EMS. The 'learning curve' included the use of credit facilities together with a community loan scheme, and the improvement in national monetary policy co-ordination *vis-à-vis* other states, via the Committee of Central Bank Governors and the institutionalized procedures of the European Monetary Cooperation Fund.

'A zone of monetary stability' — the EMS

Commission President Roy Jenkins, in direct consultation with European leaders such as Schmidt and Tindemans, put forward his idea for a relaunch of the integration process: to move towards an economic and monetary union, in the first instance as a response to and partial solution of the perennial economic and monetary crises plaguing the EC during the 1970s, and also as a political and pro-integrationist move, designed to promote confidence and interest in the continuation of the EC.

However, by the Bremen Council of July 1978 governmental opinion had shifted more in favour of a method to stabilize European monetary problems rather than in favour of an outright move toward EMU; the Schmidt/Giscard proposal for a European Monetary System (EMS) was agreed upon, and eventually came into being in March 1979.

First of all, it must be stressed that there were substantive differences between the expectations underlying, and the procedures of, the EMS and the earlier 'snake'. Perhaps the most important was the shift in economic and political priorities by the late 1970s; the problem of inflation and the use of methods to reduce it, were of greater significance than the earlier emphasis upon full employment.

Another vital difference concerns the underlying expectations of those parties setting up the EMS. Unlike the earlier Werner Report with its explicit goal of EMU by 1980, the EMS was more of an institutional and procedural mechanism to create 'a zone of monetary stability', as President D'Estaing described it in April 1978.

In other words, the actual EMS in itself was not designed to bring about EMU; the EMS, by definition and content, could only ever aspire to its stated aims of facilitating closer co-operation between European Community member states and hopefully, by so doing, ensure a stable monetary environment within and between the EC members: acting as a phase of transition.

So what exactly is the EMS? The EMS is built around three distinct elements:

- the Exchange Rate Mechanism (ERM);
- the European Monetary Cooperation Fund (EMCF);
- the EC-wide embryo currency, the European Currency Unit (ECU).

The ERM acted as a parity grid, where national currencies would be tied together, similar to the previous snake. However, weaker currencies, it was argued, would be better served by a 'basket' method, since intervention under this system would be unilateral. Not surprisingly the FRG preferred the grid system which would require all participating members to intervene if an exchange rate suffered from wild swings in value. However, the ERM differed from the snake in that the ECU would act within the grid as a 'denominator' or as a measurement of the central rate within the grid, and also thereby send a vital signal to all participants — a divergence indicator — if a currency was moving away from its designated parity value.

This room for movement of currency values was set at a maximum of 2.25 per cent either side of the central ECU value. However, Italy — and the UK since eventually joining the ERM in November 1990 — are permitted a wider room for movement which is 6 per cent either side of the central parity value. If a currency moves more than 75 per cent of the maximum allowable fluctuation rate, the government and central bank of that country are expected to intervene to stabilize the currency's movement: the methods available range from intervention on foreign exchange markets, to changes in domestic economic and monetary policy, such as adjusting interest rates.

On the whole this system was favoured by Germany, since intervention would most probably be undertaken by the country with its exchange rate at the lower limit of the parity grid, whereas for the country with the stronger appreciating currency, there would be less pressure for central intervention. Given that the Deutschmark has been and is set to continue as the strongest European currency, the ERM as a parity grid exchange rate stabilization scheme would be of greater utility to Germany.

The ECU acts within the ERM as a basket currency — it is composed of all ERM participating currencies' value, each currency being weighted.

Therefore, as the values of some currencies rise, so too does the overall value of the ECU.

The other element of the EMS, the European Monetary Cooperation Fund (EMCF), was based closely on the earlier credit facility of the snake, FECOM. The EMCF would act as a pool for approximately 20 per cent of participating members' gold and dollar reserves, in exchange for which members would receive ECU deposits in order to settle any internal debts arising from intervention over exchange rate fluctuations.

The final element of the EMS was expected to constitute a number of credit facilities, available to all participants. The question of credit being made available to those states with weaker currencies was an important area for negotiation: resource transfers in general — comprising short-term or medium-term credit, guaranteed loans, or even increases in regional aid via the ERDF — were seen as vital if weaker currencies were to survive the ERM, and for example, Eire and Italy made it clear that these conditions would be an essential precondition of their re-entry into the snake, prior to the EMS being created. So 'very short-term', 'short-term' and 'medium-term' loans were instigated, in order to provide states with the wherewithal to intervene over their currency fluctuations, and were repayable over different time periods according to their nature. It was expected that over time, the administration of these credit facilities would be assumed by the EMCF.

There is general agreement that, on the whole, exchange rate volatility has been lessened, and that exchange rates under the EMS are more stable than before. Despite being adjusted intermittently there have been only twelve realignments, the last being in 1987 concerning the French franc. In other words, the volatility of exchange rates has decreased sharply since the EMS has been in existence: this point can only really encompass participating EMS members, as exchange rate fluctuations have continued to be widespread outside the EMS.

However, there is also evidence to suggest that after the 1979–80 oil shock currency volatility lessened internationally, and for OECD states the relevance of conservative or monetarist administrations, it has been argued, helped to stabilize exchange rates and control inflation. However, in recent years the increasing expectations of economic and political advantage have led non-EC member states to link their currencies to the ERM — such states include Norway, who joined the ERM just prior to UK entry, and Sweden and Finland who joined during 1991.

This brings us on to the related question of whether the EMS has brought about economic policy and performance convergence, that is, closer levels of economic growth and inflation. If so, results are lower prices, increased confidence of trade and healthier balance of payments. Therefore one cannot arbitrarily examine whether the EMS has helped to create a 'zone of monetary stability' unless one also examines the extent to which closer economic and monetary activity has been fostered. Again the evidence suggests that inflation rates between participating EMS members have declined since 1979, and have tended to congregate loosely at this lower level; so not only has inflation in an absolute sense been reduced, its differential between participating members has also been eroded.

However, regarding the question of economic policy convergence and interest rate stability within the EMS: there is little clear agreement that the EMS in itself has brought about the reduction of inflationary tendencies within its members, and what tends to be stressed as more relevant here is the political desire of both EMS and non-EMS member states to control and reduce their inflation rates during the 1980s.

Within the EMS, this political intention resulted in high-inflation states such as Italy and France agreeing to adopt Germany's economic and monetary discipline, and this is known as 'policy credibility' whereby inflation-prone economies can 'borrow' credibility from their close links to a low-inflation economy. Perhaps one of the more fundamental constraints of the EMS concerns both its structure and process: its asymmetric nature and its description as a 'Deutschmark Zone'.

During the negotiations for the creation of the EMS symmetry or equality of participation was heavily stressed, in order to place the onus of intervention on more than one set of shoulders. However, as the EMS has developed, it has taken the form of an asymmetrical system. Such developments include the fact that the ECU has not been widely adopted as the preferred currency for intervention, nor has the 'divergence indicator' or 'rattlesnake' lived up to expectations. Also, EMS membership was for over a decade relatively unbalanced, although Spain and Portugal joined in 1989 and the UK in October 1990.

In essence, the problem of an asymmetric EMS is perhaps not so surprising: it is clear that a country with low inflation, good terms of trade and a strong currency would dominate any monetary system, irrespective of any political desire not to do so. Such economic and monetary discipline can be useful to other members, and for the functioning of the system itself, 'a system of fixed but adjustable exchange rates needs a firm anchor, which in present circumstances can only be provided by a major partner currency and the monetary policy that stands behind it' (Rieke 1990, p. 30).

In addition to the general perception of asymmetry as a possible constraint upon the EMS, a more specific problem exists with regard to *exchange controls*. These instruments of national monetary policy are essential for the limitation or liberation of movements of foreign capital, vital in instances of exchange rate intervention, as well as for balance of payments deficits and freedom of movement of capital.

Exchange controls were not outlawed by the EMS, and have been used extensively by some EMS members, notably Italy and France, as methods of protecting their currencies from wild fluctuation as a result of speculation. The question of whether capital controls can be continually employed to protect domestic money markets and exchange rate values, especially since the White Paper on Completing the Single Internal Market was adopted in 1985, has become increasingly important.

The opposing views on the utility of exchange controls spans the spectrum from those who argue that their abolition could result in either greater exchange rate fluctuations or instability in domestic money markets, to those who argue that abolition of capital controls can encourage speculation.

This is an important element of the debate surrounding the EMS, given both the SEM of 1992 with the related liberalization of capital movements and financial services and the agreement at Maastricht in December 1991 on the Treaty on European Union.

Another issue concerns the question of narrowing the margins of permissible fluctuation for ERM currencies. This, it is argued, would render the EMS even more anti-inflationary and reduce even more the presently low levels of exchange rate volatility, but could result in further unemployment or regional economic disparities, therefore strengthening the traditional argument of real resource transfers. And, finally, the EMS of course operates within the parameters of the international economic and financial system, and is therefore affected by strengths and weaknesses of the US dollar and US trade and budgetary deficits.

There has thus been a school of opinion suggesting a radical overhaul of the EMS and a 'relance' of the concept of EMU, rather than a continuation of piecemeal tinkering with the dysfunctional elements of the present EMS: '. . . the problem will emerge of the contradiction between full trade integration, complete mobility of capital, fixity of exchange rates, and as yet unchallenged national autonomy in the conduct of monetary policy . . . the only solution to this contradiction that does not entail the undoing of the common market is to move toward a monetary union' (Padoa-Schioppa 1989, p. 383).

The Community and EMU into the 1990s

The present developments concerning a possible EMU within the EC, unlike the original Werner Report, were not initially characterized by a sense of urgency or crisis within the global economic and monetary system; the interest in and debate over the content and structure of an EMU owe more to political considerations and expectations concerning the future direction and competence of EC integration.

Therefore it is not just the obvious economic and monetary 'contradictions' of the EMS in relation to a single market which have spurred the debate on — although this is an intrinsic element — it is the political aspirations and expectations of national groupings and supranational institutions, concerning the nature of European integration. Although formally obliged to instigate EMU since 1972 — that is since the Council adoption in March 1971 of the

Werner Report — the Community has only recently taken steps to realize that aim.

The German Presidency of the European Council in 1988 was responsible for a number of initiatives; in this context the decision of the Hanover Summit to create a committee, chaired by Jacques Delors, the President of the Commission, whose role was to devise and submit a plan for EMU. The Committee reported in 1989, and its original blueprint for EMU was composed of three stages:

(1) Stage I, where all EC member states would be full members of the ERM,
   • where the maximum permissible range of fluctuation for all participating currencies would be 2.25 per cent;
   • where exchange controls would be removed to allow the free movement of capital;
   • where monetary policy co-ordination would be increased under the aegis of the Committee of Central Bank Governors;
   • where a European Reserve Fund would be created to pool 10 per cent of national foreign exchange reserves, in order that intervention would be facilitated by either national authorities or the fund.
   In short, Stage I of the Delors Report on EMU is intended to increase national co-operation and co-ordination over monetary policies, exercise uniform discipline over all EMS currencies and begin to develop the ECU.

   Stage I is therefore a vital first step toward EMU: fundamental political and economic interests have to be reconciled, both within national boundaries and between national and supranational centres of power: this is evidenced clearly in the British Parliament's debates over loss of sovereignity as a result of any further federal integration.

   Stage I was also defined as coming into effect from 1 July 1990 — decided upon at the 1989 Madrid Council — and in June 1990 the Dublin Council set the starting date for the IGC leading to Treaty revision as December 1990.
(2) Stage II, as envisaged in the original Delors Report, would involve limited intervention within the ERM: in other words, only in special circumstances, and would present an important and intensive stage for the development of institutional mechanisms for EMU — Eurofed, or the European System of Central Banks, would be set up gradually to assume control of national monetary policy as laid down in the revised EEC Treaty.

   This stage was initially agreed to commence in 1994, although Britain did not support this date.
(3) Stage III of the Delors Report is characterized by the permanent fixing of exchange rates which would ultimately be replaced by a single European

currency — the timing and characteristics of which, the Delors Report envisaged, would be agreed to during the Treaty revisions of the IGC, and the Eurofed would assume total control of national monetary and economic policy.

At the Rome Council in December 1990 the EC's member states, except for the UK, agreed that the move toward Stage III should be discussed by 1997.

First of all, what are the technical and political justifications for European EMU? For the EC Commission, the benefits of a full and economic and monetary union include:

- a more efficient economy, for example, by achieving and maintaining the stability of prices, by reducing if not eliminating the uncertainties and speculative activity associated with exchange rate fluctuations, and by eliminating transaction costs involved in changing currencies. Although this last point can only be truly effective if EMU is characterized by a single currency, as envisaged by the 1989 Delors Report, but not by the 1971 Werner Report;
- a more effective platform from which to tackle the underlying economic problems of inflation and unemployment — for example the Delors Report sees EMU as the primary tool of the Community to reduce interest rates and levels of public debt;
- as a more powerful framework to address regional economic divergence and underdevelopment, which cannot be wholly met by the present EC instruments of regional policy: for example, the Commission's argument that 'unduly large regional imbalances would pose an economic as well as a political threat to the union . . . the exchange rate can no longer be used by individual member states as a policy instrument to deal with a loss of competitiveness or to adjust to adverse economic shocks' (Communication of the Commission, 21/08/90, pp. 25–6);
- finally, returning to the European experiences of the 1970s and early 1980s, another technical argument in favour of EMU is that it would enable the EC not only to assume a stronger world role in the international economy, but that an economic and monetary union of EC states could act as a cushion against the effects of serious external events. No doubt the economic and financial costs associated with the Gulf conflict of 1991 were important in this context.

Another strong argument put forward by the EC Commission has concerned itself with the effects of the completion of the internal market upon the functioning of the EMS: it suggests that as the '1992' completion date nears, the effects of some of the internal market legislation, especially the removal of exchange controls and the creation of a single financial area, will constrain the ability of the EMS to manage exchange rate fluctuations. As far as the Commission is concerned, the more desirable option in this situation is to move as rapidly as possible to full EMU, rather than attempting to refine the EMS — and particularly the ERM.

Thus the agenda for the present EMU debate has been set by the notion of a single currency as the epicentre of a monetary union and, as a result, the IGC on EMU tended in media terms to concentrate on the implications of monetary union, rather than economic union, given that many characteristics of an economic union have already been adopted as a result of the 1992 programme.

As the Delors Report of 1989 suggested, it would be Stage II of EMU when the monetary institution would be established — referred to officially as the European System of Central Banks, and composed of the national control banks and a new European Central Bank (Eurofed).

This institution, according to the Report, was necessary in Stage II since national central banks would still retain ultimate authority for monetary policy in this period. The Eurofed would require a period of 'learning' as it increasingly assumes day-to-day responsibility for managing the EMS, incorporating the work of the European Monetary Cooperation Fund and increasingly playing a central role in co-ordinating national monetary policy, such as determining interest rates, managing foreign exchange reserves and so on.

Stage II, for the Delors Report, would also mark a significant period of change for the ECU as it moves toward becoming Europe's single currency. In this sense, Eurofed would also be involved, as it would encourage wider use of the ECU and the ever-closer relationship between it and national currencies. And, by Stage III, Eurofed is expected to assume control of all nominally independent monetary policy, during which national exchange rates would be permanently fixed, to be ultimately replaced by the ECU as the single currency.

However, although there is 'room for manoeuvre' on how member states wish to revise the Treaties, the Report made clear its own views on this matter: that the Eurofed should be politically independent both from national governments and EC authorities and that it should be democratically accountable for its activities.

On its specific functions and powers, the Report envisaged

- Eurofed management of the ECU's exchange rate *vis-à-vis* non-Union currencies such as the dollar and yen;
- the formulation of a European monetary policy and thus the issuing of ECUs;
- its role in banking and capital markets, for example as guarantor.

A number of these expected powers and functions owe much to the persistent German diplomacy within Europe: both Chancellor Kohl and the former Bundesbank President Karl-Otto Pohl, amongst others, stressed the anxiety of the German government and monetary authorities regarding a possible outcome of EMU within the EC.

Their views, that they were not ready to commit a stable German economy and currency to a system of EMU where the political independence of the Eurofed was not guaranteed, or where stringent prerequisites of closer economic convergence, fiscal harmonization and price stability were lacking have paid off in the sense that the political implications of EMU were as fiercely debated as the economic.

The fear that the present EMS and the future EMU could be jeopardized both by the nature of the transition to '1992', and the effects of international events, appears to have played a major part in the desire that EMU should be achieved as quickly as possible. The Luxembourg Presidency of the Council of Ministers, not unlike the previous Italian Presidency, recognized this and in the 'Luxembourg Non-Paper', suggested that a 'council' of EC Central Bank Governors should begin co-ordinating national economic policy by mid-1993 and that its technical arm, the 'Eurofed', could be in operation by 1996, although the 'Delors Compromise' — directed notably at the British Government — was included, whereby no member government should be bound to the introduction of a single currency unless its national Parliament agreed. The outcome, for the agreed economic and monetary union in the Maastricht Treaty on European Union, is contained in two broad areas — new Articles relating to economic and monetary policy and in several Protocols appended to the Treaty.

The new Articles (102a–109m) replace the original Part III, Title II of the Treaties. Article 102a lays down that the 'Member states and the Community shall act in accordance with the principle of an open market economy with free competition, favouring an efficient allocation of resources'.

Article 103 goes much further by elaborating the responsibilities chiefly of the Council of Ministers in overseeing the period of convergence: 103.1 stresses that 'member states shall regard their economic policies as a matter of common concern and shall coordinate them within the Council'. Article 103.2 gives the Council, acting on a qualified majority basis, responsibility to 'formulate a draft for the broad guidelines of the economic policies of the Member states and the Community'. This broad guideline will then be discussed by the European Council after which the Council of Ministers will adopt some form of recommendation.

Article 103.3 supplements this function by endowing the Council with a monitoring role — such 'multilateral surveillance' also includes the Council assessing the extent to which national economic policy is consistent with the goals laid out in 103.2 above. Article 103.4 states that where 'the economic policies of a Member State are not consistent . . . or that they risk jeopardizing the proper functioning of economic and monetary union', the Council may use qualified majority procedures to 'make the necessary recommendations to the Member State concerned'. Significantly, the Council also has the power, if a qualified majority vote on a Commission proposal is accepted, to make its recommendation public.

In general terms, then, Article 103 is clearly seeking firm political commitment to the process of achieving EMU − and the role of the Council in monitoring economic policy and potentially rebuking any member state for failing to meet its obligations is an important departure from the conventional role of the Council. However, Article 103a does allow for the Council to vote unanimously on granting financial assistance to a member state 'seriously threatened with severe difficulties caused by exceptional occurrences'.

Articles 104–104b specify the need for financial prudence by Community institutions including the European Central Bank in relation to overdraft or credit facilities and liability for debts. Article 104c states that 'Member States shall avoid excessive government deficits' and allows the Commission to monitor budgetary compliance and levels of debt. If an excessive deficit exists, or is likely to exist, both the Commission and Council may intervene. Importantly, if a member state 'fails to comply' with any recommended course of action, the Council may invite the EIB 'to reconsider its lending policy towards the Member State concerned' or 'impose fines of an appropriate size' amongst other forms of punitive action (Article 104.11).

Articles 105–109k are concerned with monetary policy − Article 105 stipulates that the 'primary objective of the European System of Central Banks shall be to maintain price stability' and its major tasks are 'to define and implement the monetary policy of the Community'; 'to conduct foreign exchange operations'; to 'hold and manage the official foreign reserves of the Member States'; and to 'promote the smooth operation of payment systems'. Also, the ECB shall 'have the exclusive right to authorize the issue of bank notes within the Community', according to Article 105a.

Article 109 sets out the procedures by which the Council of Ministers may 'conclude formal agreements on an exchange rate system for the ECU in relation to non-Community currencies' − an important point given that one of the weaknesses of the EMS was its lack of a dollar or yen policy.

Article 109j.4 states that 'if by the end of 1997 the date for the beginning of the third stage has not been set, the third stage will start on 1 January 1999', before which time the Council of Ministers will confirm which 'Member States fulfil the necessary conditions for the adoption of a single currency'.

It is equally important to remember the Protocols concerning economic and monetary union attached to the Treaty. Protocol 3 details the Statute and Constitution of the ECSB and ECB; Protocol 4 covers the Statute of the European Monetary Institute, the forerunner in Stage II of the ECB, Protocol 5 'on the excessive-deficit procedure' quantifies the precise deficit which, under Article 104.c, the Commission is required to investigate: an actual or planned government deficit; GDP ratio of 3 per cent, or a government debt; GDP ratio of 60 per cent.

Protocol 6 'on the convergence criteria' is an extremely important one. In summary, the elements of national economic and monetary policy which must converge in order for EMU to proceed include:

- 'a price performance that is sustainable and an average rate of inflation, observed over a period of one year before the examination, that does not exceed by more than 1.5 percentage points' that of at most the three best performing Member States in terms of price stability;
- no excessive government deficit;
- no movement outside the 'normal fluctuation margins' of the EMS;
- no unilateral devaluation;
- no nominal long-term interest rate more than 2 percentage points in excess of the 'three best performing states'.

In conclusion, it is first of all extremely clear that the new Treaty's contents relating to the achievement and functioning of the economic and monetary union are designed to be comprehensive and stringent — political uncertainties of many EC members concerning the present recession, the future role of a united Germany, and the prospects of further enlargement were no doubt equally vital factors in the shaping of the EMU, as were existing economic and commercial interests.

Secondly, the Treaty on European Union is not necessarily one carved from stone: Article N Final Provisions confirms that in 1996 'a conference of representatives of the governments of the Member States shall be convened' in order to review the provisions of the Treaty — for example, in order to reform the EC's institutions further, or to revise the Treaties in accordance with enlargement.

In any case, in Article 109j.3, the Council of Ministers acting by qualified majority voting procedures must, by 31 December 1996 at the latest, decide whether a majority of member states 'fulfils the necessary conditions for the adoption of a single currency' and also decide 'whether it is appropriate for the Community to enter the third stage' of economic and monetary union.

As this chapter hopes to have shown, there is a heritage, for the Community, of earlier aspirations for EMU and a variety of methods which have been employed to bring about conducive conditions for such union. What the Treaty on European Union has illustrated very effectively is that the broad political consensus within and between EC member states is the key towards achieving what it originally set out to accomplish in 1969, albeit under qualitatively different domestic and global conditions.

References and further reading

Artis, M., 1990, 'The UK and the EMS', in de Grauwe, P. and Papademos, L. (eds), *The EMS in the 1990's*, Longman, London.

Commission of the EC, 1990, *Communication of the Commission on Economic and Monetary Union 21 August 1990*, Office for Official Publications of the EC, Luxembourg.

Davies, G. *et al.* (eds), 1990, *EMU: the issues*, IPPR Economic Study #4,

Davies, G., 1989, *Britain and the European monetary question*, IPPR Economic Study #1, London.

Emerson, M. and Huhne, C., 1991, *The ECU Report*, Pan/Commission of the EC, London.

House of Lords Select Committee on the European Communities, *Economic and monetary union and political union*, House of Lords Session 1989–90, 27th report, HL Paper 88–II, Volume II evidence.

Ludlow, P., 1982, *The making of the EMS*, Butterworth, London.

Padoa-Schioppa, T., 1989, 'The EMS: a long term view', in Giavazzi, F. *et al.* (eds), *The EMS*, CUP, Cambridge.

Padoa-Schioppa, T., 1985, *Money, economic policy and Europe*, Commission of the EC, European Perspectives series, Brussels.

Rieke, W., 1990, 'Alternative views on the EMS in the 1990's', in de Grauwe, P. and Papademos, L. (eds), *The EMS in the 1990's*, Longman, London.

Russell, R.W., 1977, 'Snakes and sheiks: managing Europe's money', in Wallace, H., Wallace, W. and Webb, C. (eds), *Policy making in the EC*, John Wiley & Sons, London.

Statler, J., 1979, 'The EMS: from conception to birth', *International Affairs*, 55 (2), 206–25.

Story, J., 1988, 'The launching of the EMS: an analysis of change in foreign economic policy', *Political Studies*, 36, 397–412.

6

Regional policy

The development of the Communities' regional policy, albeit in a relatively short period of time, is a good illustration of the various types of political interests at work in the EC: the policy since its inception in 1975 has also undergone a number of structural revisions and has increased in political importance in the face of major political and economic change during the 1980s.

The role and functions of the regional policy look set to increase in terms of political visibility and national economic performance, in the post-Maastricht EC, given the variety of pressures upon the integration process which include the realization of the 1992 process, the moves toward economic convergence prior to the introduction of a single currency, and the pressures for expansion of Community membership in the medium term from a number of other European states.

The development of EC regional policy

The motivation underlying the negotiations over, and the creation of, the European Regional Development Fund (ERDF) in 1975 have been documented elsewhere (see, for example, Wallace, H. *et al*. 1983).

In general, however, the creation of an explicit financial mechanism to promote regional economic development administered at a Community level, sprang from a number of somewhat overlapping existing Community and national approaches.

The ECSC Treaty and the Treaty of Rome had provided for what were in effect regional regeneration measures via such bodies as the ECSC (European Coal and Steel Community), the EIB (European Investment Bank), the ESF (European Social Fund) and the Guidance section of the EAGGF

(European Agricultural Guidance and Guarantee Fund). At the national level, member states pursued regional policies or procedures according to different political and economic criteria, and it is widely accepted that the British Government during accession negotiations sought to create a means of recompense for its contributions to the EC budget. It was perhaps the relative convergence of Community aspirations for the development of the integration process, together with the concern that structural regional economic imbalances and backwardness could possibly hamper any benefits won by deepening and widening the integration process, which stimulated the search for a Community-level regional policy.

In a number of respects, the concerns of the Community by the early 1970s, leading to the response of the ERDF, are not radically different, on the surface, to the concerns of the early 1990s, these being the repercussions for the health and vitality of the Community of economic and monetary union (EMU) and the probability of enlargement.

Nor, in a general sense, have the underlying regional problems altered from those in the early 1970s involving backward rural regions and those based upon declining primary industry. However, in the present decade, the Community has an increasingly robust and visible regional policy framework, and in order to analyse how the challenges of the 1990s may require new approaches, it is important to clarify what existing regional policy is and why it has undergone a series of reforms.

The Paris Summit in late 1974 took the decision to create the European Regional Development Fund (ERDF), after several years of discussion within the EC as to the precise structure and aims of any Community regional policy. In Regulation 724/75 the ERDF was to comprise the policy's funding mechanism, a Regional Policy Committee was created to bring together national and Community representatives primarily to examine national regional policy programmes and interests, and the EC's Commission had been partially reorganized in 1968 to create a new Directorate-General and Commissioner responsible for regional policy matters, DGXVI.

The ERDF, upon creation, accounted for a modest 5 per cent of the Community Budget, smaller in real terms than one of its major supporters, Commissioner Thomson, would have wished. The method by which these monies were disbursed for regional programmes was a relatively simple one of national shares or quotas. This was a result of the initial negotiations over the creation of the regional policy, with some states wishing to secure tangible transfers of resources from the Community. Thus, each member state was allocated a share of the monies, based partly on adroit national bargaining and Commission identification of regions in need of investment and development. On the whole, Britain, Ireland, France and Italy were the major beneficiaries prior to enlargement in the 1980s; these were the member states with the highest quotas or shares. However, one important characteristic of the policy, which remains politically contentious today, concerns the concept of 'additionality'. In other words, monies received from the ERDF were not to be used instead of pre-existing national financial commitments to regional development, but were instead intended to complement or top-up such national measures.

Hence, the ERDF and national shares of it were 'additional' to national projects, and thus the monies available to member states were intended to provide, at a maximum level, 50 per cent of the costs of national funding.

So, right from the start, it was never intended that the ERDF or the wider recommendations of the EC's regional policy should supplant and replace national commitment to regional development, but rather that by creating such a policy, the political and economic importance of regional well-being could be recognized at the Community level. Alternatively neither was the ERDF to be used by national governments to cut back their own expenditure.

In regard to the specific type of projects which could receive, or at least become eligible for, ERDF monies, the 1975 decision limited the Fund's application to two types of projects; industrial or service sector investment which may create new employment or maintain existing employment structures, and infrastructure investments which could again be linked to industrial needs, or which were required in particularly unusual areas such as remote or mountainous ones.

Another important characteristics of the EC's regional policy in this early phase was the identification of a 'region', or in other words the physical, economic or socio-political characteristics of the recipient units which were intended to gain from the policy.

In short, the EC had little if no discretion in trying to influence the identification of 'regions' or the identification of 'priority' regions; this remained securely within the remit of national governments. As a result, the notion of what constituted a 'region' differed markedly from one member state to another; some regions being defined by degrees of political and legal autonomy such as the German *Länder*, and others identified in terms of national economic planning characteristics, such as in Britain, where Scotland, N. Ireland and Wales were treated as single units, and England was broken down into such units as the North-West and West Midlands. In addition, the policy as constituted in 1975 relied upon national governments to identify priority areas and to sift applications for investment programmes, and due to the fixed quota system of ERDF monies, national governments then submitted a number of projects which would fulfil their national quota.

The decision in 1975 to create the EC's regional policy, financed through the ERDF, allowed for a three-year period of operation, after which time assessment could be made as to any further continuation and refinement of the policy. During this period, a number of problems and weaknesses in the operation of the policy became apparent, and as early as 1977 the Commission began to propose a number of changes. Formal revision of the EC's regional policy occurred in 1979, with the most significant change being in the composition of the ERDF. Instead of the entire ERDF monies being earmarked for national quotas or shares, 5 per cent of the ERDF was now to be labelled as 'non-quota'.

In theory, this 'non-quota' section of the Fund marked an important shift in emphasis to the EC itself, and the Commission in particular, given that it allowed the EC somewhat greater powers to identify projects in need of ERDF assistance, and particularly that it could identify projects of Community, as opposed to national, significance. In reality, however, the amount of money available for non-quota disbursement was miniscule, given the limited share of the ERDF in the wider EC budget and the non-quota section was ultimately relying upon national governments to come forward and propose projects which would be held up to scrutiny by the Commission, a practice which many states did not prefer to undertake.

None the less, this change in philosophy and direction was important for the continuation of further reforms. In addition, the 1979 reform attempted to revise the basic political interests underpinning the regional policy: the Commission suggested that member states view regional policy as an essential component of economic policy, rather than merely as a means of 'juste retour', or 'getting back what one pays in'. In this sense, the Commission suggested that the ERDF should no longer serve all member states, in terms of individual quotas or shares, but that some of the more affluent members' quotas be scrapped, given that these member states — such as France and Germany — could adequately fund their own regional aid schemes without requiring any financial intervention by the ERDF.

Perhaps not surprisingly, debate over the purposes, structure and procedures of the EC's regional policy continued, again to culminate by 1984 in a major reform package. On this occasion, however, the reforms proved more far-reaching and were subsequently aided by related developments such as the Single European Act and the 1988 Inter-Institutional Agreement concerning amongst other things, reform of the structural Funds. (For an in-depth examination of the 1984 reforms, see for example Croxford *et al.* 1987.)

The EC's regional policy was in effect overhauled in terms of its scope and direction and, it was hoped, restructured in order to provide a more effective solution to the ever-present regional imbalances in the context of existing EC member states attempting to accelerate out of the 1979–81 recession, and a Community facing a long period of accession, from Greek entry in 1981 and Spanish and Portugese negotiations at the time.

What were the effects of the 1984 Regulation? Firstly, the aims of regional policy were redefined more precisely, to promote the 'structural adjustment of regions whose development is lagging behind' and in the 'conversion of declining industrial regions'. This essentially recognized the socio-economic differences and inequalities, almost in terms of a North-South divide, which in the EC had become increasingly visible due to the enlargement mentioned above. Almost inevitably linked to this clarification of regional policy aims was the strengthening of the role of the Community itself. Hence the Regulation stressed the need for the co-ordination of different EC policies, some or all of which impacted in varying degrees upon regional conditions, as well as stressing the need for complementarity between EC and national policies in order that they may converge in their aims and level of support. Secondly, perhaps one of the most significant aspects of the Regulation concerned the abolition of the earlier quota-based system, and introducing a new approach to funding. The new system now operates ERDF funds according to a series of minimum and maximum ranges for each member state. These ranges apply for three-year periods, at the end of which they are reconsidered within the Regional Policy Committee and DG XVI.

In other words, the 'share' of the ERDF going to each member state was no longer a flat, non-negotiable or rigid sum, but a looser and more flexible arrangement, according largely to the severity of the particular regional problems in each member state. In addition, to maximize receipt of funds between the minimum and maximum ranges, national governments were forced to justify such further applications according to reasonably stringent criteria as laid down in the Regulation.

Overall, the effect of removing the original quota system and introducing the min-max ranges led to ERDF spending, and the national prioritization of regional projects, undergoing somewhat stricter control and management.

Thirdly, the Regulation increased the earlier 'non-quota' section of the ERDF to a ceiling of 20 per cent of total ERDF funds, a large increase on the previous 5 per cent. This Community-determined element of EC regional policy has increased in importance both in relation to the effectiveness of the policy itself, and also to public awareness of the Community's activity, given that many projects assisted under the 'non-quota' section — as well as those under the min-max range system — are publicly identified with the EC flag symbol.

This 'non-indicative range' of the ERDF has been accompanied by the Commission's greater stress upon the need for a continuity of approach, favouring a programme approach for funding, rather than a one-off project emphasis. The type of applications which are eligible for assistance under EC-determined criteria fall into one of two categories:

- similar problems facing regions in more than one member state, or in other words, issue-specific Community-initiated action;
- 'National Programmes of Community Interest', submitted by national government.

In the first category, early programmes initiated and funded by the EC included VALOREN, concerning the development and strengthening of local energy resources, and STAR, designed to promote high-tech telecommunications provision. Subsequent initiatives have focused upon the problems faced by regions characterized by declining heavy or primary industry, such as RESIDER for steel industries and RECHAR for the conversion of the coal sector. Also within this category are the Integrated Development Operations (IDOs) and Integrated Mediterranean Programmes (IMPs).

The second category of 'National Programmes of Community Interest' combines national and Community input, so that national governments forward applications which they feel will be accepted according to the Commission's assessment of their utility and long-term contribution to restructuring and regeneration.

In addition to this 1984 reform package which, it was hoped, would improve the efficiency of allocations and the identification of serious regional problems, the Commission lobbied hard to increase total ERDF resources within the wider EC budget. However, the problem for the now-reformed and streamlined ERDF is that the 1986 accession of Spain and Portugal diluted the impact of the funds, and in practice ERDF monies had to be stretched further to accommodate the new members.

Given that the total amount of monies available for the ERDF (approximately 8.5 per cent of the EC budget by the mid-1980s) and the fact that, at most, ERDF monies can account for only 50 per cent of the expenditure incurred by national government regional policy, the utility of EC regional policy continued to give rise for concern, despite the reform package outlined above.

It is important to review the nature of the changes made to the EC's regional policy framework in the subsequent Single European Act (SEA), and which also have concerned the operation of the remaining structural Funds all of which, as mentioned previously, contain regional dimensions, as it is these changes, beginning with the Single European Act (SEA), which have assumed immense political importance in the present Stage I of economic and monetary union (EMU). Title V was added to the EEC Treaty by the Single European Act (SEA) signed during 1986 and which entered into force in 1987.

In a very broad sense, the SEA was intended to clear away some of the political and institutional 'cobwebs' which had built up within the decision-making process, to clarify Community competency in a number of specific policy areas, and generally to provide a clear constitutional way for the completion of the single internal market, or the 1992 programme.

Title V concerns Community recognition of the need for 'social and economic cohesion', and the necessary action required to strengthen such cohesion. Hence the stress upon 'cohesion' was a result, particularly of the Commission's and Parliament's concerns that the completion of the internal market could marginalize poorer or weaker regions even further, and that in some cases, the existence of a large section of the EC lacking in adequate socio-economic and infrastructural capacities could compromise the effective functioning of the single market.

Article 130b of Title V stressed the need for close co-ordination of national economic policies in order to facilitate the closer economic integration of regional disparities, and also emphasized the necessity for other EC policies, including the internal market, to 'take into account' the objectives of regional social and economic cohesion.

Article 130c specifically laid down that the ERDF was to 'help redress the principal regional economic imbalances in the Community through participating in the development and structural adjustment of regions whose development is lagging behind and in the conversion of declining industrial regions'.

Title V also included a commitment by the Commission to propose a 'comprehensive' overhaul package (Article 130d) and final agreement on this and any further decision was to include the use of the co-operation procedure between the EP and Council of Ministers (Article 130e).

The Commission subsequently produced a response to Article 130d during 1987 and the final Regulations concerning the reform of the structural Funds came into effect in January 1989. This is the most recent and wide-ranging reform package to date, although by late 1991 the Commission was preparing its report on the effectiveness of these reforms, and particularly their budgetary requirements, with a view to proposing further legislation on the EC structural Funds during 1992/93.

The primary reason for the present discussions concerns the fact that the 1988 Brussels summit which reformed the Community budget by restraining CAP expenditure, also agreed to double progressively the proportion of the structural Funds to 25 per cent of the EC budget by 1993. With such expenditure levels only in place for a further few months, the Commission was under pressure to review those spending ceilings. So, given the impact of the SEA and the 1988 Regulations which entered into force in 1989, what is the current state of the EC's regional policy?

---

(1) Objective 1 is concerned with the 'development and structural adjustment of regions whose development is lagging behind', and at present covers the entire states of Greece, Portugal and Ireland, and areas of Italy, Spain, Britain (Northern Ireland) and the French overseas departments. (The main criteria in assessment is where GDP per capita is at least 25 per cent below the EC average.)

(2) Objective 2 concerns those regions seriously affected by industrial decline, covering northern EC member state regions, and areas in Italy and Spain. (The primary characteristic in assessment concerns levels of structural unemployment.)

(3) Objective 3 aims to countenance long-term unemployment.

(4) Objective 4 is to encourage the integration of young people into the local economy.

(5) Objective 5(a) is to reform the structure of the agricultural sector, and Objective 5(b) is to promote the development of rural areas.

However, the above objectives cannot be entirely classified as coming under the aegis of Community regional policy: the SEA's Article 130c did state the specific purpose of the ERDF, the sole funding mechanism associated with regional policy per se, was to cover, in essence, objectives 1 and 2 above.

Therefore, in reality, whilst the ERDF is seen as the major tool for regional redistribution of aid, the wider problems faced by European regions have been clearly laid down, and the remaining structural funds — the ESF and the Guidance section of the EAGGF — as well as the Community's lending mechanism, the EIB, have been allocated the remaining objectives.

This is essentially what is meant by the SEA's phrase of 'economic and social cohesion' — where the cohesion of the Community can be promoted by a variety of tools and policies, regional policy being the single most important but not the sole means.

Apart from trying to concentrate the uses of the structural Funds by way of the above objectives, the 1988 Regulations introduced a number of important parallel changes. Perhaps the most significant in terms of the relationship between member states — the governments — and the Community, was the introduction of a system to ensure that the management and implementation of regional policy was more rigorous. This system is known as a Community Support Framework (CSF), which is drawn up between the member state and the Commission based on member states having submitted regional development and conversion plans.

This, it was hoped, would begin to introduce more efficiency and long-term commitment, on both sides, in terms of achieving what the regional policy had set out to do since 1975; to reduce disparities and inequalities between regions and promote the genuine cohesion of the Community.

Another important development within the package was the strengthening of the relationship between political and economic regional representatives and the Community institutions — in part facilitated by the changes in the method of identifying the territorial boundaries of the regions. The Commission not only sought to reformulate the objectives of the structural funds as mentioned above, but also introduced new criteria for defining regions across the Community, and therefore the identification of those regions falling under Objective 1 and 2 status. Two of the most important elements in the new criteria were the measurement of GDP per capita and levels of structural long-term unemployment.

Obviously, these changes have impacted upon the role and function of regional actors — local government, development agencies, business groups and so on — and increasingly they have been encouraged to play a greater role in the determination of regional programmes, in addition to the traditional role of national governments — this being the 'partnership' emphasized by the 1988 Regulations.

The clearest example of this was the setting-up in 1988 of the Consultative Council of Local and Regional Authorities, which liaises closely with the

Commission and its various Directorate-Generals, which is involved in regional policy processes, and which benefited from earlier close relations between the Council of European Municipalities and Regions (CEMR) and the International Union of Local Authorities (IULA) in relation to the Commission. In a more general sense, regions themselves have increasingly set up offices or bureaux in Brussels in order to lobby the Community institutions and to maintain their awareness of new initiatives — these representatives range from elected local politicians to development agencies and Chambers of Commerce — for example in Britain, Metropolitan authorities such as Manchester and Birmingham, as well as the Welsh Development Agency, have set up offices.

A related development is the agreement to create the Committee of the Regions (Articles 198a–c, Treaty on European Union) where representatives of regional and local authorities will enjoy advisory status, similar to the Economic and Social Committee. This will no doubt result in a greater and more visible role for debate over regional policy matters.

Having examined the development of the Community's regional policy framework since its formal inception in 1975, it is useful to conclude by briefly assessing the prospects for such policy initiatives, since imminent changes are likely to be made to the structural funds financial ceilings, during 1992/93.

Present trends and issues concerning the efficacy of EC regional policy activity

One perennial criticism made of EC regional policy concerns its share of the EC budget. During the 1980s the ERDF increased relative to its original proportion of 5 per cent of the EC budget, and despite the 1988 budgetary reforms which promised to double the amount awarded to the structural Funds so that they would account for 25 per cent of the EC budget — from 7bn ECU to 14bn ECU — criticism remains. It is often argued that the impact of accession in the 1980s, together with the effects of inflation on real spending, combined to dilute the efficiency expected of the often-reformed ERDF. (The Commission acknowledged that only one-fifth of the ERDF increases represent additional real resources: Commission of the EC 1991a, p. 60.)

The Commission's Fourth Report on the regions (1991a), therefore, noted a number of disturbing trends, that in the least prosperous regions of the Community (35 regions show GDP data which is 25 per cent below the EC average) employment prospects, income disparities and differences in provision for education and training have not much improved or have worsened during the 1980s. The disparity between income levels in the EC being twice as large as disparities in the USA is an often-quoted example. Whilst the Commission acknowledges that although much of regional policy programmes and investment are long term, and therefore there is often a time-lag between intensive regional policy measures and increased competitiveness and growth in regions, there remain immense structural problems in some of the weakest EC regions, with high rates of growth and inward direct investment necessary for many years in order for these regions to reach the EC average.

This point therefore raises many questions relating to the redistribution effect of the present policy, and whether the resources of the EC budget should be increased beyond its present level of approximately 1 per cent of EC GDP, in order that the structural funds may be in a stronger position to effect a meaningful transfer of resources. However, linked to this criticism of insufficient resources for the ERDF and thus the relative inability of the EC to reduce inequalities and provide greater cohesion, is the level of funding maintained by national governments for domestic regional policies.

On the whole, it has been suggested that in most EC member states, national expenditure on such policies has declined steadily during the 1980s: one figure suggesting it may be as much as 40–80 per cent between 1979 and 1987 (Bachtler 1990, p. 6). In addition, the Commission's Fourth Report pointed out that national subsidies to particular economic sectors or industries may also 'maintain and even reinforce the existing pattern of inequalities in the Community' (Commission of the EC 1991a, pp. 61), hence the issue of 'additionality' has been highly visible.

Therefore the relationship between the EC's regional policy framework financed by the structural Funds, and national regional policies remains interdependent; as national expenditure had declined during the period due to domestic political and economic concerns over levels of public expenditure, the reforms of the ERDF intended to concentrate spending and political management upon those regions with the most serious problems (Objectives 1 and 2), and the EC's desire to involve more directly the political and commercial actors in the regions' economic and entrepreneurial capacity, can be more readily understood.

This point brings us to another current issue which has also influenced the efficacy debate over regional policy — the completion of the single market. On the whole the Commission and increasingly the newer EC members sought to deploy the regional policy and structural funds in order to encourage broadly similar economic attributes and capabilities, certainly for the worst-off regions, in order that the vast bulk of the European regions, if not all, could gain equally from direct inward investment, job creation, productivity and competitiveness.

Earlier fears expressed by some northern EC member states over wide discrepancies between labour costs, educational levels of workers, basic infrastructures such as telecommunications and transport links, differing levels of indirect taxation and government policies towards attracting investment, resulted from what some feared would be a movement of capital and production away from high-cost northern EC members to the EC's periphery states.

None the less, regional policy initiatives, in practice, are attempting not only to remove or reduce these differentials in order that the operation of the single market is not compromised or undermined, but also to promote positive initiative and entrepreneurship within regions in order that they may become, at some future date, reasonably self-sufficient and capable of taking their place within the wider European market. In other words, the weaker regions must not act as an economic drain upon others. The EC Commission has argued that the restructuring of European production and service sectors may have somewhat disadvantageous repercussions for weaker regions, as the expectation, backed by present practice, is that the major urban areas will be the major beneficiaries of such corporate activity. However, specialization by weaker regions on particular markets and labour-intensive industries is not a long-term practice to be recommended, not least because of the challenge posed to such sectors by Central and Eastern European states, not to mention the various Republics of the former USSR, as they attempt to develop and strengthen their economies by exports of agricultural, textile and other goods (Commission of the EC 1991b, pp. 67–9 and also Mellors and Copperthwaite 1990, pp. 65–71).

Ultimately, much depends upon priorities and policies enacted by national governments in relation to their weaker regions — as mentioned earlier the EC's regional policy efforts are of necessity limited in their financial ability and there is a strand of thought which suggests that, in any case, regional policy may be more effectively conducted at the national level than the EC level (see for example Nevin 1990, pp. 344–5). Hence national government intervention in economic matters can be vital to the overall success of regional aid programmes.

However, one increasingly visible issue for the regions in the EC, which together with the potential effects of liberalizing the European economy, may require a fundamental change in approach to resolving regional economic inequalities is the question of how economic and monetary union (EMU) will impact.

The existence of an economic and monetary union managed by common, and in some cases politically independent, institutions will constrain the independence of national economic policy-making and, in this context, the ability of governments to use fiscal and economic tools to protect or promote regional economic activity. Economically, the discipline necessary to achieve far closer convergence between EC economies, and in the medium term the probable introduction of a single currency, may also affect the performance of regional economic growth and productivity. On balance it appears that those regions qualifying under Objective 1 status (in fact the entire states of Greece, Ireland and Portugal, as well as areas of Italy and Spain) may face the most serious problems of restructuring, whilst the single market programme and EMU convergence policies are being carried out. Whereas in other member states, with less severe problems, the effects of monetary discipline through interest and exchange rates may be dispersed and any high-growth regions may help to shoulder the short-term impact.

It has been suggested that for the regions 'seriously lagging behind'

(Objective 1) the most important aspects of EMU concern the replacement of the national currency by the single European currency — in the sense that the exchange rate value no longer exists — and the abolition of certain types of taxation of revenue (Emerson and Huhne 1991, pp. 164–7). This is due to the fact that exchange rates and the ability of a government to revalue or devalue will no longer exist and hence governments can no longer employ such methods to protect economic sectors or regions within the country. Moreover, as their report shows, some of the poorer EC states may lose a certain element of national GDP for governments can no longer increase revenue through issuing currency.

At the present time, the political desire of the southern EC member states to accelerate the process of economic convergence — by attracting investment to speed economic growth, by tackling inflation rates and budget deficits — in order that they will be able to support the introduction of a single currency, gives rise to expectations that the effects of completing the economic union or single market, as well as the constraints imposed by monetary union, may not be as drastic upon their weakest regions as feared. However, this expectation does rely upon high-growth rates being present in the European economy — a relatively long-term prospect in any recessionary climate.

Weaker states and regions, then, do face genuine pressures upon domestic political and economic policies in the early 1990s and, perhaps not surprisingly, during the Inter-Governmental Conferences (IGCs) of 1990/91, there was support among the southern member states for greater financial assistance in order for them to overcome structural economic problems, and for them to reap the benefits of EMU as soon as possible. The Commission had acknowledged prior to the IGCs that 'in the final stage of EMU there might be a need to further strengthen Community structural policies' (Communication of the Commission 1990b, p. 26).

The Treaty on European Union initiated at Maastricht in December 1991 incorporated these aspirations, to a certain extent, by including a commitment, incumbent upon the Council of Ministers, to set up a Cohesion Fund by December 1993, which would provide financial assistance for projects concerning environment and trans-European networks for transport infrastructure policies (new Article 130d). This development was opposed particularly by Germany, Britain and France who were concerned over increased EC expenditure and thus doubts remain over the future financing of the EC budget. However, the Cohesion Fund owes much to the efforts of the Spanish Prime Minister, Felipe Gonzalez, and the EC Commission.

Furthermore, the fifteenth protocol to the Treaty also provides for budgetary reform and additional regional finance to be awarded for a wider range of needs (education, training, health research and development) rather than being concentrated as at present on primarily infrastructure projects.

There was also a hint in the negotiations that the principle of 'additionality' may be revised in the future: with the weaker member states arguing that it is very difficult to match EC spending on regional policy in the present climate of reducing public expenditure and debt in order to comply with EMU convergence criteria.

Despite much economic and political argument over the extent to which the EC's policies for cohesion are contrary to the philosophy underlying the Treaty of Rome — in other words redistributive and interventionist aims versus free market and free competition — the fact remains that the Community has for some time pursued the goal of reducing regional disparities and encouraging the social and economic cohesion of its members.

It is clear from both the long-standing political commitment by the EC institutions and the increasing involvement of other Community actors, that the future debate over reform of the structural funds accepts as a necessary factor the interventionist role of the Community, within the broader political concerns of a 'Europe of regions' and the nature of the integration process itself, no longer concerned exclusively with the 'negative' aspects of integration, but increasingly with promoting political and economic equity and diversity between its members.

References and further reading

Bachtler, J., North versus south in European regional policy, 1990, *European Access*, 6; 9–11.

Commission of the EC, 1991a, *The regions in the 1990s*, fourth periodic report on the social and economic situation and development of the regions of the Community, Office for Official Publications of the EC, Luxembourg.

Commission of the EC, 1991b, *Europe 2000: outlook for the development of the Community's territory*. Communication from the Commission to the Council of Ministers and EP, Office for Official Publications of the EC, Luxembourg.

Commission of the EC, 1991c, *Guide to Community initiatives* (taken under the reform of the structural Funds), Office for Official Publications of the EC, Luxembourg.

Croxford, G. *et al.*, 1987, 'The reform of the ERDF', *Journal of Common Market Studies*, 26 (1), 25–38.

Emerson, M., and Huhne, C., 1991, *The ECU Report*, Pan Books/Commission of the EC, London.

Keating, M. and Jones, B., 1991, 'Scotland and Wales: periperhal assertion and European integration', *Parliamentary Affairs*, 44 (3), 311–24.

Kellas, J., 1991, 'European integration and the regions', *Parliamentary Affairs*, 44 (2), 226–39.

Martins, M. and Mawson, J., 1982, 'The programming of regional development in the EC: supranational or international decision making?' *Journal of Common Market Studies*, 20 (3), 229–44.

Marques Mendes, A., 1990, 'Economic cohesion in Europe: the impact of the Delors Plan', *Journal of Common Market Studies*, 29 (1), 17–36.

Mellors, C. and Copperthwaite, N., 1990, *Regional policy*, Routledge (University of Bradford/Spicers Centre for Europe Ltd), London.

Nevin, E.T., 1990, 'Regional policy', in El-Agraa, A.M. (ed.), *The economics of the EC* (3rd ed.), Philip Allan, London.

Wallace, H., Wallace, W. and Webb, C. (eds), 1983, *Policy making in the EC* (2nd ed.), John Wiley & Sons, Chichester.

7

Social and environmental policies

To a certain extent, the development of Community policies in these fields is similar to the development of the EC's regional policy — all are linked to the EC's search for political legitimacy and authority, and to the way in which many have sought to define union and thus widen the scope for 'positive' integration between the states of Europe.

Another similarity linking these policy areas has been their increased political saliency during the 1980s — both at domestic and EC levels. However, it has been EC attempts to increase its competency in the area of social policy which has proved to be one of the most contentious and visible areas of European political debate — notably between the third Conservative Government and the EC Commission characterized in terms of Thatcher-Delors disputes, and most recently evident in the British Government's negotiating position during the IGCs, over the 'Social Chapter'.

Social policy

On the whole, until the mid-1970s, EC legislation and Treaty commitments to social goals could not reasonably be defined as a policy, as the 1957 Treaty of Rome contained only disparate and relatively few articles concerning social matters. In addition, the term 'social' was also rather narrowly defined in terms of employment and 'workplace' interests, rather than encompassing other social activities and needs.

So, the rationale underlying the Rome Treaty was economic integration, albeit for long-term political purposes, but it was not until the late 1960s and 1970s that social policies became more prevalent in both domestic and Community politics.

Hence the original provision for social legislation concerned itself with

Community competency in the free movement of workers (Articles 48–51) and more generally in Title III of the Treaty, where 'member states agree upon the need to promote improved working conditions and an improved standard of living for workers' (Article 117), upon equal pay for equal work between men and women (Article 119), upon creating common social security provisions for migrant workers, and upon the creation of a European Social Fund (ESF), as it 'shall have the task of rendering the employment of workers easier and of increasing their geographical and occupational mobility within the Community' (Article 123).

Until the first enlargement of the EC in 1973, the Community instituted much of the secondary legislation necessary to meet these aims, although on the whole the rather vague and bland principles in the Rome Treaty were secondary to the achievement of the customs union, common market and common policies, such as the Common Agricultural Policy.

However, the first enlargement posed additional questions as to the extent of social protection in the EC, and along with issues such as foreign policy co-ordination and economic and monetary union (EMU), the Community was keen to seize new opportunities to extend the integration process, hence the profile of social policy increased — the Hague Summit of 1969 yet again proved to be an important step forward.

By 1972, political support for the extension of Community social policy led to the first in a series of Social Action Programmes (SAPs) beginning in 1974. Similar to the later Environmental Action Programmes (EAPs — see later section of this chapter) the Social Action Programmes were intended to provide a relatively coherent plan of action for a four-year period. The first Programme clarified the aims of subsequent social policy legislation and was directed at unemployment, which had risen rapidly due to the oil crisis induced recession. It aimed at an upgrading of the role of the ESF to counteract the impact of EC policies upon employment patterns, and to retrain redundant workers in regions characterized by declining heavy industry and manufacturing. Youth unemployment became increasingly visible as a common European problem, although this particular problem was not directly addressed until the cumulative effects of the 1979/81 recession prompted a major reform of the ESF.

In the same way that the EC's regional policy deficiencies and future prospects had encouraged the reform of the ERDF by 1984, so too were the ESF's capabilities and direction addressed. The ESF became increasingly focused upon the specific educational retraining and employment skills require-ments of young people, as well as the long-term unemployed, women and several other social groups.

The Commission also sought to upgrade the relationship between theoretic-ally separate policy areas, prior to the outright reform of the structural funds in 1988, by making the other ESF priority that of severely backward, or 'lagging behind', regions. Hence the regions identified as Objective 1 status not only qualify for the bulk of ERDF expenditure, but a sizeable element of the ESF's resources. These and Objective 2 status regions have increasingly benefited from guaranteed ESF resources, particularly if specific projects are incorporated into a programme approach, such as an Integrated Mediterranean Programme (IMP) or a national Community Support Framework (CSF). The wider aspects of a Community Social Policy as well as the political implications of increased EC competency in this field have assumed greater proportions since the mid-1980s, largely as a result of different political perceptions of the single market.

Whilst it is not the intention to ascribe to the White Paper on completing the single internal market ('1992') powers not existing in it, unlike the holy grail, none the less the elite and public impact of the 1992 programme has been responsible for generating much of the dynamism in the EC, and injecting deep interest in the process of redefining the nature of the EC.

Political debate over European union earlier in the 1980s and discussion of the variety of policies necessary to build a union in place of an economic community, combined with the presentation of the 1992 Programme as a comprehensive step toward achieving what the Treaty of Rome set out to do in 1957. This highlighted the role and function of several key policy areas, social policy and the desirability of 'economic and social cohesion' amongst others.

A further strengthening of the scope and direction of social policy was seen as necessary for a number of interrelated reasons:

- in terms of the completed single market, concerns were expressed over the ability of both skilled and non-skilled people to move freely or at least to perceive that they could take up work in another member state, hence a free-market concern over the genuine mobility of people;
- strategic long-term concerns, largely of organized labour in northern EC member states, of 'social dumping', or the movement of capital and services to those sectors of the European economy with lower wage costs and social security provisions;
- the importance of ensuring that the effects of a single market were not concentrated, in decision-making terms, in the hands of political and business elites — hence the 'tripartism' or corporatist approach, to involve labour and business interests as well as consumer, women's and regional interests in the formulation of social legislation.

The revisions made to the original social policy competency of the Community, laid out in the Single European Act (SEA), reflect some of these concerns. A revised Article 118a committed member states to harmonizing the health and safety conditions of the workplace; Article 118b stressed the formalization of the tripartite or corporatist policy network, whereby the 'dialogue between management and labour at European level could, if the two sides consider it desirable, lead to relations based on agreement'.

Social policy was also reinforced to the SEA's commitment to 'economic and social cohesion' which led in the reform of the structural funds including the ESF (see previous chapter on Regional Policy). Although the revisions made to the Community's social policy may appear somewhat unconvincing or insufficient, this may be due partly to the EC's reluctance to promote a vigorous revision, given the political objections of particularly one member state at the time and, more importantly, because the SEA in itself, as with any treaty governing EC activity invariably relies upon secondary legislation to flesh out more detailed policy. Thus, the SEA's importance lies not so much in its omission of any detailed legal responsibility to conduct social policy, but in the fact that it represented a legal codification of EC activity in this field.

Thus the development of social policy legislation was reliant upon further political momentum generated by the Commission, increasingly together with the European Parliament, and the Economic and Social Committee. By 1988 the Commission, although generally supportive of any increased role for social policy, was facing pressure from a number of bodies in addition to the EP and the Committee — such as the European Trades Union Confederation (ETUC), the labour representative in the social policy dialogue mentioned above.

By May 1989 the Commission presented its draft Social Charter which was accepted at the Strasbourg European Council in December 1989, although not by the British Government.

Until Maastricht and the Treaty on European Union it was this document which acted as the basis for Community legislation in the social field — although it had not been uniformly supported either by member states or by the Community institutions, notably the EP, which has remained dissatisfied with the fact that the eventual 'Community Charter of the Fundamental Social Rights of Workers' or Social Charter has in any case concentrated upon employment-related social rights and that, in some cases, these 'rights' are not seen by the EP as sufficiently clear in intent or effective in practice, in order to safeguard the interests of employed people. The 'Social Charter' as it is commonly referred to, is a declaration of the basic principles and rights which operate throughout the Community and thus covers such themes as the free movement of workers, fair remuneration, right to social protection and 'adequate' levels of social security benefits, freedom of association and collective bargaining, information consultation and participation of workers, and others — see COM (89) 471 final.

The Commission subsequently drew up a new Social Action Programme (SAP) in order to advance legislation according to these principles. Certain proposals within this SAP have featured heavily in national politics and media, particularly in Britain, latterly the common maternity leave and pay proposal.

Before reviewing the impact of the 'Social Charter' included in the European

Union Treaty, it is useful to summarize the areas in which EC social policy operates. As mentioned previously, the primary focus of social policy legislation remains employment-centred:

- the ESF's role in providing additional funding for national programmes to combat long-term and youth unemployment, and since the 1988 reform of the structural funds, to aid the funding of projects designed to enhance 'economic and social cohesion';
- the provision of vocational training such as the Eurotecnet scheme to promote vocational training in the area of new information technologies; schemes such as LINGUA and ERASMUS to facilitate the linguistic skills and educational mobility of students in higher education; and COMETT which stimulates the placement of university students in industrial and business sectors;
- the improvement of living and especially working conditions, such as legislation providing for equality between the sexes over pay, social security benefits and most recently over private pension schemes; the protection of migrant workers allowing them equivalent rights to free movement and settlement; health and safety legislation particularly in relation to toxic or dangerous substances such as asbestos and lead; Social Charter proposals for health and safety requirements in sectors such as transport and quarrying; limited measures on poverty; industrial relations legislation since the 1970s focusing upon the right to appeal against unfair dismissal, and the protection of pay claims against collapse or bankruptcy; and Social Charter proposals over freedom of association and collective bargaining, and principles of co-determination such as workers' rights to information, consultation and participation in their place of work — these latter proposals having formed the bridgehead of political disagreement during the 1980s between the Commission and the British Government, as to the definition of accompanying legislation for the single market — cohesion and partnership — and the long-term implications of any increase in the competency of the EC over social affairs.

Increasingly, however, along with the strengthening of the somewhat more traditionally-defined scope of Community social policy, is the evidence of Community aspirations to widen the direction and impact of social policy. For example, issues such as childcare provision for working parents, protection of children from economic exploitation, initiatives concerning groups such as the elderly and the disabled, and 'social protection' measures not confined to employment-related matters such as a minimum wage, but increasingly to consumer affairs such as credit, food additives and tobacco advertising — these are but indications of the future trends for social policy determination at the European level.

With regard to the protracted and divided political debate, during the latter 1980s, over the social dimension of '1992' — which also marked perhaps the most bitterly contested example of British divergence of opinion over the nature of the integration process — this too has entered a new phase.

For many EC member states, during the IGC negotiations of 1990/91, there existed a broad political consensus on the desirability of increasing EC competency over social affairs, and this consensus may have been strengthened in part by persistent British antipathy.

In early 1991, the Luxembourg Presidency of the Council of Ministers issued the so-called 'non-Paper' — a negotiating text for the IGCs on economic, monetary and political union. In the non-Paper, the Luxembourg Presidency suggested a number of revisions to the Treaty of Rome's Title III concerning Social Policy. In many respects, the revised Articles urged a greater role for the EC — via the Commission — in setting the objectives of Community social policy, in promoting consultation between organized interests, and in implementing a common vocational training policy.

In most cases, although not all, the non-Paper envisaged the use of majority voting in the Council of Ministers and the continued use of the co-operation procedure with the EP (see Agence Europe, Europe Documents 1709/1710, pp. 6–7). By December 1991, the Treaty on European Union initialled at Maastricht, introduced firstly a revision of the EC's social policy competency (Title III to be replaced with the new Title VIII) and secondly, the fourteenth Protocol on Social Policy.

The new Article 123 upgraded the function of the ESF beyond the original aim of rendering 'the employment of workers easier and to increase their geographical and occupational mobility within the Community' to include facilitating 'their adaptation to industrial changes and to changes in production systems, in particular through vocational training and retraining'.

New Articles 126 and 127 make up a new chapter concerning education, vocational training and youth — qualified majority voting will be used for Commission proposals covering the development of 'the European dimension in education', as well as mobility schemes, youth exchanges and distance learning. The non-Paper's suggestion of a common vocational training policy has been incorporated, especially to facilitate 'adaptation to industrial changes' and the 'vocational integration and reintegration into the labour market'.

The fourteenth Protocol to the Treaty concerned social policy — this being the Protocol signed by the eleven member states without British participation. The Protocol stated that the eleven member states 'wish to continue along the path laid down in the Social Charter of 1989'. The Protocol also stated that 'the United Kingdom shall not take part in the deliberations and the adoption by the Council of Commission proposals made on the basis of this Protocol and the above-mentioned agreement'.

The Agreement subsequently clarified the objectives of EC social policy — 'the promotion of employment, improved living and working conditions, proper social protection, dialogue between management and labour, the development of human resources with a view to lasting high employment and the combatting of exclusion'.

The Council of Ministers would vote unanimously on specific legislation covering, for example, 'representation and collective defence of the interests of workers and employers, including co-determination'. The Agreement also covered other issues, such as allowing for positive discrimination measures for women in employment, and the strengthening of labour-management dialogue over social matters.

The significance of this Agreement and Protocol, in legislative terms, enables the eleven mainland European states to develop policy without the participation or influence of the British Government — in the Council of Ministers, Britain would not be permitted to vote on any legislative initiative stemming from the Protocol and, in the EP, British MEPs' views would be largely irrelevant, given that such legislation would not in any case be implemented by the British authorities.

In political terms, the concern of such a divergence of opinion leading to what appears to be a 'two-tier' or 'two-speed' Europe is a valid one — apart from the domestic political constraints appearing to prevent the British Conservative Government from accepting the social 'acquis', which may or may not be a temporary political issue for the government of the day — given that social policy has thus become a political football within the integration process. During the Maastricht Council, the issue of social policy was largely marginalized until it became apparent that British objections to Community development were not just confined to the notion of a single currency or the use of the word 'federal'.

The methods by which other member states sought to stress their commitment to the deepening of the integration process therefore concerned the signing of the Protocol on Social Policy, as well as attempting to meet other British reservations.

It is clear from the debate over EC social policy competency that the parameters of the debate have moved on, by now far removed from the earlier Thatcher Government dislike of 'socialist superstates' and its fears of increased trade union power.

Social policy in the Community, or Union, will increasingly concern the protection and advancement of basic employment and social rights for all groups and, as the Protocol is at pains to stress, this will take into account differing national traditions and practices.

Environmental policy

This is one issue area which has developed its political visibility at all levels of public policy-making — national, Community and global. The question of natural and physical environments, such resources, their use and abuse, and the relationship between economic and human growth in terms of the planet's environmental or 'carrying' capacity have increasingly become integrated into socio-political activity since the late 1960s and early 1970s.

In this context, Community-level concern and legislation in this area are no different — along with individual states and international organizations, the EC reacted to the 1972 United Nations Conference on the Environment, which gave global publicity to the variety of environmental problems in existence at that time, by beginning to consider the state of Europe's natural environment, and the potential impact that a common, Community-wide environmental policy could have.

By October 1972 the Heads of Government — of the original six EC members — had agreed to establish the principles, and subsequently a programme, for Community action, in the area of the environment. Amongst the principles underlying further action, were that of the prevention of pollution 'at source' rather than a wholesale commitment to cleaning up the actual problems once they were in evidence; that the costs involved with preventing or removing environmental problems should in theory be paid by the polluter; that research should be encouraged in order to discover new and effective methods of environmental protection; that consideration of environmental issues should be built into technical planning and decision-making procedures; and that Community policy in this field should aim to co-ordinate and harmonize national environmental policies, although this aim was not to compromise the working of the common market. Specific legislative proposals to promote and achieve such objectives have subsequently been laid out in Environmental Action Programmes (EAPs), which began in 1973 and generally speaking cover a five-year period. Similar to the social action programmes, the EAPs are designed to provide a co-ordinated and wide-ranging statement of Community goals. Before examining the scope and nature of the Community's environmental policy, it is important to note the significance of the Single European Act (SEA). It is clear, from previous chapters, that the amendments made to the original EC Treaty — the Treaty of Rome — in the SEA, were in many cases far-reaching and pragmatic.

In the context of environmental policy, the SEA first of all created a new section — Title VII — within the Treaty, specifically concerning the environment. This brought the legal recognition of Community concern over the environment into line with other policy areas covered in the original Treaty, such as the free movement of goods, persons, service and capital, and agricultural and social policy. Within this new Title, Article 130r stated the objectives of Community environmental policy — the preservation, protection and improvement of the quality of the environment, the protection of human health, and the 'prudent and rational utilisation of natural resources'.

Article 130r.2 suggested that Community action also be based upon preventive action, rectification at source, and that the polluter should pay. Or in other words, Article 130r.2 formalized some of the principles initially agreed by the Heads of Government back in 1972. Article 130r.4 stressed that 'the Community shall take action relating to the environment to which the objectives referred to in paragraph 1 can be attained better at Community level than at the level of the individual member states'. This was an important addition to the new Title, because it was stressing the principle of 'subsidiarity', which had proved problematic in that, on occasion, member states had disputed the right and the utility of Community-level policy-making in this policy area. On the whole, although many environmental problems were transnational and/or global in their impact, there were political differences of opinion over whether the Community had the right or capability to address some aspects of environmental damage, particularly when EC environmental legislation had repercussions for the level or direction of government expenditure.

So Article 130r.4 hoped to clarify the debate by stressing that if the nature of some environmental problems required joint action — Community and member state — then the Community would take the initiative, whereas if other problems or issues could be more effectively managed at national or local level, then the way was clear for such action.

Other important aspects of the SEA's new Title concerning the environment included Article 130s which stipulated that EC environmental legislation would be subject to unanimous voting procedures in Council, although Council could choose to use qualified majority voting procedures if it so desired.

Finally, Article 130t stipulated that despite any common measures agreed to under Article 130s, member states were permitted to introduce or maintain 'more stringent, protective measures compatible with this Treaty'. In theory this particular Article was perhaps designed to allay the concerns of some member states that Community-level action might introduce lower standards of environmental protection, and thus such states had the ability to require higher standards in their own countries.

In practice, however, this Article could prove contentious, with disputes over whether high environmental standards could, for example, constitute a barrier to the free movement of goods within the single market; a similar dispute arose in 1989 when the Dutch Government offered tax-breaks on cars fitted with US-style catalytic converters, because the US converters brought about higher exhaust emission standards than the European emission standards. The Commission dropped its claim that these tax-breaks constituted an illegal form of state aid or subsidy, but maintained that the Dutch Government's preference for stricter environmental standards constituted a distortion of trade by discriminating against products meeting EC standards.

In overall terms, the significance of the SEA for the Community's environmental policy lies in the fact that, for the first time, the Community's involvement in matters concerning the environment had been legally recognized and legitimized.

The Treaty on European Union, signed at Maastricht in February 1992, has developed this legal competency. The new Article 130r added another objective to the EC's environmental policy — to promote 'measures at international level to deal with regional or worldwide environmental problems'.

The new Article 130s states that the Council acting unanimously and after consulting the EP, shall adopt certain legislation 'of a fiscal nature', thus having financial implications for environmental policy; 'measures concerning town and country planning, land use . . . and management of water resources'; and measures 'significantly affecting a member state's choice between different energy sources and the general structure of its energy supply'.

Article 130s.5 also importantly laid down that, apart from the principle that the polluter should pay if any measures agreed to by Council 'involves costs deemed disproportionate for the public authorities of a member state', then Council is permitted to allow temporary derogations and/or 'financial support from the Cohesion Fund' — a Fund created by the new Treaty, to be set up before 1993, to contribute to environmental and trans-European transport programmes.

Article 130t also clarified the earlier flexibility of national environmental policy, so that any legislation adopted under Article 130s 'shall not prevent any Member State from maintaining or introducing more stringent protective measures. Such measures must be compatible with this Treaty'.

Having briefly examined the political significance of the Community's environmental policy, it is important to consider the scope of the Community's policy — the issue areas it covers and the way in which the vast bulk of such legislation is intended to complement and reinforce national environmental policies.

The scope of environmental policy is necessarily large: environmental damage and resource scarcity can occur in all areas of our physical surroundings, including land, sea and air. For example, on the issue of atmospheric pollution, the Community has introduced a number of Directives to cover acceptable content levels of lead and benzene in petrol; the introduction of lead-free petrol across the EC was prioritized as early as 1985; a 1982 Directive addressed the need for co-operation to strengthen national monitoring of types of air pollution. Increasingly since the late 1980s, a number of Directives have concerned acceptable emission limits from cars below 1.4 litre engine size, and from industrial combustion plants such as coal-powered electricity stations, and a 1989 Directive made mandatory the fitting of catalytic converters on all new cars below 2.0 litre engine size.

In addition, Community policy in the area of atmospheric pollution has been strengthened by a number of multilateral environmental agreements, such as the 1985 Vienna Convention on the Protection of the Ozone Layer, with its follow-up Montreal Protocol (1987) which suggested an initial 20 per cent reduction in use of chlorofluorocarbons (CFCs) by 1994, with a further 50 per cent reduction by 1999. In 1989 the Community agreed to take this commitment further by agreeing to eliminate CFC production by 85 per cent before 2000.

On the issue of water pollution — freshwater and seawater — the Community has also introduced a wide range of measures: largely concentrating on harmonizing minimum standards for water quality, for a variety of different purposes. A number of Directives in the mid to late 1970s laid down standards for bathing water, drinking water and shellfish waters; the so-called 'bathing water Directive' — 76/160/EEC — has continued to attract much political disagreement largely between Britain and the Commission, although other member states have also been involved, over the notification of clean beaches.

Other legislation has concerned the limiting of certain toxins and chemicals discharged into Community waters, particularly oil but also cadmium and mercury. A number of Directives have also covered the wider question of waste management, involving specific types such as sewage sludge, and more generally the transportation and disposal of industrial and radioactive wastes in order that contamination or spillage can be more readily prevented both on land-based sites and, in this context, also in terms of river, estuary and marine pollution. Recycling, wherever possible, of these waste products including the reprocessing of nuclear fuels, has become another issue within the Community, with a number of environmental groups stressing that Community policy on this issue could be greatly improved.

Again, the Community is a signatory to a number of international agreements concerning water pollution, such as the 1976 Barcelona Convention to protect the Mediterranean, and the earlier 1963 Berne Convention, which established a Commission to deal with the pollution of the Rhine.

EC environmental policy from its early beginnings has also spanned the issues of flora and fauna protection: initially this involved international agreements such as the 1973 Washington Convention on trade in endangered species (CITES) and the later 1979 Bonn Convention on the conservation of migratory species. This latter agreement was produced within the EC as the 1979 Birds Directive, and is notable for the fact that all the, then nine, EC member states were brought before the Court for non-implementation of the Directive. The Community has also upgraded its policy in response to major international environmental concerns — in addition to legislation covering the use and manufacture of CFCs, the EC responded to highly publicized media campaigns in the early 1980s concerning the slaughter of seals and seal-pups for their pelts, by banning all Community imports of these, and also whale, products. Complementary legislation, perhaps not concerning specific environmental problems as mentioned above, is also a component of EC environmental policy, Complementary in the sense that it is attempting to strengthen the scientific, technical and political dimensions of environmental policy, examples include the 1985 Directive on Environmental Impact Assessment, where assessment is compulsory prior to major infrastructural construction projects such as dams, roads, power stations and refineries, and the creation in 1990 of the European Environmental Agency, ultimately charged with the provision, to the EC and member states, of reliable and comparable data on environmental and meteorological patterns. However, the politics of the creation of the Agency provides a useful example of divergent political interests in the EC, in that the Parliament withheld its opinion for some time, concerned over what it perceived to be the lack of powers for the Agency, which the EP had felt should resemble the US Environmental Protection Agency. The eventual function of the European Agency differed from the Parliament's preference, although the EP secured a review clause for two years after the entry into force of the legislation establishing the Agency.

Prospects for the short-term development of the Community's environmental policy will involve not only further international or global agreements, and the United Nations Conference on Environment and Development later this year — 1992 — may well result in further EC legislation on carbon dioxide emissions as part of the Conference's emphasis on a climatic convention, but within the Community itself, environmental policy may well continue to overlap with other EC policies as the SEA intended, for example in the promotion of economic and social cohesion, in research and development programmes, and energy policies — the latter potentially involving the introduction of an EC-wide carbon or energy tax.

In conclusion, there are a number of issues which may face the future develoment of 'flanking' policies, such as social and environmental policies.

In a general context, it has become clear in recent years that there is often a great deal of 'overlap' between separate policy areas — for example, environmental standards for the use and handling of chemicals will have repercussions on the provision of health and safety legislation, technically within the ambit of social policy, whilst there may theoretically be conflicts of interest between environmental protection and regional development and regeneration programmes. These very generalized illustrations, however, demonstrate Community policies and commitments must complement one another to promote the most desirable outcome. This issue was recognized by the Commission in the SEA — with its emphasis on 'cohesion' and the way in which all the structural funds were subsequently linked and co-ordinated in order to provide maximum assistance to those areas of the EC in greatest need. Also, within the SEA's Title VII on the environment, it was stipulated that 'environmental protection requirements shall be a component of the Community's other policies' (Article 130r.2).

Thus, Community legislation in areas such as agriculture, or single market legislation, or even in external agreements with other states or bodies, should take into account any environmental considerations.

This broad issue of the interdependence between theoretically separate policy areas is important for a number of reasons: not only must Community institutions and decision-makers ensure that the policies they create are consistent with one another, they must also consider the nature and function of national and local authorities and agencies.

Because much EC legislation is delegated to other levels of decision-making for implementation and monitoring, the repercussions of a particular decision taken at Community level will, increasingly, be felt at other levels, such as national ministries or government departments, and regional or local government. This has had and will continue to have effects upon the organization of these bodies and the effectiveness of the links between them and the other levels of decision-making. For example, the decision to create a consultative Committee of the Regions (European Union Treaty, 1992) will have a direct effect upon both the nature of Community-level decisions, given the input of this Committee upon relevant draft legislation, and upon the functioning of cohesion policies in the Community.

Similarly, the desire on the part of the Commission to involve both business and labour representation in discussing 'social dimension' legislation for the single market has marked an important shift away from the historical pattern, for the most part, of national government and Community institutions dominating the arena of Community decision-making.

References and further reading

Commission of the EC, 1987, *The EC and the environment*, Office for Official Publications of the EC, Luxembourg.

Commission of the EC, 1989, *Community Charter of Fundamental Social Rights*, draft, Commission of the EC, Brussels.

Commission of the EC, 1990, *1992 — the social dimension*, Office for Official Publications of the EC, European Documentation series, Luxembourg.

Dankert, P. and Kooyman, A. (eds), 1989, *Europe without frontiers: socialists on the future of the EEC*, Mansell Publishing for Cassell, London.

Haigh, N. and Baldock, D., 1989, *Environmental policy and 1992*, Institute for European Environmental Policy, London.

House of Lords Select Committee on the EC, 1989, *A Community Social Charter*, HMSO, HL Paper 6–I, London.

IEA Readings 29, 1989, *Whose Europe? Competing visions for 1992*, Institute for Economic Affairs, London.

McCarthy, E., 1989, *The EC and the environment*, PNL Press, European Dossier Series, London.

Roberts, B.C., 1989, *Delors versus 1992?*, The Bruges Group, Occasional Paper 1, London.

Taylor, C. and Press, A., 1990, *Europe and the environment*, The Industrial Society, London.

Tyszkiewicz, Z., 1989, 'European social policy — striking the right balance', *European Affairs*, 3 (4), 70–5.

8
The Lome Convention: the EC-ACP relationship

These Agreements, signed between the EC and the group of African-Caribbean-Pacific (ACP) states, began in 1975, although the Community's relationship with member states' former colonial territories began with the 1957 Treaty of Rome. It is often a simple mistake to equate the EC's Lome Conventions with EC-developing state relations — the ACP group forms a sizeable bulk of the total group of developing or Third World states, and their special relationship via the Conventions is derived mostly, although not entirely, from their former colonial 'possession' status with a number of EC member states. Specifically, the members of the ACP Group are primarily the non-Asian ex-colonies of France and Britain: with only two states, Ethiopia and Liberia, having had no prior colonial status.

In order to view the Lome Conventions more effectively and assess their major characteristics, it is useful to review the earlier structures created to bind the EC with, initially, French colonial territories. The Treaty of Rome contained a chapter devoted to laying out the nature of the Community's relationship with colonies and ex-colonies associated with some of its member states: France being the prime mover, during the negotiations to create the EEC, in pursuing a Community-level relationship largely for French dependencies, but which eventually also included Italian and Belgian colonies. This enthusiasm for linking colonial interests with the creation of the Common Market has been explained by reference to France's historically close, not to say almost dominating, political links with its overseas departments, and its desire to maintain advantageous economic and trading links within the context of the Common Market's rules and procedures.

Part Four of the Treaty of Rome created the 'Association of the Overseas Countries and Territories'. Article 131 suggested that 'the purpose of association shall be to promote the economic and social development of the countries and territories and to establish close economic relations between them and the

Community as a whole', and to 'further the interests and prosperity of the inhabitants of these countries and territories in order to lead them to the economic, social and cultural development to which they aspire'.

Article 132 then laid out in more detail the nature of Association as far as the Community and its member states were involved: with the Community and the Associates agreeing to a de facto recognition of Most Favoured Nation status between each other, and where the principle of non-discrimination was applied to the right of establishment for citizens and business ventures for both Community and Associate states. Article 133 concerned itself with the direct repercussions of Association, such as the abolition of customs duties on goods imported from the Associates, and although Article 133.3 did permit the Associates to levy duties for development purposes, it was implied that these should be of only a temporary nature and should eventually be reduced to the general tariff levels in existence.

Under Article 134 if such tariff levels caused trading problems for any Community member state, that state did have the right to ask the Commission to propose a solution.

Article 136 delegated the specific tasks of bringing the Association into being, to an Implementing Convention, which although not greatly widening the scope of the relationship to include social and political aspirations of the Associates — such as independence — did nonetheless make some attempt to suggest that the Community could take a greater role in promoting the rounded development of its Associates.

The Convention also laid down a five-year time period for the workings of the Association, whereas the Treaty of Rome suggested that, as with the creation of the EEC itself, the relationship with the Associated countries would be indefinite; hence the European Development Fund was created and expected to operate for five years, primarily to offer grants to Associates, in addition to regular bilateral overseas assistance or aid.

The net effects of this initial five-year period of Community-associated countries have been documented at length elsewhere (see, for example, Lister 1988, pp. 18–30). In general though, there were some positive developments such as the contribution of EDF monies for basic infrastructure projects, and the invaluable experience gained by colonial administrations in the day-to-day operation of the Associate system. There were, however, a number of problems too: the long-term nature of some provisions, such as freedom of movement or establishment as well as expected trade creation and increased trade flows within and between the parties to the relationship, did not materialize as quickly as some had expected, and in some cases, was negative.

On the whole, the political significance of the EC's early attempts to create and sustain its first major external relationship, however limited, lies in the fact that both parties sought to maintain a formal relationship, despite many Associated countries receiving their independence by the mid-1960s and despite the growing closeness between the Community and its member states as the Common Market emerged.

The 1960s were characterized by a revised set of agreements between the EC and the former Associated countries and territories, now mostly independent. These eighteen newly independent states, entirely African, took the title, under the new Convention, of the Association of African and Malagasy States (AAMS) — they included Chad, Cameroon, Senegal, Somalia and Togo amongst others. The first Yaounde Convention of 1963, followed by a second in 1969, did not in many respects differ markedly from the previous Treaty of Rome Associates relationship.

These Conventions maintained the system of association, albeit this time between the EC and a group of sovereign states — rather than between the EC and colonial administrations previously — and the aims of the Association continued to focus upon economic development, although general references to the importance of social and cultural progress were not precluded. Thus the exports of the AAMS members continued to enter the EEC under the same rules as before: duty-free and with no quotas or quantitative restrictions unless these were applied within the Community.

Another shared characteristic was the system of mutual trade preferences, where AAMS products received preferential access to the EEC market and similarly where the EEC received preference in AAMS markets for its exports. However, the first Yaounde Convention introduced a set of joint AAMS-EEC institutions which would direct and manage the relationship — these bodies composing a Council aided by a Committee, a Parliamentary Conference and a Court. These institutions not only provided a valuable seat for 'learning' but also could take major decisions affecting the Association, such as the accession of any further AAMS member states.

Another change, to the volume and purposes of the European Development Fund (EDF), was a reflection of growing concern that some AAMS members could be over-reliant upon the production or processing of a primary commodity. Therefore the EDF was enlarged in volume by approximately 20 per cent, and was available in the form of both grants and loans, in order for example to encourage trade diversification and the stabilization of key commodity prices.

The second Yaounde Convention, in a political context, was perhaps not as straightforward a process of transition as the first Convention had been. Increasingly the AAMS members stressed their own, largely economic, problems and the measures necessary within the Association system which they felt were necessary — especially in the development of industrial and manufacturing capability. The overriding characteristic of the political relationship between the parties prior to Yaounde II was that the AAMS was not entirely prepared to accept the presentation of Association conducted almost exclusively by EC interests.

The EEC itself underwent major changes in the 1960s: the early divergence of opinion between de Gaulle and other Community members over issues such as British accession and the furtherance of the supranational character of the Community; the achievement of the Common Market ahead of schedule; and the political issues posed by the late 1960s again relating to EEC enlargement, this time interposed with debate over the 'widening' or the 'deepening' of the Community. So perhaps to some degree the EEC was preoccupied by interests closer to home, those interests not only pertaining to internal political developments but to the Community's evaluation of its role in relation to its direct neighbours — hence the EEC's links by the late 1960s and early 1970s with Greece and Turkey — in the form of Association, with Mediterranean states and the North African Maghreb and Mashreq groups of states. However, the second Yaounde Convention was eventually signed — the obligations and provisions of this latter agreement were not substantially altered, except for one important area: the Group of 77 and the wider global grouping of developing states within the UN's Conference on Trade and Development (UNCTAD) were successful in gaining partial acceptance of their case for a Generalized System of Preferences (GSP) to be extended multilaterally, in order that developing states could attempt to penetrate markets without necessarily having to extend this freedom to developed nations. This GSP did therefore affect the previous mutual or reciprocal preference system in existence since the Treaty of Rome's Associate system.

An important factor shaping the continuation and adaptation of the Community's previous relationships with developing states was the general shift in political and economic relations between North and South during the early 1970s: the increasingly vocal calls by developing states for a 'New International Economic Order' (NIEO) in order to restructure global economic relations along more equitable and less divisive lines, as well as the political nourishment given to developing states by the OPEC states' use of oil as economic leverage against dependent Northern states, contributed to the broad climate of assertiveness and concern for the long-term economic future of developing states. Thus as far as the developing states were concerned there was every good reason to maintain close links with the EC, especially if those links could be reformed in accordance with the 'wants' of the time.

Specifically, another factor prompting the re-evaluation of the Yaounde Conventions was the accession of Britain, as well as Ireland and Denmark, to the EC. Britain, like France, had historically maintained a large prosperous Empire upon which independence in the post-1945 period, transformed itself into the Commonwealth. Britain had long valued its trading relationships with ex-colonies and Dominions, and sought to maintain these links, as had France, through a Community-level relationship.

However, it was to be African and Caribbean members of the Commonwealth who were accepted into the new agreement, and the Asian members of the Commonwealth — such as India, Pakistan and Singapore — were instead linked to the Community in separate agreements, due to the overwhelming European-African nature of previous relationships, and the fact that in terms of demographic and economic factors, it was felt that their incorporation into the new Lome Convention would be unduly difficult to achieve.

The Lome Convention

The Lome Convention, setting out a new phase in the relationship between Europe and a number of developing states, was signed in Lome, the capital of Togo, early in 1975. Instead of referring to the Community and its Associates, the Convention referred to the EEC-ACP Group: the African-Caribbean-Pacific Group, comprising the original Treaty of Rome Associates and Yaounde Associates (mostly ex-colonial areas of France) and the newest British Commonwealth members, with some states not previously a colonial possession, such as Ethiopia. The Group initially comprised 46 states, stretching from the Bahamas and Barbados, Fiji to Ghana, Grenada and Jamaica, and from Nigeria to Zambia (see end of chapter for complete list).

What did this new agreement encompass? Firstly, it covered co-operation over a number of issues such as trade and trade-related measures and the question of development aid and secondly, it created a number of institutions designed to facilitate contact and negotiation over the operation of the Convention.

The incorporation of the British Commonwealth states did produce some effects: some have argued that, for example, their determined negotiation over the nature of trade reciprocity resulted in one of the Lome's major characteristics. Unlike the earlier types of relationship where trade between the two parties was deemed mutual or reciprocal, the 1975 Convention resulted in a non-reciprocal trading relationship — or in other words, a system whereby the ACP Group were not obliged to offer special access to Community exports and where ACP exports were granted trade preferences for entry into the Community market. Another trade issue concerned EEC tariff barriers to ACP exports: although the Treaty of Rome Associates system and the Yaounde Conventions had progressively reduced tariff barriers and other quantitative restrictions applying to developing country exports, the position was initially unclear on the question of Commonwealth exports, previously having enjoyed UK trade preferences and tariff reductions. Under the Lome Convention, all ACP members were essentially offered the same rights created by the earlier EEC relationships — so that whilst the EEC did not necessarily reduce even further the barriers to ACP goods, neither were these barriers increased or applied haphazardly.

Other trading and economic issues directly linked with prospects for further economic development in the ACP Group were also addressed. For example a separate Protocol covering sugar production was included in the Lome Convention: sugar being one of the most significant export products originating from ACP states, especially the Commonwealth members. The Protocol was intended to provide a guarantee of EEC purchase of ACP sugar, in terms of both a negotiated price and quantity: the price being linked to the price paid to the Community producers under the CAP. This single-commodity deal worked in favour of the EEC, who were guaranteed steady supplies of sugar, and generally in favour of the ACP sugar producers, who were similarly guaranteed market access and export revenue. However, the EEC's Common Agricultural Policy did promote the production of sugar, as well as a number of other agricultural products, so that by the 1980s domestic sugar production in the Community enabled it to compete as an exporter in world markets.

Linked to the concept underlining the Sugar Protocol was another novel aspect of the Lome Convention: a procedure whereby export revenue earnings of ACP states could be 'stabilized', if the state was heavily dependent upon several primary export products.

This procedure, known as STABEX, was novel in the wider context of North-South economic relations, where no other industrialized state had created a similar scheme, although it was not essentially a radical or new departure in so far as the Community was concerned — similar funds for aid in special circumstances had been a feature of the previous Yaounde Conventions.

The STABEX procedure covered a number of primary products — coffee, tea, cocoa, cotton, groundnuts, coconuts and palmnuts, bananas, timber products, iron ore and animal hides. Generally speaking, ACP states that depended heavily on revenue raised from these exports could apply for reimbursement if they suffered from more than approximately 7.5 per cent loss of export earnings, whilst the poorest ACP states could be reimbursed if they lost revenue over 2.5 per cent. STABEX was itself identified as a separate fund within the wider European Development Fund (EDF).

In a broad context both the Sugar Protocol and the STABEX mechanism could serve to bring a relative sense of security to ACP producers, given that although cash crops were seen as useful revenue-raisers for domestic economies, many ACP states sought to diversify their economic structures and if revenue, in any one year, could be maintained, then the hope was that long-term economic restructuring could take place in a more conducive environment.

The Lome Convention thus undertook to promote industrial co-operation between the EEC-ACP Group, largely funded by the EDF but also by the European Investment Bank (EIB), and in which the accompanying Centre for Industrial Development would act as a forum for identifying and debating individual projects. However, this was not necessarily a highly-articulated feature of the Convention, so its significance lay in the hopes for a long-term or successive commitment to industrial development. So far the major trade-related features of the Lome Convention have been stressed. None the less, another significant aspect worth noting is the aid provisions of the relationship.

Given that the membership of the new ACP Group had more than doubled since the earlier Yaounde system, the question of the volume of aid, as well as its purpose and direction, became an important characteristic of the negotiations. Under this first Lome Convention, total EC aid was set at 3,390m UA (Units of Account) which represented, in real terms, a doubling of the amount of aid allocated to the second Yaounde Convention. The vast bulk of this was directed at the EDF and the remainder was allocated to the EIB.

Perhaps not surprisingly, the ACP Group lobbied for higher net sums and although they were disappointed in that context, nevertheless most seemed to see that it was the best possible arrangement, given the problems in the global economy at the time. What was important, rather than the overall net volume of aid, was instead the management and political influence over how, where and why aid monies were spent. On the whole, it was the Community again which ultimately controlled the management of the EDF: although the Lome Convention did introduce a greater degree of participation and influence for the ACP Group in this context, for example in their presentation and priority-setting of particular development projects best suited to their needs.

Finally, another major characteristic of the Lome Convention was its adaptation of institutional procedures, begun under the Yaounde system, to represent the views not only of EC-ACP governments, but of the EC's institutions themselves and parliamentary representatives from both parties to the agreement. So under Lome, a joint Council of Ministers, a joint Committee of Ambassadors and the joint Consultative Assembly were formed. Also, the ACP Secretariat was created, based in Brussels, and acts as an important focus for ACP diplomacy and consultation.

The Council of Ministers comprised both EC member state Ministers and senior members of the EC Commission, with the Ministers of the ACP states. Similar to the EC's Council of Ministers, the EC-ACP Council was to fulfil a legislative role or, in other words, it had the final power of taking decisions. However, unlike the EC Council which for domestic political reasons shifted towards unanimity procedures in the mid-1960s, the EC-ACP Council was expected at the outset to reach an effective consensus on any given issue and thus take decisions on that basis. No doubt this was intended to avoid precisely those problems inherent in the EC's Council of Ministers when absolute agreement could not be reached.

The Committee of Ambassadors, despite its rather grandiose title, was nevertheless an important adjunct to the workings of the Council — the Ambassadors and their staff were expected to complement and back up the infrequent meetings of the Council of Ministers, essentially to provide some continuity and in-depth examination of problems, issues or day-to-day workings of the Convention.

The Consultative Assembly, however, was not endowed with any meaningful powers or functions in the way that the above institutions were. Similar to the early EC Assembly, later the EP, the Lome Assembly was credited merely with the function of consultation and debate — the other Lome institutions were under no obligation to take Assembly views into account. However, the institutional framework was not completely static as it has also been pointed out that 'informal elaboration' of this institutional framework was subsequently carried out: regular meetings between social and economic organized interests from both the Community and the ACP Group hoped to sustain a form of dialogue (Lister 1988, pp. 101–2).

Having briefly considered the major characteristics of the first Lome Convention in a largely uncritical light, it is important to consider what the EC-ACP relationship has achieved, and to what extent the relationship, as its preamble was at pains to emphasize, was based on 'equality' and 'partnership'. Under the first Lome Convention, the volume of trade entering the EC from the ACP Group was not substantially affected by the Convention's provisions concerning preferential arrangements such as lower tariffs — largely perhaps as a result of the conservative provisions of Lome which essentially perpetuated the preferences enjoyed by the Yaounde Associates and which were then extended to the wider membership of Lome. In other words, the same preferential treatment applied to the same products as before. However, what was noticeable under the first Lome Convention was the overall increase in ACP exports, very largely the function of the new members, and that this increase was represented in terms of increased oil exports to the Community from new Lome members such as Nigeria and several Caribbean states.

Increasingly, too, the ACP Group during the 1970s found themselves competing with other developing states who had negotiated bilateral trade and co-operation agreements with the Community: China, India and a number of Latin American states, in addition to the EC's economic relations with Mediterranean and North African states. By the 1980s this resulted not so much in trade friction between ACP and other developing states (although this was occurring due to ACP and non-ACP textile exports to the EC), but gave rise to ACP concern that many other developing states had diversified their economic base and were thus no longer directly competing for an EC market share in an identical product.

The STABEX mechanism, although generally praised for its efficient and quick disbursement to ACP states having suffered from the relevant losses in export revenue, was criticized by ACP members in that its coverage of products designated as important for export revenue-raising purposes could be widened, notably in respect of minerals exports. Although the STABEX coverage was widened, it did not incorporate primary materials or minerals to the extent that the ACP had wished.

Another criticism of the STABEX mechanism was that some of the poorest ACP states (LDCs) did not benefit from the STABEX transfers largely as a function of the nature of products covered by STABEX rules, as a number of these LDCs did gain significantly from payments where their primary exports coincided with the list of STABEX products. In the area of development aid, along with the stated desire to promote industrial co-operation, the Lome Convention did not escape criticism. The aid programme within the EDF was, and continues to be, raised solely from the EC's General Budget, so in this sense the EC's aid programme could only ever be complementary to bilateral official development assistance, and other aid programmes managed by, for example, the International Monetary Fund or World Bank. In this context, EDF funding has long been seen as insufficient in volume, given the diverse and often pressing needs of ACP members — for example the present Lome IV has a total aid package of 12 billion ECU worth approximately US $15bn, which is available for the first five years of the ten-year life-span of the Fourth Convention.

In relation to the application or specific purposes for which EDF monies were available, it was envisaged that the ACP states themselves would be responsible for identifying development priorities and for advancing projects and programmes to the EDF Committee. The procedure for being awarded aid was criticized for, in practical terms, being over-bureaucratic, time-con-suming and subject to political manipulation and influence. Thus the 'public image' of some EDF projects was poor, with connotations of wastefulness, corruption or personal empire-building. However, it would be incorrect to assume a thoroughly bleak view of the purposes of EDF aid, as many ACP states benefited from their broad quota of aid when used for small-scale local projects, such as health and rural development programmes.

EDF aid also tended to be given on a 'soft' basis, whereas multilateral agencies such as the IMF and World Bank tended to impose much stricter conditions on donor countries. However, a criticism of EDF agricultural and rural programmes, similar to criticisms made of earlier World Bank projects, was that they tended to stress the growth of cash crops for export-driven economic restructuring in developing states — and socio-environmental costs of such policies, amongst other issues, had on many occasions failed to be considered. Hence one of the potential areas for aid programmes, notably the promotion of industrial and manufacturing development, was considerably marginalized, given that basic social and economic infrastructure requirements of ACP states were not completely or effectively met by the EDF.

However, although the practical results of the first Lome Convention may not have matched the earlier aspirations of 'equality', 'partnership' and the beginnings of a new 'economic order', none the less subsequent Lome Conven-tions have been introduced — Lome II signed in 1979 to cover the period 1980/85, Lome III signed in 1984 to cover 1985/90, and the most recent Lome IV, signed in December 1989, this time due to cover a ten-year period, 1990–2000.

These further Conventions have added new mechanisms and dimensions to the EC-ACP relationship. Lome II, in addition to an increased membership of 57, introduced a complementary scheme to the STABEX mechanism — SYSMIN (also referred to as MINEX). SYSMIN, in many respects, sought to address the earlier concerns of ACP minerals exporters, by acting not necessarily as a method of stabilizing export revenue, but which instead sought to maintain the 'export capacity' of these mineral producers (the more important minerals covered include aluminium, uranium and cobalt). A fall in the 'capacity' of mineral exporters of at least 10 per cent would ensure that the particular state concerned would receive aid, thus preventing any capital equipment or distribution facilities linked to the extraction process being downgraded. Lome III (again, increased to 65 ACP states by 1984) was characterized in terms of the tightening-up of some of the procedures of the STABEX mechanism, notably the scrutiny of how ACP governments spent the monies received under STABEX in compensation for their loss of revenue. The EC suggested that monitoring the expenditure of the monies in the sector for which they were originally intended was a necessary reform. Lome III also attempted to strengthen previous policy towards promoting 'self-reliant' and regional development, and during the Lome III period began to address the massive problems of debt repayment faced by developing states — extra and reallocated Lome funds were made available to those extremely affected by the debt crisis.

Important in Lome III, also, were the beginnings of a shift in emphasis of development aid — as the visibility of multilateral agencies such as the IMF and World Bank increased in the economic and political decision-making processes of developing states, the Lome Convention began to reflect this, with mention being made of 'structural adjustment', 'conditionality' provisions and sectoral long-term aid programming. All these factors thus marked the beginnings of a new approach to the methods and processes by which the Lome Conventions had sought to sustain the EC-ACP relationship.

Lome IV, the most recent Convention to date, has attempted to clarify some of these points. By 1992 the 70 signatory states (including Haiti, Dominican Republic, and Namibia after gaining its independence) displayed a number of serious reservations concerning the utility of the Lome relationship. On the whole trade preferences were not substantially altered, except for a Rum Protocol, allowing increases of ACP rum exports to enter free of customs duties. The STABEX mechanism was reformed, whereby monies disbursed for lost revenue no longer require repayment to the EC, although the Community maintained a degree of control over the purposes of the STABEX disbursements, for example by encouraging STABEX funds to be used to diversify domestic economies. Lome IV also included a separate fund to help those ACP states undertaking 'structural adjustment' measures, invariably as a result of receiving a Structural Adjustment Loan (SAL) from the IMF. The Lome fund is intended to provide speedy assistance for import requirements such as fuel or for technical assistance in carrying out economic reforms.

Importantly Lome IV explicitly recognized the environmental dimension of development and the costs associated with it: the Convention has attempted to highlight such problems as resource depletion and desertification. Also within its coverage of the natural environment, the Convention banned all exports of toxic and radioactive wastes from the EC to any ACP state. These provisions may not necessarily be as comprehensive or as financially robust as would prove desirable — nevertheless they too mark an important shift in focus.

Regional economic development, and the uses as well as co-ordination of Lome funds to encourage regional economic initiatives were also features of successive Lome Conventions: under Lome III funds accruing to each individual ACP state, especially in Southern Africa, began to be linked with other Lome grants and funds, in order to promote regional co-operation and development programmes, covering infrastructure projects and technical assistance. This form of EC-ACP co-operation, through the Southern African Development and Coordination Conference (SADCC), also became increasingly politicized, in relation to South Africa's acts of destabilization and the 'frontline states' economic dependency upon the Republic of South Africa.

Prospects and summary

The Lome Conventions have for much of their existence been characterized by criticism — from ACP states, development NGOs, independent commentators, and from within the EC.

Criticism, in a general sense, has concerned the basic fact that the existence of the Lome Conventions have for the most part failed in their aims of promoting the political equality and partnership of its members and, even more importantly, have not essentially altered the structure and nature of international economic relations between developed and developing states.

Evidence to support this claim is found in the institutions and processes governing the relationship — where, although in some cases the ACP states do have the prerogative to act, in most cases it is the Community's view or position of strength that may offset any notions of partnership. This has tended to become more prominent in the 1980s as many developing states have undertaken structural adjustment measures for debt repayment and economic growth purposes, in line with the Bretton Woods institutions of the IMF and World Bank — increasingly there have been ACP complaints that the EC, through the Lome Conventions, has sought to discipline the use made of Lome aid in this context.

In economic terms, the Lome Conventions have also faced criticism over their inability to deal effectively with the debt crisis of developing states, to empower ACP members to diversify and strengthen their economic activities by lessening their dependency on primary exports and more generally to prevent the marginalization of developing states in the international economic system.

For a long time, the Lome Conventions were praised and heralded for their liberal, peaceful and relatively non-partisan characteristics, as they enabled both the ex-colonial powers and their ex-dependent countries and territories to adjust to changing world conditions. Essentially seen as benevolent and liberal, the Conventions provided a degree of political and economic security, free from any superpower connotations, and which constituted a fundamentally different relationship between developed and developing states.

Again, the various trade preferences extended to ACP states, especially in terms of Lome's non-reciprocity: the creation of the STABEX and later the SYSMIN mechanisms; and Lome III's emphasis upon basic human rights and the apartheid system in the Republic of South Africa, are often seen as evidence of the liberal 'harmony of interest' nature of the Conventions.

There are perhaps elements of truth in both viewpoints — what is equally important to bear in mind are the present problems and issues facing developing states, and a consideration of whether the Lome Conventions are an adequate or effective framework through which to address them.

In EC terms perhaps the most obvious issue facing the ACP states, that of the repercussions of the single market programme, has in many respects been politically eclipsed in terms of the structural changes experienced by the former Eastern bloc states of Central and Eastern Europe as well as the former Soviet Union itself. Specific concerns of the EC's 1992 programme for ACP states have included the future for special marketing arrangements between individual ACP and EC member states which may be abolished and thus may hit the export earnings of some ACP states comparatively severely; the effects of harmonizing health and environmental standards especially for foodstuffs may mean that ACP goods will not be able to compete effectively against products from other countries which do meet the necessary requirements; and the effects of other internal policies in the EC which may have an impact upon EDF funding, such as the EC's 1988 emphasis upon the doubling of the structural Funds, or the effects of a single European currency as an element of EMU.

Underlying these issues is the wider concern that ACP goods will increasingly be forced to compete with products from other developing states as a result of EC trade agreements since the 1970s with China, Israel and Latin America amongst others — to a certain extent this is an existing feature in ACP trade with the EC, having lost ground to other developing states since the late 1970s.

In relation to the effects upon the EC of a 'new Europe', not only may the ACP states be affected by cheaper Central European imports, such as textiles or semi-manufactured goods, but also may well be concerned over the direction of investment, especially when a large number of ACP African states are already classified as the least-developed countries (LDCs) and thus have difficulties in attracting investment or relocation of business.

None the less, criticism apart, the Lome Conventions have both positive and negative characteristics — it is largely true that no other state, group of states or international organization has maintained such an economic framework and political relationship with developing states.

The Conventions have much to commend them: they contain elements which could be upgraded and extended to meet their aims effectively. It does not appear a likely scenario that the fourth Lome Convention will not be renewed; however, it appears equally unlikely that the EC-ACP relationship will be maintained in a benign fashion. In order for the Lome Convention framework to meet, in however incomplete a fashion, the needs of developing states in the 1990s and beyond, the framework may increasingly adopt the political and economic criteria advanced by the multilateral institutions of the IMF and World Bank.

Current ACP membership (1992)

Angola	Liberia
Antigua	Madagascar
Barbuda	Malawi
Bahamas	Mali
Barbados	Mauritania
Belize	Mauritius
Benin	Mozambique
Botswana	Namibia
Burkina Faso	Niger
Burundi	Nigeria
Cameroon	Papua New Guinea
Cape Verde	Rwanda
Central African Republic	St Christopher and Nevis
Chad	St Lucia
Comoros	St Vincent and Grenadines
Congo	Sao Tome and Principe
Cote d'Ivoire	Senegal
Djibouti	Seychelles
Dominica	Sierra Leone
Dominican Republic	Solomon Islands
Equatorial Guinea	Somalia
Ethiopia	Sudan
Fiji	Suriname
Gabon	Swaziland
Gambia	Tanzania
Ghana	Togo
Grenada	Tonga
Guinea	Trinidad and Tobago
Guinea Bissau	Tuvalu

Guyana	Uganda
Haiti	Western Samoa
Jamaica	Vanuatu
Kenya	Zaire
Kiribati	Zambia
Lesotho	Zimbabwe

References and further reading

The Courier, magazine for EC-ACP Group.

Gruhn, I., 1976, 'The Lome Convention: inching toward interdependence', *International Organization*, 30 (2), 241–61.

Journal of Common Market Studies, 1990, Special Issue on Europe 1992 and the developing countries, 29 (2).

Lake, M., 1985, 'The Lome III Convention — Europe's new model for dialogue and development', *Yearbook of European Law*, 5, 21–56.

Laurent, P-H., 1983, 'Partnership or paternalism: a critical view of the EC-ACP Conventions', *The Round Table*, 288, 455–65.

Lister, M., 1988, *The EC and the developing world: the role of the Lome Convention*, Avebury Press, Aldershot.

Notzold, J. *et al.*, 1990, 'Lome IV: a chance for black Africa's return to the world economy?', *Aussenpolitik*, 41 (2), 181–92.

Ravenhill, J., 1985, *Collective clientelism: the Lome Conventions and North-South relations*, Columbia University Press, New York.

Taylor, P., 1983, *The limits of European integration*, Croom Helm, London.

9
The EC and EFTA

The early history of the division between the European Communities and the European Free Trade Association (EFTA) is covered in Chapter 1 (pp. 15–16). The creation of a European Economic Community in 1957 with just six members meant that most of the countries of Western Europe were excluded from this innovation. Certain countries — Greece, Iceland, Ireland, Portugal, Spain — were not economically developed enough by the end of the 1950s for such an experiment, but others — the United Kingdom, the Scandinavian states and the Alpine republics of Austria and Switzerland — had other reasons for their exclusion. Their governments seemed unprepared for participation in an organization with supranational institutions (that is, ones that could overrule national decisions) and which espoused a Common Agricultural Policy and a Common External Tariff. Their failure, by the end of the 1950s, to persuade the Six to set up the European Economic Community within the framework of a wider West European free trade arrangement, meant that by 1960 the trade division of Western Europe was unavoidable. The establishment of the European Free Trade Association in May 1960 by 'the Seven' — Austria, Denmark, Norway, Portugal, Sweden, Switzerland and the United Kingdom — formalized that divide. Since then, relations between the organization and the EC have been through four phases and are entering a fifth.

EC-EFTA: four phases

The first phase was brief: it lasted until summer 1961, barely two years after the EFTA treaty had been signed. During this period EFTA attempted to reach a bilateral understanding — trade bloc to trade bloc — with the European Economic Community. From the start the Seven pressed for reciprocity of tariff cuts between the EEC and EFTA. The hope was, with the creation of a new Western trade forum — the Organization for Economic Cooperation and Development — in 1960, that the two groupings would move towards each other. Instead the EEC accelerated its July 1960 tariff cuts, obliging EFTA to speed up its tariff reductions to keep in step (Archer 1990, p. 128; Miljan 1977, p. 148).

The second period was that from summer 1961 until the end of 1972, during which time leading EFTA members attempted to negotiate entry into the EC. The United Kingdom government had decided — in early summer 1961 — to apply for membership negotiations with the EEC (Charlton 1983, p. 252), thereby giving the impression that EFTA would be ditched. To improve the situation, the British agreed at the London EFTA Ministerial Council in June 1961 that the EFTA states would 'remain united throughout the negotiations' with the EEC, that EFTA would be maintained until agreements had been reached with the EEC to meet 'the various legitimate interests of all members of EFTA, and thus enable them to participate from the same date in an integrated European market' (*EFTA Bulletin* 1961, p. 1). This allowed each EFTA state to decide on its own approach to the EEC, but also hinted at a 'convoy' strategy to ensure that, in the end, all the Seven were accommodated by the Community, though not necessarily by full membership. Indeed, only Denmark, Norway and the United Kingdom applied for this option, with Austria, Sweden and Switzerland requesting talks about associate membership, mainly because of concerns about their neutrality.

After the French veto of the United Kingdom application (see Chapter 1, p. 16), EFTA returned to the task of creating an industrial free trade among its members, which it achieved in December 1966 — a year earlier than planned (Archer 1990, p. 127). A second attempt by the United Kingdom and some of its EFTA colleagues to apply for EC membership in 1967 was also vetoed by the French Government. There was little progress that EFTA could sensibly make after its mainstay member had twice indicated its intention to join another organization. Indeed the Nordic states decided to negotiate a Nordic Economic Union (NORDEK) to supplement their EFTA membership (Miljan 1977, pp. 102–10). However, events intervened. In 1969 a new government in France accepted the idea of extending membership of the EC and in 1970 negotiations opened with the British, later joined by the Danes, the Norwegians and the Irish (the latter not being EFTA members). From 1 January 1973, the United Kindom, Denmark and Ireland became full members of the EC, the Norwegian people having rejected membership at a referendum in September 1972.

The period that began in 1973 and lasted until 1984 has been described as one of 'pragmatic bilateralism' (Pedersen 1991, p. 13). From 1972 to 1973 the remaining EFTA countries (which by then included Finland and Iceland) signed individual industrial free trade agreements with the extended EC. These allowed for a period up to July 1977 within which the EFTA states and the EC would dismantle their tariffs on industrial trade, and those on processed agricultural imports, from each other. Goods would only be traded freely if they had been 'wholly produced' in the area of association between the EC and each of the EFTA states, or if they had undergone 'sufficient transformation' within that area (Curzon 1974, p. 235).

The seven remaining EFTA states' individual agreements with the EC were to be overseen by joint committees of the EC and each of the EFTA states, and all the agreements, except that with Finland (which was still concerned about its relations with the Soviet Union), had an 'evolutionary clause' which allowed matters not covered by the free trade arrangement to be discussed. In May 1977 the EFTA leaders, meeting in Vienna, decided that they wanted closer co-operation with the EC, especially on economic matters. This raised little interest in Brussels.

The fourth phase started in 1984 after the few remaining tariffs between the EFTA states and the EC had been swept away. In April 1984 the EFTA governments, those of the EC members and the EC's Commissioner for External Affairs met in Luxembourg at a 'Jumbo' meeting. They discussed a long agenda, including non-tariff barriers, co-operation in agriculture, fisheries, transport and energy, and common action in international forums (*EFTA Bulletin* 2/84, p. 7). The President of the EC Council of Ministers, Claude Cheysson, advanced the idea of further dialogue between the EC and EFTA, with a view to creating a 'European Economic Space' with co-operation on research and development, industrial matters, action at the international level especially on international monetary questions and relations with the third world (*Agence Internationale*, 9–10 April 1984).

The 'Jumbo' meeting resulted in increased goodwill and some concrete action. One of the two meetings of the joint commissions each year was upgraded to the political level with a member of the EC Commission present, and by 1986 the EC had signed framework agreements on technology with all the EFTA states except Iceland.

The considered response of the President of the Commission — Jacques Delors — to this flirtation came in his address to the European Parliament in January 1989. He pointed out that the Commission's view was that internal development of the EC had priority over enlargement, but that this had not stopped the strengthening of agreements with the EFTA states. However, he saw two options for future EC-EFTA relations:

we can stick to our present relations, essentially bilateral, with the ultimate aim of creating a free trade area encompassing the Community and EFTA; or ... we can look for a new, more structured partnership with common decision-making and administrative institutions ... to highlight the political dimension of our cooperation in the economic, social, financial and cultural spheres (European Parliament 1989, 2–373, p. 75).

The stark option that Delors gave the EFTA states was either to mark time or to go forward. The latter choice, he suggested, would be easier if EFTA 'were to strengthen its own structures' which would then allow the framework for co-operation to 'rest on the two pillars of our organizations'. Otherwise any advance would be made on the basis of Community rules being extended to the EFTA countries. He then expressed misgivings about EFTA 'being allowed to pick and choose' from elements of EC co-operation, which involved a Common Commercial Policy, harmonization, supervision by the European Court and social conditions of fair competition, not to mention closer co-operation on social and foreign policy (ibid.). This interpretation proved to be far-sighted.

For the EFTA states, two events between the 'Jumbo' meeting and Delors' January 1989 speech had affected their calculations. First, the EC had expanded southwards by taking in Spain and Portugal as members in 1986, thereby enlarging — and making more attractive — the potential market represented by the EC. Secondly, the plan for a Single European Market accepted at the Milan EC Council of 1985 and the consequent 1986 Single European Act, meant that the Communities were deepening as well as widening and increased the economic cost for those outsider states (Krugman 1988, pp. 1–4).

The response of the EFTA states to Delors' démarche was twofold. First, they increased their contact with the EC. There had already been a joint EC-EFTA ministerial meeting in February 1988 and the European Council had declared its wish in December 1988 for stronger and expanded relations with EFTA. There followed an informal ministerial meeting between the EC and EFTA in Brussels in March 1989 and an agreement at a High Level Steering Group of officials in April 1989 to examine the possibilities of a more structured partnership between the EC and EFTA based on the four freedoms of movement — of goods, services, capital and persons — and on other areas of co-operation, the so-called 'flanking policies'. In May 1989 officials from the EFTA states met the EC Commission and agreed progress on export restrictions, Trade Electronic Data Exchange Systems (TEDIS), public procurement and simplification of rules of origin. Advances were made in other areas such as technical barriers to trade, the environment and education (*EFTA Bulletin* 3/89, pp. 18–20). All these developments were viewed with a certain amount of satisfaction when Commissioner Christophersen met with the EFTA ministers in June 1989.

The second response by the EFTA countries was to work more closely together, as recommended by Delors. This was given a political impetus by the March 1989 summit of EFTA heads of government. Although this meeting did not agree any change to EFTA's structure, it was decided that — to be effective — EFTA had to speak ' "with one voice", thus following a wish expressed by the Community to deal with one partner only' (*EFTA Bulletin* 3/89, p. 1).

The climax of the frenetic activity throughout 1989 came in December with three meetings. The Strasbourg European Council (8–9 December) concluded that there should be a comprehensive agreement between the EC and EFTA. The EFTA Council, meeting in Geneva on 11–12 December, welcomed this move by the Communities and, recalling 'that the EFTA countries have spoken with one voice during the high-level talks, they stated their intention to continue to do so' (*EFTA Bulletin* 4/89–1/90, p. 4). It seemed that the EFTA dual-track approach to the EC was paying off. This line had evolved throughout 1989: they would continue with the sort of practical co-operation presaged by the 1984 Luxembourg meeting but would also plan for a more general EC-EFTA settlement, as outlined by Delors.

The third meeting was a joint one in Brussels (19 December) between the EC ministers, the Commission of the EC and EFTA ministers. Working on the basis of the preparation done by a Commission-EFTA High Level Steering Group, the meeting agreed to commence formal EC-EFTA negotiations in 1990 with a view to creating the European Economic Space — which during these negotiations was renamed the European Economic Area — of eighteen countries (nineteen when Liechtenstein became a full member of EFTA in 1991) as from 1 January 1993. The aim was to achieve the four freedoms of movement between the two groups on the basis of the acquis communautaire — the EC's existing stock of legislation — and to strengthen and broaden co-operation in the context of EC action in areas such as education, social welfare and consumer protection. It was recognized that exceptions — justified on the grounds of fundamental interests — and transitional arrangements would be matters for negotiation, but that equal conditions of competition should be ensured. Furthermore, as recognition of the differences between the rich members of EFTA and the poorer southern members of the EC, economic and social disparities between regions should be reduced (*EFTA Bulletin* 4/89–1/90, pp. 5–6).

Negotiations started on 20 June 1990 and seemed to be making good progress by the time of the joint EC-EFTA ministerial gathering in December 1990, partly because EFTA countries had withdrawn almost all of their requests for permanent derogations from the four freedoms of movement. It was hoped that an agreement would be signed by the summer of 1991 (*EFTA Bulletin* 1/91, pp. 22–5). This proved a little optimistic as the final few sticking-points needed another bout of negotiations in the autumn. An agreement was reached on 21 October 1991.

The EEA agreement

The agreement of association fulfilled the aims set by the EC and EFTA at their joint meeting of 19 December 1989. It set down provisions to create a homogeneous European Economic Area with free movement of goods, persons, services and capital; by ensuring that competition is not distorted and rules are equally respected; and by providing for closer co-operation in other areas such as research and development, environment, education and social policy. There is to be no discrimination on the grounds of nationality for the citizens of the nineteen countries party to the agreement. Common institutions are to be established.

The free movement of goods added to what had been achieved by the existing EC-EFTA bilateral treaties. Further duties on processed agricultural products are to be removed, as are non-tariff and technical barriers to trade in line with the EC's drive towards a Single European Market (see Chapter 3). However, the EEA is not meant to become a customs union like the EC: the EFTA states can still maintain their own tariffs towards the rest of the non-EEA world. Also the EFTA states can keep their agricultural and fisheries policies, with limited free trade in these products between EFTA and the EC. Free trade in fish and fish products (salmon excepted) was exchanged for greater access to Norwegian waters for EC vessels. EFTA is to enforce state aid and competition law to comply with EEA rules, and public procurement is going to be opened up on the basis of EC directives (DTI 1991, p. 1).

Free movement of workers between the EC and EFTA states is to be established under the EEA. This would allow the right to accept offers of employment actually made and to move freely within the EEA states for that purpose, to stay in that territory for employment under conditions governing the nationals of that state, and to remain there after having been employed. Exceptions are made for employment in the public service and limitations can be justified on the grounds of public policy, public security or public health. To make such movement easier, aggregation of social security benefits is secured, as is the mutual recognition of diplomas and certificates of qualification.

While this free movement of labour has been planned to take place for the beginning of 1993 for most of the EEA area, there are some exceptions. In addition to the ones already existing within the EC (for example, for Spanish workers), a five-year transition period has been accepted for the deregulation of the tight Swiss labour market where the issue is 'politically explosive' (Gemperle 1991, p. 7) and may cause opposition to any close arrangement between Switzerland and the EC.

The agreement also allows for freedom of establishment of agencies, branches and subsidiaries in the EEA area by any national of an EC or EFTA state, as part of the freedom of movement of persons. This also includes the right to undertake self-employed activities. The EEA countries are to afford the nationals of other EC and EFTA states the same treatment as their own nationals, a constant theme in the agreement.

Freedom to provide services within the EEA territory for the nationals of EC and EFTA states established in a state other than that of the person for whom the services are intended, is also allowed. For example, a German firm could, after 1 January 1993, employ a Swedish carpet cleaning company without any interference from the authorities on the grounds that the Swedes were not EC members, and the Swedish company could pursue its service activities in Germany under the same conditions as those imposed on German nationals.

The free movement of capital again removes the restrictions based on the nationality or the place of residence of those involved, in so far as they might be EC or EFTA residents. Again there are some exceptions: for instance, Norway can maintain its national legislation for fishing boats to which fishing rights are attached, and Iceland has been allowed to prohibit foreign investment in its fisheries and to subject purchase of land or property to national legislation (*News from Iceland*, November 1991, p. 1). The Swiss negotiated a five-year transition period for the elimination of the Lex Friedrich, their law preventing acquisition of land by non-Swiss (Gemperle 1991, p. 6). Furthermore, safeguard clauses were written into the agreement allowing EFTA states to take measures in the event of serious economic disruption.

Transport is also dealt with under the heading of the freedom of movement within the EEA. Again the general rule is that there should be no barriers established on the basis of national citizenship as far as EC and EFTA states are concerned. Neither should there be different rates or conditions for the same goods on the same journey, on the grounds of country of origin or destination. Separate from the EEA agreement — although linked to its outcome — were bilateral Swiss-EC and Austrian-EC agreements on transit arrangements through those Alpine states for the EC member countries. The two states promised to increase the permits for lorries in transit, though Switzerland was allowed to maintain its 28-ton limit on trucks. Switzerland will also invest 24 billion Swiss francs in two new transalpine rail tunnels (DTI 1991, p. 1).

The nineteen countries established a number of common rules to ensure that competition within the EEA territory would not be distorted by monopolies, cartels or restrictive practices, or by impermissible state aid. Further rules covered public procurement regulations and the laws on intellectual property.

If serious economic, societal or environmental difficulties of a sectoral or regional nature arise, a signatory can take certain measures unilaterally to remedy the situation. However, other EEA states can take their own counterbalancing measures.

The EEA agreement includes a section on 'the horizontal policies relevant to the four freedoms' which is meant to support the good functioning of these freedoms. Under the heading of social policy, the parties agree to promote improved work conditions and the health and safety of workers, and to maintain equal pay for equal work for men and women alike. Provisions are to be made for consumer protection and the preservation, protection and improvement of the quality of the environment is given high priority.

A strengthening of co-operation between the EC and EFTA states is to come about in a number of so-called 'flanking policies' which include: research and development; information services; education, training and youth; social policy; consumer protection; small and medium-sized enterprises; tourism; and the audio-visual sector. In particular, joint programmes, exchange of information and parallel legislation is to be encouraged. The EFTA states also agreed to set up and run a fund to help the poorer EC regions, especially those in Greece, Ireland, Portugal and Spain. The fund is to consist of 500 million ECU in grants to be disbursed over five years, and 1.5 billion ECU in low-interest loans (DTI 1991, p. 1).

The EEA institutions mirrored some of those of the EC. The EEA Council is to lay down guidelines and give a political impetus to the implementation of the agreement. Thus it is to assess the functioning and development of the agreement and decide on amendments. It is to consist of members of each of the EFTA governments, of the EC's Council of Ministers and of the EC Commission, with decisions to be taken by agreement between the EC on the one hand and the EFTA states on the other. The Council is to meet at least twice a year.

An EEA Joint Committee is established to ensure the effective operation and implementation of the agreement, and any matter causing a difficulty can be raised in the Committee by one of the parties. The Committee is to consist of the representatives of the contracting parties (EFTA states, EC states and the Commission) and is to meet at least once a month. Decisions are by agreement between the EFTA states 'speaking with one voice' on the one side and the Community on the other.

Two EEA courts — an independent EEA Court and an independent Court of First Instance — were in the original October 1991 agreement, but were later dropped. The intention was that an 'independent EEA Court, functionally integrated with the Court of Justice' should consist of five judges of the EC's Court of Justice and three nominated by the EFTA states. Its competence would have covered the settlement of disputes between the contracting parties; actions concerning the surveillance procedure regarding EFTA states and appeals initiated by the EFTA Surveillance Authority (see below, p. 143). Its rulings would have been binding. The independent Court of First Instance was to have legal control of the decisions of the EFTA Surveillance Authority relating to competition rules for undertakings.

These plans for two EEA independent courts were jeopardized when the Commission of the EC asked the Court of Justice for an opinion on the EEA judicial machinery. The Court's critical judgement of December 1991 caused the EC and EFTA negotiators to revise the agreement by cutting out the section on the EEA courts (Articles 95–103).

The main reason given by the EC Court for their criticism was that as the EEA Court would be dealing with the settlement of disputes between the agreement's signatories — the EFTA states, the EC and the EC states — it would have to rule on the respective competences of the EC and the EC member states in EEA matters. That would be an interference into internal

EC matters and would prejudice the autonomy of the EC legal order, the respect for which the EC Court is supposed to ensure.

The Court further pointed out that the EEA Court would be obliged to take account of the Court of Justice's rulings before the signature of the agreement but not those after. The Court feared that its judges sitting on the EEA Court would treat the same matters in a different fashion depending on whether they came before the EC Court of Justice or the EEA Court. The Court also criticized the provision for courts and tribunals in EFTA states to use the EC Court of Justice. Nor did it believe that an amendment of the EEC Treaty would solve the problem of the incompatibility with EC law of the system of courts proposed by the EEA agreement (Court of Justice Information Office 1991, pp. 3–5).

This was a damning indictment of the EEA agreement which effectively prevented its signature as it stood. The negotiators had to re-examine the text and find a new formula that would not only satisfy the parties to the agreement but which would not be hostage to a further attack from the Court of Justice or, indeed, from the European Parliament.

The outcome, which was agreed in February 1992, was to scrap the idea of EEA courts and instead replace it by a new division of labour between the EFTA and EC parties to the agreement. The EFTA states were to establish an EFTA Surveillance Authority (see below, p. 143) and an EFTA court (Article 116 bis). This EFTA court would have competence over actions concerning the surveillance procedure regarding the EFTA states, appeals about competition initiated by the EFTA surveillance authority, and in disputes between two or more EFTA states. Under Article 117 the EC or an EFTA state could bring a dispute about the interpretation or the application of the Agreement before the EEA Joint Committee for settlement. In a matter of certain case law issues if the Committee has not settled the question within three months, the parties to the dispute can take it to the EC Court of Justice for a ruling. Failing this, a party can trigger a safeguard measure to protect its interests from what it might regard as unfair imposition of the rules. A dispute about such safeguard measures can be taken to arbitration (Article 117.4).

To ensure as uniform as possible an interpretation of the agreement, it was decided that courts within the EEA network should establish — through the EEA Joint Committee — a system of exchange of information on the judgments of the EFTA court, the EC Court of Justice and its Court of First Instance and the EFTA courts of last instance (their highest courts) (Article 104). Also Protocol 34 allowed the EFTA states to allow their courts to ask the EC Court of Justice to interpret an EEA rule, and Protocol 35 stated that the EFTA countries would make sure that EEA rules would prevail in any conflict between them and other statutory provisions. All this represented a fairly tight legal supervision of EEA matters by the EC Court of Justice.

An EEA Joint Parliamentary Committee is to be established consisting of an equal number of members of the European Parliament and of the members of parliament of the EFTA states. Its aim is to contribute to a better mutual understanding, and it can express its views in reports and resolutions. An EEA Consultative Committee is to represent the social partners in the EC and EFTA — the workers and employers — and is to be composed of an equal number drawn from the EC's Economic and Social Committee and from EFTA's Consultative Committee.

Concerning decision-making, the agreement lays down that the EC Commission should informally seek expert advice from within the EFTA states when it is preparing new legislation in a field governed by the EEA agreement, and that a copy of its proposal should be transmitted to EFTA governments as well as to the EC Council. A continuous process of consultation should follow, especially using the EEA Joint Committee where every effort should be made to find mutually acceptable solutions. If agreement cannot be reached, new legislation can be suspended, though this leaves open the possibility of an interested party taking counter-measures if it feels such a move has altered the balance of EEA rights and obligations.

An EFTA Surveillance Authority shall be established to ensure the fulfilment of the agreement's obligations. Acting together with the EC Commission, the Surveillance Authority is to ensure a uniform surveillance policy throughout and both will receive complaints about the application of the agreement. The division of the workload of the two surveillance bodies — the EFTA Surveillance Authority and the EC Commission — is set out under Article 56, and Article 63 bis lays down the procedure to be followed when one of the bodies considers that the implementation by the other surveillance authority is not in conformity with the agreement. The EEA will attempt to find a commonly acceptable solution.

All the changes agreed to the EEA agreement in February 1992 were accepted by the EC Court of Justice.

A final phase?

The EEA agreement, with all its imperfections, represented the end of the fourth phase of the EC-EFTA relationship, that started in Luxembourg in 1984. However, an alternative outcome to this saga can be traced back to 1989 when Austria filed its application for full membership of the EC. It was followed in June 1991 by Sweden and by early 1992 Finland, with the Swiss and Norwegian governments considering similar moves.

This places the EEA agreement in a different light. It no longer appears to be a solution to the EC-EFTA divide that can endure into the next century, but more an interim arrangement that will see the main EFTA members through the period after 1 January 1993. It allows them access to the Single European Market from the beginning, thus providing them with transitional economic arrangements until decisions are made about their full membership. The upset with the Court judgement, seen from this perspective, merely reminded the EFTA states of the unsatisfactory nature of the EEA arrangement that placed them 'half in, half out of the Community' (Buchan 1992, p. 2).

Either way, an EFTA-EC arrangement can provide the EC with not just 32.5 million more consumers, but ones with an average per capita income of $26,485 (compared with the EC's $18,324). Also EFTA was in 1990 the EC's largest export market, taking 26 per cent of its goods and also providing 23.5 per cent of its imports (Gemperle 1991, p. 6). The EEA agreement meant the EFTA states accepting some 1,200 EC rules and regulations, but some of the EFTA states (such as Norway, Iceland and Switzerland) will feel less able to go along with federalist thinking dominant in the governments of most EC states. Also the neutral and unaligned countries (especially Sweden, Switzerland and Finland) will have reservations about the European Union's emerging defence competence. Despite this, the EFTA states could be rich and stable members of the EC.

References

Agence Internationale D'information pour la presse, April 1984, Brussels.

Archer, C., 1990, *Organizing western Europe*, Edward Arnold, London.

Buchan, D., 1992, 'EC tackles legal hurdle to 19-state trade area', *Financial Times*, 4 February, 2.

Charlton, M., 1983, *The price of victory*, British Broadcasting Corporation, London.

Court of Justice, 1991, *Press Summary 16 December 1991*, Information Office of the Court of Justice of the European Communities, Luxembourg.

Curzon, V., 1974, *The essentials of economic integration*, Macmillan, London.

DTI, 1991, Department of Trade and Industry, *Single Market News*, 13.

EFTA Bulletin, August/September 1961; 2/84; 3/89; 4/89–1/90; 1/91.

European Parliament, 1989, *Debate of the European Parliament No 2–373*, 1988–89 Report of Proceedings from 16 to 20 January 1989, Official Journal EC No. 2/373.

Gemperle, R., 1991, 'The European economic area: an integration milestone', *Swiss Review of World Affairs*, 41/9, 7–8.

Journal of Common Market Studies, 1990, 28 (4), special issue — the European Community, EFTA and the new Europe.

Krugman, P., 1988, *EFTA and 1992*, Occasional Paper No,. 23, EFTA, Geneva.

Miljan, T., 1977, *The reluctant Europeans*, Hurst, London. *News from Iceland*, November 1991.

Pedersen, T., 1991, 'EC-EFTA relations: an historical outline', in H. Wallace (ed.), *The wider western Europe*, Pinter, London, 13–27.

10
The EC and the rest of Europe

As shown in the previous chapter, the EC has developed a 'special relationship' with the EFTA states and this is likely to develop into closer economic integration, if not membership of the EC by a number of the EFTA countries, throughout the 1990s. There is, however, part of Europe that is not yet covered by either the EC of the twelve or by EFTA. What can be called 'the rest of Europe' includes the East and Central European states that were members of the Warsaw Treaty Organization (WTO) — the members of the Commonwealth of Independent States/former Soviet Union; the three Baltic states of Estonia, Latvia and Lithuania; Poland; the Czech Slovak Federal Republic (CSFR); Hungary; Bulgaria; Romania and Albania — the remains of Yugoslavia and its successor states; Cyrpus, Malta and Turkey. This chapter will examine the EC's relations with the former Soviet bloc, with Yugoslavia and with Cyprus, Malta and Turkey.

A layer of relationships

The EC has ordered its dealings with the rest of Europe in a form that demonstrates the effect of past relations and the expectation of future arrangements. The closest relationship would be that of EC membership and it is against this standard that these other states' 'proximity' to the Communities can be measured.

The EFTA countries form an inner ring of rich, traditionally democratic states most of which would have little trouble in becoming full EC members with a relatively short transition period. They would make good additions to the EC in trade and economic terms and would add to its democratic values and environmental concerns. Whether they would be enthusiastic supporters of a European Union with a defence competence is perhaps the only qualification on their contribution.

The three Mediterranean candidates for membership — Turkey, Cyprus and Malta — form the next ring. They are associates of some years' standing. They have been used to some of the rigours of a market economy, though all of them have economic and social problems as well as some political dislocation that could make them uneasy partners within the EC.

The next ring — that consisting of the Czech Slovak Federal Republic (CSFR), Poland and Hungary — may indeed be placed in a position inside that of the three Mediterranean applicants. These three states represent the most advanced — in economic and political terms — of the former WTO countries, and this status has been recognized by the EC in treating them together and ahead of other East European states. EC membership may be some way off, but at least it is on the agenda. For the time being that cannot be said for Bulgaria, Romania and Albania. Their state of economic and political development would place them near the back of the line for EC membership — presuming they wanted it. The three Baltic republics and Slovenia and Croatia may be able to 'jump the queue' through political pressure, though none of these countries are economically attractive for the EC. The CIS/ex-Soviet states must be in the outmost ring as far as EC membership is concerned. These groups of countries and their relations with the EC will now be examined separately.

Turkey

Turkey's relations with the EC have been difficult for a number of reasons. After the First World War the reformist government in Turkey decided on the adoption of Western ways. Now, with a foothold on the European continent and membership of NATO and the Council of Europe, Turkey regards itself as a European state as well as one situated in Asia Minor. The population is Islamic though the state is secular. Its level of development is high compared to its neighbours, though below that of the EC members where many Turks are resident as 'guest workers'. It has developed democratic institutions, but the army has seized power on a number of occasions (in 1960, 1971 and 1980). It has been constantly in dispute with Greece, especially about the seas between the two countries and over the island of Cyprus (see below, p. 148). Turkey can be seen either as a bastion for Europe against the unrest and Moslem fundamentalism of the Middle East or as an area of possible instability that could impinge on Europe.

Turkish relations with the EC until Greek membership in 1981 demonstrate an anxiety not to be treated any less favourably than their Greek rivals. After several false starts in negotiations, Turkey obtained associate membership of the EC in 1963, partly as a response to a similar Greek move. The idea was for a 22-year transitional phase from December 1964. The Turkish invasion of Cyprus in 1974 lowered the country's estimation in the eyes of the EC leaders, especially as an EPC-EC démarche was upset by further Turkish action. Greek application for EC membership in 1975 led Turkey to seek — and obtain — assurances that Turkey would be kept informed of the progress of the Greek negotiations. The period from 1975 until 1981 saw EC-Turkish relations take on an erratic nature, especially as the prospect of Greek membership came closer (Tsakaloyannis 1980, pp. 46–54).

The military take-over in Turkey in January 1980 froze relations with the EC until civilian government returned. With a partial restoration of democracy in 1983 and in expectation of full parliamentary elections, the Turkish government felt confident enough to apply for membership of the EC in April 1987.

Turkey had to wait for over two and a half years for a Commission opinion on Turkish membership and, when it came, it was unfavourable. First, the Commission said that the EC could not consider starting negotiations with any candidates before 1993 at the earliest, because of the priority attached to the creation of the Single European Market. Next they stated that, because of its economic and social situation, Turkey 'would find it hard to cope with the adjustment constraints with which it would be confronted in the medium term if it acceded to the Community' (*Bulletin of the European Communities* 1989, 12, p. 88). Other problems were mentioned such as those of political pluralism and human rights, 'the persistence of disputes with a member state' (Greece), and 'the lack of solution of the Cyprus problem' (ibid.). The Commission proposed a set of measures to help Turkey to modernize politically and economically, in line with the 1963 association treaty. These involved the completion of the customs union with the EC, more financial, industrial and technical co-operation, and the strengthening of cultural and political links. In June 1990, the Council of Ministers adopted the Commission opinion on Turkish membership and called for specific proposals such as the completion of the customs union by 1995, co-operation as outlined to reduce the development gap between Turkey and the EC and the re-establishment of financial co-operation suspended in 1981.

Turkey's role in the Gulf conflict from August 1990 to February 1991 and in the subsequent operations among the Kurds, reminded EC members of the importance of the country in Middle East affairs but also of its vulnerability to outside factors and internal rifts. Despite Turkey's clear wish to join the EC, there seems little hope that it can do so while Greece holds a veto on its entry and is prepared to exercise it. Not that it has had to. Concern about the social and economic effects of Turkish membership and of possible political instability in the country have meant that the other countries have not pushed for its membership. However, those same concerns have caused the EC not to turn Turkey down flat and instead to encourage it to develop towards the stage when its membership might be more acceptable.

Cyprus and Malta

President of the Commission, Jacques Delors, referred to these Mediterranean countries (together with Yugoslavia) as 'the orphans of Europe', presumably because they did not belong to any trade — or defence — group. Both received their independence from the United Kingdom in the 1960s and have precarious economies based on tourism and agricultural exports.

In 1974 Cyrpus was invaded by Turkey, one of the island's guarantor powers, after a coup had brought to power a group that wished to join the country to Greece — always a Turkish fear. The Turks claimed that they were defending the Turkish minority in Cyprus and established a republic led by the local Turkish politicians. This republic has not received international recognition and a solution to both the international and internal aspects of the Cyprus question has eluded both NATO and the UN, let alone the EC and EPC.

Cyprus signed an association agreement with the EC in December 1972, in preparation for entry into the Communities by the United Kingdom, one of the island's major trading partners. One consideration in 1973 was that the arrangement should not work exclusively to the benefit of the Greek Cypriot majority to the detriment of the Turkish minority. After the Turkish invasion in 1974, an element of turmoil was introduced into the workings of the agreement. The second stage — originally planned to start in 1977 — of transition to a customs union with the EC was continually postponed. Cypriot trade was given some concessions by the EC but more generous treatment was opposed by the EC's Mediterranean members with whom the Cypriots would compete. Furthermore, the practical arrangements of how to implement a customs union for the Turkish-occupied areas of Northern Cyprus arose.

A unilateral declaration of independence by the northern area was condemned by the foreign ministers of the EC and by the European Parliament and gave some impetus to EC-Cypriot relations (Tsardanidis 1984, pp. 352–76). It was hoped that the second stage of the association agreement would lead in about fifteen years to a complete customs union that would benefit the whole island. By 1990 progress towards an EC-Cyprus customs union was still being discussed between the two sides (*Bulletin of the European Communities* 1990, 3, p. 59). By July of that year the Cypriot government had decided it wanted eventual full membership of the EC though it does seem that this will be difficult as long as the division of the island remains unresolved.

The Maltese government signed a treaty of association under Article 238 of the EEC Treaty in 1970, in time for British entry in 1973. This was part of the strategy of orientation away from dependence on Britain that had been initiated by Malta's left-wing government. During the 1970s and 1980s the Maltese government attempted to play off the EC against its neighbour to the south, Libya. However, a change of government in 1987 brought Malta closer to the EC and by 1990 the country had expressed its intention of seeking full membership of the European Communities.

The Eastern European background

The European members of the former Council for Mutual Economic Assistance (CMEA or Comecon) were the Soviet Union, Bulgaria, Czechoslovakia (now CSFR), the German Democratic Republic, Hungary, Poland and Romania. In the first fifteen years after the signing of the Treaty of Rome in 1957, the governments of these countries — taking their lead from the Soviet Union — considered that the EEC was just a capitalist enterprise and refused to recognize its competence in trade matters. Even after the EC took over the right to conclude commercial agreements from its member states in 1973, ways were found round this seeming monopoly by individual EC members and the Comecon countries (Hiester 1983, p. 192). When the EC Commission attempted to open negotiations on a wide range of trade matters with Comecon states in 1974, they were met by silence from the east (Pinder 1991, p. 11).

The onset of détente in the late 1960s and early 1970s led to a considerable increase in trade between the EC and Comecon states, with it showing a five-fold growth from 1958 to 1971 (ibid., p. 191). However, a Comecon-EC relationship failed to develop as the EC refused to accept that Comecon was on the same level as itself. Compared with the EC, Comecon was a fairly loose-knit organization that could not bind its members in the same way that EC institutions could. Neither did the EC wish to give Comecon the opportunity to strengthen central control against the wishes of its East European members as this would certainly have meant greater Soviet influence (ibid., p. 193). Once Mr Gorbachev came to power in the Soviet Union in March 1985, attitudes changed. Contact was quickly made between the Commission and Comecon and, after relations between the EC and individual Comecon states were 'normalized', a joint declaration between the EC and Comecon was signed on 25 June 1988. It allowed for co-operation 'on matters of mutual interest' and by October 1990 agreements had been signed between the EC and all the Comecon European members (Pinder 1991, p. 25).

With the revolutions in Eastern Europe in the winter of 1989, the situation changed dramatically. The fall of the communist regimes there meant an end to their state-trading economies, their tight links with the Soviet Union, and to Comecon and its military equivalent, the WTO. The EC responded quickly to these events, sponsoring a meeting of the G24 — the industrialized countries — which established the European Bank for Reconstruction and Development (EBRD) in May 1990 to provide aid for the ex-communist states, and also established its own assistance programmes. It soon became clear that the EC would deal with these states in a variegated way.

A note on East Germany

There is one part of Comecon that is already in the European Communities. East Germany, formally known as the German Democratic Republic (GDR), was established by the Soviet Union as a state in 1949 from its post-war occupation zone in Germany. When negotiating the EEC's Treaty of Rome, the Federal Republic of Germany (FRG) — which had been formed from the three Western post-war occupation zones and whose government insisted that it was the only legal government of Germany — required that trade between the GDR and FRG should be treated as internal German trade. This meant that it remained free of tariffs.

Less than a year after the collapse of the communist regime in the GDR in November 1989, Germany was unified on 3 October 1990. The GDR ceased to exist, its territory became five new *Länder* (regional governments) in the FRG and there was economic and monetary union with the FRG (already in July 1990). From November 1989 to October 1990, the EC acted speedily to make sure that the former GDR could successfully become part of the European Communities as well as of the FRG. No revision of the EC treaties was needed as they were all signed by the FRG which regarded the GDR as legally part of its country. With the unification of Germany, EC legislation automatically applied to the ex-GDR, except where the EC Council decided otherwise, on a proposal from the Commission.

The Commission proposed that the GDR should be integrated into the Communities ahead of unification, just as it was to accept a number of FRG laws before October 1990, and a blueprint for GDR integration into the EC was taken at the Dublin European Council in April 1990. After the GDR had become part of the FRG, transitionary tariff measures were introduced to cover goods coming from the other European Comecon states under agreements signed by the GDR government. These countries were in effect given a year's grace — from December 1990 to December 1991 (*Bulletin of the European Communities* 1990, 4, pp. 5–27).

Czechoslovakia, Hungary and Poland

From the 1960s Hungary had been regarded as the most advanced Comecon country in terms of using the market economy. Its communist government was also seen as the most reformist of the group and strong tourist and border trading links were built up with the FRG and Austria. During the 1970s and early 1980s Poland was viewed in the West as a strongly Catholic country with an independent peasantry that had had a communist government imposed on it. Czechoslovakia had seen the liberal Prague spring in 1968 with a reformist communist government, but had been forced into neo-Stalinist winter by Soviet tanks. However, its inter-war democratic roots were not forgotten.

Such a sympathetic view of the three states prior to 1989 did not translate readily into EC help. Until the 1988 EC-Comecon accord, the countries were not even considered for inclusion in the EC's Generalized System of Preferences or for bilateral agreements, from which many non-European areas benefited (see Chapter 11). This was not just because of the lack of democracy or the state-trading nature of the three countries, but also because many of their exports were in direct competition with EC products (Tovias 1991, p. 291).

The EC-Comecon accord opened the way for bilateral agreements. In September 1988 Hungary signed a non-preferential trade and co-operation agreement with the EC which included Hungary among the GSP recipients and lifted some of the restrictions on Hungarian exports. This was followed by similar agreements with Czechoslovakia in December 1988 (but which excluded the element of co-operation because a hardline government was still in power) and with Poland in December 1989. The co-operation element was added to the CSFR (as it had then become) agreement after their free elections in March 1990.

The next stage in the EC's relations with the three countries was that of encouraging the move to market economies and helping with the structural changes needed. This had an early start in the PHARE programme initiated in July 1989 under an EC Commission initiative and with assistance from the G24 industrial states. The programme's original name was Poland-Hungary Aid for the Reconstruction of the Economy but Czechoslovakia (and other ex-Comecon states plus Yugoslavia) was included in September 1990. The priority areas for reconstruction were identified as being agriculture, industry, investment, engineering, training, environmental protection, and trades and services, especially in the private sector. In 1990 provision was made for 500 million ECU in EC assistance, 785 million ECU in 1991 and a planned 1 billion ECU for 1992.

In 1990 the EC Commission proposed a European Training Foundation and the Trans-European Mobility Programme for University Students (TEMPUS) for the ex-communist East and Central European states.

From 1990 the European Investment Bank was able to assist the East and Central European countries with the first finance going to infrastructure renewal schemes in Hungary and Poland (EIB 1991, p. 50). Further aid came with the creation by the G24 of the European Bank for Reconstruction and Development with the aim of fostering 'the transition towards open market-oriented economies and to promote private and entrepreneurial initiative in the Central and Eastern European countries committed to ... multi-party democracy, pluralism and market economies' (*Official Journal of the European Communities*, 1990, 33, C241, 1).

The next stage in the EC's relations with Czechoslovakia, Hungary and Poland came with the offer of 'second generation agreements' — the first generation being the ones resulting from the EC-Comecon accord. These were to be treaties of association and became known as Europe Agreements. The idea for these was advanced by the United Kingdom and adopted by the European Council in August 1990. Czechoslovakia, Hungary and Poland were identified as the three states that had advanced economically and politically enough to become associated with the EC, and all three countries have expressed the wish that the agreements should lead to their eventual EC membership (Pinder 1991, pp. 59–60). The agreements were concluded at the end of 1991 after a good deal of resistance by France and Portugal to giving concessions to the three countries for their agricultural and textile exports (Kramer 1992, p. 15).

The Europe Agreements have limitations that reflect the problems of the three countries but also the caution of the EC members. There is to be a phased creation of an industrial free trade area between the associates and the EC, with tariffs and quotas being demolished, apart from some exceptions such as textiles. Further access to EC markets is allowed for the associates' agricultural produce, but the EC has been wary of allowing free movement of labour from the three associates into the EC. The fear is that, until the three countries strengthen their economies, such freedom would allow a mass movement of economic migrants into Germany and other EC members. This could undermine economic progress in the associates — especially if their most talented citizens left — and lead to further social unrest in the Communities.

The hope of the Europe Agreements is that they will allow the three associates to prepare for membership by the late 1990s. There are dangers that if the reform process takes longer than expected, then the associates will face a number of problems in adjusting their economies ready for EC member-ship (Killick and Stevens 1991, pp. 679–96).

The Baltic republics

The three Baltic republics — Estonia, Latvia and Lithuania — had their independence in the inter-war period but were incorporated into the Soviet Union in 1940. National revivals took place in the Gorbachev period, leading to declarations of independence by the three states in 1990. After the failed military coup in the Soviet Union in August 1991, the three put their declar-ations into practice and their return to sovereign republics was soon recognized by other European states, the USA and, finally, the Soviet Union and its successor state, Russia. In June 1990 the three states established a Baltic Council based on the model of the Nordic Council.

The republics have a range of outstanding problems. They are small coun-tries — Estonia has 1.6 million inhabitants, Latvia 2.7 million and Lithuania 3.7 million — with limited natural resources and their economies have been integrated into that of the former Soviet Union. They have large non-native populations — mainly Russians involved in defence-related activities. The non-native population of Latvia was 48 per cent of the total in 1989. On the positive side all the republics have developed links with the Nordic states and there remains the possibility of their becoming part of a wider Baltic economic, cultural and environmental grouping (Aage 1991, p. 156; Joenniemi 1991, pp. 147–65).

After the re-establishment of the independence of the Baltic republics, the Commission of the European Communities recommended them for 'first generation' trade and co-operation agreements and for inclusion in the EC programmes for East and Central Europe such as TEMPUS. The 'first generation' agreements would cover industrial and agricultural products and would allow for eventual association agreements on the same basis as the Europe Agreements (*Bulletin of the European Communities* 1991, p. 70).

It is possible that the Baltic republics, because of their image in the West as small near-Nordic democracies, might find their way to EC membership (to which their governments seem to aspire) made easier, especially if they were sponsored by Germany. However, they have a number of outstanding issues that would have to be solved before consideration of membership. These include the viability of their economies, their frontiers and the question of citizenship, the presence of ex-Soviet forces on their territory, their mutual relationships and their political stability.

Bulgaria, Romania and Albania

These three countries broke loose of communist government between 1989 and 1991. However, they have had difficulty in establishing stable administrations and dealing with their adverse economic situations.

Romania was able to benefit from its independent foreign policy line under President Ceausescu when the EC offered it — alone among the Comecon states — GSP treatment on a number of products in 1974. A trade agreement followed in 1980 and negotiations began for a trade and co-operation agreement in April 1987 but were suspended because of Ceausescu's repression in July 1989. Just before the dictator fell in December 1989, the EC decided to suspend the 1980 agreement. Negotiations opened with the new government but were held up by further political unrest in the country (Pinder 1991, p. 33). Romania eventually became eligible for PHARE assistance.

Bulgaria also experienced difficulties in its relations with the EC when negotiations on a trade and co-operation agreement were suspended from May 1989 to March 1990 because of the treatment of their Turkish minority (Pinder 1991, p. 33).

Albania is perhaps the most problematic of all these states as it only returned to international relations in the early 1990s after having been isolated under an inward-looking communist dictatorship dating back to 1945. EC involvement has been in the form of humanitarian aid to what is one of the poorest parts of Europe, and to consideration of a 'first generation' treaty (*Bulletin of the European Communities* 1991, 9, p. 46).

The main concern of the EC in its dealings with these three states is to help prevent their economic and social collapse. Their grave economic problems and their political instability make them unlikely candidates for association treaties in the near future.

Yugoslavia and its successors

During the latter part of 1991 Yugoslavia, a state created after the First World War, broke apart into its component republics. Serbia and Montenegro together with the remnants of the Yugoslav army formed up against Slovenia and Croatia, with Bosnia-Herzegovina trying to remain outside the conflict. The role of the EC-EPC in attempting to bring peace to Yugoslavia is noted in Chapter 12, pp. 176–177. The EC has been involved with Yugoslavia on the trade side, though since 1991 the trade and political elements have merged.

Yugoslavia, though a communist country after the Second World War, was never a member of Comecon and always took a more open approach to the West than other East European states. Under President Tito in the 1960s and 1970s it became a leading member of the Non-aligned Movement.

Because of its precarious position between East and West and its ability to stay out of the Soviet bloc, individual EC members had granted a most favoured nation status to Yugoslav exports before the formulation of the EC's common commercial policy. The EC concluded a trade agreement with Yugoslavia in 1970 which confirmed this privileged position and established a joint EC-Yugoslav committee to deal with mutual problems. A second trade agreement in 1973 led to a reduction of some tariffs and import duties on Yugoslav exports to the EC (Pinder 1991, p. 18).

Just before Tito died in 1980, the EC moved to develop its trade agreement to include co-operation, in order to help stabilize the country in the post-Tito period (Ginsberg 1983, p. 162). This confirmed Yugoslavia's position in the EC's Generalized System of Preferences (granted in 1971), allowing many of its manufactures to enter the Communities tariff-free. It also saw the development of co-operation with Yugoslavia over finance, labour and science and technology. Loans from the European Investment Bank helped to ease transport between Italy and Greece (Pinder 1991, p. 18).

Yugoslavia's favoured position with the EC was soon eroded after the events in Eastern and Central Europe in 1989–90. The Yugoslavs only received a small share of the PHARE programme and the EC's interest in co-operation was no longer determined by Yugoslavia's strategic position in the East-West struggle but was informed by the requirements to move to multi-party democracy and a market economy. Yugoslavia's journey along that road proved hazardous in 1990 and it found itself being overtaken in the EC's Eastern policy by the CSFR, Hungary and Poland. The disintegration of Yugoslavia in 1991 changed the country from being — in EC eyes — an object of its commercial policy, albeit for political reasons, to being the subject of political debate, but with economic implications.

Of the Yugoslav successor states, Slovenia is in the most favourable position in relation to the EC. It has avoided much of the disruption of inter-ethnic violence, has the advantage of bordering Italy (and Austria), and has been the most economically advanced part of Yugoslavia. Croatia suffered badly in its war with the Serbian forces and is less viable as an economic entity than Slovenia. It has also received German support in the conflict and may expect economic assistance or investment from there. Serbia and other republics that may wish independence (such as Montenegro) have few friends in the EC and are regarded as being politically and economically unreformed. It may be that the successor republics will be offered first generation trade agreements with a co-operative element depending on 'good behaviour' in the areas of human rights, treatment of minorities and non-belligerence.

The Soviet Union and its successors

Because of the Soviet Union's antipathy in the pre-Gorbachev period to the EC, trade relations remained on the basis of the arrangements made with the Soviets by each individual EC member state. After the Soviet Union recognized the EC in 1988, this situation changed and by the end of 1990 the European Council had decided to offer the Soviets a far-reaching agreement — covering economic, political and cultural co-operation — to expand on that signed in Brussels in December 1989.

However, the repression by Soviet forces of the Baltic republics in January 1991 led to a suspension of EC aid. By the spring of 1991 it was clear that the Soviet reform process was in deep trouble and after the failed August coup the structure of the Soviet Union collapsed. The response of the EC since then has been on the diplomatic front (see Chapter 12, p. 177) and in the form of food aid. Total EC aid by the end of 1991 was estimated at 2 billion ECU, about the sum planned by the United States.

Of the Soviet successor states, Russia is the largest and most important and the EC will direct much of its concern to that country. However, there are new states that are emerging on to the international scene — Ukraine, Belorus, Georgia, Armenia, Azerbaijan and the central Asian states such as Kazakhstan. Some of these — the Ukraine and Kazakhstan for instance — are more viable than others. It may be in the interest of the EC to encourage regional groupings. It will certainly wish to tie human rights and market economy records to any trade and co-operation agreements.

Depending on the size and imagination of assistance to these states, the European Communities may find itself as the leading external civil power in the European states of the ex-Soviet Union. This will increase the pressures for a strong and common foreign policy for the emerging European Union.

Conclusion

With the end of the Cold War — and of the Soviet Union — the line to join the EC has lengthened. Between two and seven of the EFTA states could become full members by the next century, and the three central European states of CSFR, Hungary and Poland might join soon after (if not earlier). Cyprus and Malta might find sponsors and creep in. Then the EC could have a membership of twenty-four. Other anxious states would be waiting at the door.

Such an extension may take Europe along the road of being 'united and whole' and it will no doubt strengthen the economic — and political — clout of the emerging European Union in the world. But there are three other aspects that should be considered. First, would an increase in membership change the nature of the European Union and would this be desirable? Some existing members may hope that extension takes the European Union away from any federalist aspiration and toward a confederation, while others fear expansion for just that reason.

Secondly, what would such an extension do to the countries excluded? Would it persuade them to increase their efforts to be worthy of EC membership in economic and political terms or would it leave them bitter at being on the outside of a rich-man's club?

A final consideration is that the question of prospective membership has been seen in terms of sovereign states adhering to the European Union. It is possible that the nature of this union — and of politics in Europe as a whole — may change so significantly that this no longer would be an appropriate model. If a Europe of the regions developed, or if the states currently members of the EC broke up into their constituent parts, of if some members created their own federation and non-members formed other regional associations, then different modes of relationships would have to be considered.

References

Aage, H., 1991, 'The Baltic republics', in R. Weichhardt, (ed.), *The Soviet economy under Gorbachev*, NATO, Brussels, 146–66.
Bulletin of the European Communities, Supplement 12/89, 3/90, 4/90, 9/91, 10/91, Commission of the European Communities, Brussels.
Commission of the European Communities, *Information memo*, 6 November 1991, 9 January 1992.

EIB (European Investment Bank), 1991, *Annual report 1990*, EIB, Luxembourg.

Ginsberg, R.H., 1983, 'The European Community and the Mediterranean', in Lodge, J. (ed.), *Institutions and policies of the European Communities*, Pinter, London, 154–67.

Hiester, D., 1983, 'The European Community and the east bloc' in Lodge, J. (ed.), *Institutions and policies of the European Communities*, Pinter, London, 190–5.

Joenniemi, P., 1991, 'Regionalization in the Baltic area; actors and policies', in Joenniemi, P. (ed.), *Cooperation in the Baltic sea region; needs and prospects*, TAPRI, Tampere, 147–65.

Killick, A. and Stevens, C., 1991, 'Eastern Europe: lessons on economic adjustment from the Third World', *International Affairs*, 67 (4), 679–96.

Kramer, H., 1992, 'The EC and the stabilisation of eastern Europe', *Aussenpolitik*, 43 (1), 12–21.

Pinder, J., 1991, *The European Community and eastern Europe*, Pinter, London.

Tovias, A., 1991, 'EC-eastern Europe: a case study of Hungary', *Journal of Common Market Studies*, 29 (3), 291–315.

Tsakaloyannis, P., 1980, 'The European Community and the Greek-Turkish dispute', *Journal of Common Market Studies*, 19 (1), 35–54.

Tsardanidis, C., 1984, 'The EC-Cyprus association agreement: 1973–1983', *Journal of Common Market Studies*, 22 (4), 351–76.

11
The EC and the world

The EC's relations with the non-European world have so far been described in terms of a small section of the rest of the world's population — that of the ACP states (see Chapter 8). This chapter will outline relationships between the EC and the United States, Latin America, the North African states, the Middle East, ASEAN members (in South-East Asia), India, China, Japan and Australasia.

The member states of the European Communities have had relationships of differing form and intensity with all these areas. This chapter will not deal with the political relations existing between the EC governments and the rest of the world but will concentrate on the commercial and trade links that the EC itself has forged with countries and groupings outside Europe and the ACP states. By the end of the 1980s the EC was providing over a third of world trade and with the EFTA states the figure is 44 per cent. This represents a sizeable partner for any state or group of states.

It should be noted that most of the world's trade relationships since the immediate post-war period have existed within the framework of the General Agreement on Tariffs and Trade (GATT) which has tried to liberalize trade by breaking down existing barriers to trade and preventing new ones arising. This was the aim of the last three sets of GATT negotiations, the Kennedy round (1962/67), the Tokyo round (1974–79) and the Uruguay round from 1986 to the early 1990s. EC economic relations with non-European countries should also be seen in the context of their other policies and in the light of the development by the EC and the European Union of a common commercial policy by which they take over existing commercial agreements that the member states have with other countries. The EC-Union will increasingly place these commercial arrangements in the framework of their external political aims such as the encouragement of peace and stability in regions of conflict, the furtherance of human rights and economic reforms, and the underwriting of regional economic co-operation.

United States

The main points of the political relationship between the EC and the United States are covered in Chapter 12 (see especially p. 175). The history of the dealings between the two is ambiguous: US governments have been most supportive of the process of European integration from the beginning, but have often complained about its economic effects on their country. Furthermore, the United States has been anxious to make sure that any trade disagreements with the EC states did not adversely affect the vital strategic relationship built up within NATO and through bilateral links.

From the start of American involvement in post-war reconstruction with the Marshall Plan in 1947, the United States encouraged the Europeans to maximize the gains from Marshall Aid by intensifying their own economic co-operation, including forming customs unions. During the 1950s US governments saw the idea of a European Community — first the European Defence Community and then the Economic Community — as a way of uniting the West Europeans into a bastion against the Soviet Union. An economically viable Western Europe would not only provide a market for American industry but would also be able to take on its share of the defence burden. An adverse side of the creation of the European Economic Community was that it was a customs union and the formation of its common external tariff was bound to impinge on existing trade patterns, often to the detriment of partners such as the US. The United States used the GATT Kennedy round in the 1960s to try to blunt the effect of the EEC's policies by agreements to reduce the world tariff level, but it found the Community a tough negotiator that was prepared to defend the Common Agricultural Policy to the extent that no deal was reached in that area. The US had already felt the effects of the CAP in the 'Chicken War' of 1963/64 when the inclusion of poultry into the CAP regime adversely affected US exports of chickens to the six EEC states.

After the Kennedy round US-EC relations settled into a state of general unease with particular issues often souring the atmosphere. The Nixon administration took a series of unilateral actions from 1971 to 1973 that changed the nature of the world's economic framework. Until then, the basis of world trade had been the Bretton Woods system, maintained by just the economic growth and stability it encouraged, and the United States dollar, to the value of which most currencies were fixed. The US, hit by economic stagnation and inflation, devalued the dollar, and the value of currencies started to fluctuate more (Spero 1990, pp. 67–102). The US no longer had the control over trade matters it had had in the twenty-five years after the war and, with British entry in 1973, the European Communities became more important in world economic affairs.

During the 1970s and 1980s the United States attitude towards the EC became generally more hostile and political opinion in the US Congress hardened against what was seen as the protectionist 'fortress Europe' policies of the EC which they contrasted to their own free-trading image (Ginsberg 1989, pp. 139–49). Despite this, the 1974 Gymnich agreement led to the US having closer contact with the EPC process.

A fuller examination of the US-EC economic relationship shows the two blocks to be substantially interdependent. By the start of the 1990s their trade amounted to some $190bn with the EC taking 23 per cent of US exports and the US 18 per cent of EC exports. Since the start of the EEC in 1958 the US has had a visible trade surplus with it, apart from a period in the 1980s. Almost a third of US service exports went to the EC by 1989 and in 1990 about 38 per cent of US foreign investment was in the EC with the EC accounting for 58 per cent of foreign direct investment in the US. This represents a 'high degree of transatlantic economic interdependence and industrial interpenetration' (Woolcock 1991, pp. 7–10).

This closeness has three important consequences for EC-US relations. First, the two sides need each other. The EC, EFTA and the US provide well over half of the world's trade and any breakdown in relations between Western Europe and the US would have severe consequences for both. Secondly, the US and the EC are competing against each other — in trade, investment, intellectual property — and any edge that one can gain over the other is thus important. This explains the often vigorous language each side uses against the other when discussing trade matters. Finally, the future framework of economic relations is important as it could help to decide the relative strength of the two blocks and the destination of international investment capital. Disagreement in the GATT Uruguay round focused on the desire of the US to open up markets to American products and to get concrete agreements, pitted against the EC requirement that GATT disciplines should be strengthened and its rules extended (Woolcock 1991, pp. 111–23). Domestic pressure groups encouraging American trade unilateralism and EC agricultural protectionism threaten the wider health of EC-US economic relations. This can be seen in the warnings given in February 1992 by congressional leaders and Vice President Dan Quayle that, if Europe blocked GATT trade liberalization, it would lead to an American protectionist response with the danger of US troops being pulled out of NATO (*Financial Times*, 10 February 1992, p. 1). Furthermore, the Bush administration pressed on with negotiations for a North American Free Trade Area including Canada, the United States and Mexico. If formed, this entity would provide a sizeable counterweight to the EC in any trade forum.

Judging the costs and opportunities of their mutual relationship, members of the Bush administration made suggestions in 1989 of a closer relationship between the US and the EC and a greater world role for the EC. This led to the two sides signing the Transatlantic Declaration in November 1990 which expressed the common goals of assuming responsibility for the world-wide mediation of conflict, of contributing to a healthy world economy, of backing political and economic reform in developing countries, and of providing the necessary assistance to Central and Eastern Europe. They also agreed on the need to strengthen and liberalize multilateral world trade and reaffirmed the principles of GATT and OECD.

The US President is to meet the Presidents of the Commission and the Council of the EC twice yearly; there are to be meetings of the EC foreign ministers, the EC Commissioner for External Affairs and the US Secretary of State at a similar interval. Consultation in a crisis situation will be facilitated and the US government and the EC Council will meet at ministerial level twice a year. The Gymnich arrangement whereby the EPC informs the US of its activities will continue and there are to be joint meetings of the European Parliament and the US Congress (Krenzler and Kaiser 1991, pp. 363–72).

Latin America

Latin America has been an area with which EC co-operation has been notably weak. The reasons are that it is traditionally seen as a region of US interest and, until Spanish and Portuguese EC membership in 1986 Latin America only had Italy as an interlocutor in EC councils advancing its case (Muniz 1980, pp. 55–7).

The main aim of the EC in its relations with Latin America has been to sign trade co-operation agreements with the republics there and to encourage the regional groups. For example, under the first heading, early agreements were signed with Argentina (1971), Brazil (1974) and Uruguay (1973) and new economic co-operation agreements were signed with Chile, Mexico, Uruguay and Paraguay in 1990. Contact with regional groups included that with the Andean Group resulting in a Joint Declaration in 1980 and a later decision jointly to combat illegal drugs, and the effort made in 1990 to assist Central American states — with the help of Colombia and Venezuela — in their economic and political development (*Bulletin of the European Communities*, Supplement 1/91, p. 23). Other concerns have been shown, such as the 1990 programme for the protection of the tropical rain forests agreed with the eight Amazon countries (*Bulletin of the European Communities*, Supplement 1/90, p. 35). On the political side, the European Parliament sent a delegation of observers to the Nicaraguan elections of 25 February 1990 which were lost by the incumbent Sandinista government. Despite the growing intensity of EC-Latin American activity, the link between the two still remains, as in 1980, 'a relationship to be defined' (Muniz 1980, p. 55).

North Africa

The EC has been especially concerned with North Africa both because of the colonial links with the countries there and because it bounds the southern side of the Mediterranean, the northern shores of which have increasingly become Communities' territory. The EC has developed individual agreements with the North African countries, has included them in its Mediterranean strategy and in its EC-Arab dialogue (see Chapter 12, p. 174). The EC's main concern in its dealings with North Africa was well expressed by the Commission President, Jacques Delors, in 1990: 'We must make it our concern, firstly because of traditional trade flows and cultural and historic links, and secondly because we cannot ignore . . . the urgent development needs of countries faced with a steep rise in population, the environmental pressures on the sea we share, and the flashpoints of social and religious tension which are a major source of instability' (*Bulletin of the European Communities*, Supplement 1/90, p. 9).

For the 15 years after the signing of the Treaty of Rome in 1957, the EC's relations with the Mediterranean area generally 'lacked a framework for cooperation' (Ginsberg 1983, p. 160). This had changed with British entry in 1973 and the renegotiation of previous individual agreements, and with the Arab oil embargo of October 1973 to March 1974 which made the EC more conscious of its dependence on raw material — especially oil and gas — from the southern Mediterranean states (ibid., pp. 160–1). By the start of the 1980s, the EC had developed a Mediterranean policy whereby Greece (which joined in 1981), Cyprus, Malta and Turkey had association agreements which could lead to a customs union and possible membership, and Israel, Maghreb states (Algeria, Morocco and Tunisia) and Mashreq states (Egypt, Jordan, Lebanon and Syria) had co-operation accords. Spain and Portugal also had such accords but became members in 1986.

Spanish and Portuguese accession to the EC changed the balance of Communities' policy on North Africa. Also by 1986 the fear of the Arab world holding the EC to ransom by use of the oil weapon had faded. Evidence suggests that Greek, Portuguese and Spanish membership of the EC led those countries — not surprisingly — to redirect their trade towards their fellow members, including each other. This weakened any solidarity between the southern EC members and the North African states, especially as the latter quite often wished access to the EC for products that would compete with those of Greece, Portugal and Spain (Aliboni 1990, p. 159).

In 1989 the European Council urged the Commission to flesh out a policy 'of neighbourly relations' with the newly-formed Arab Maghreb Union (*Bulletin of the European Communities*, Supplement 1990, 1, p. 9). This seemed partly in response to a Moroccan hint that it wished to apply for EC membership. Further to the Gulf conflict of 1990/91, the EC Commission negotiated its fourth financial protocol with Maghreb and Mashreq, increasing the aid and loans available, perhaps hoping that this would help stability in the region.

However, the problems of the North African countries are more deeply embedded, as Delors' speech suggested, and are connected with factors such as the increasing youth — and size — of their populations, the desertification of their lands, and the spread of fundamental religious ideas.

Middle East

The Middle East mirrors in an enlarged way the problems of the North African states. Added to these have been inter-state wars between Israel and its neighbours (1948, 1956, 1967 and 1973), Iran and Iraq (1980/88) and between Iraq and its neighbours (1990/91).

However, the EC has found partners that are oil-rich, regionally organized and have only been in the last war mentioned above, and then — as were EC countries — on the side of the alliance against Saddam Hussein's Iraq. These are the states of the Gulf Cooperation Council (GCC) — Bahrain, Kuwait, Qatar, Oman, Saudi Arabia and the United Arab Emirates. A co-operation agreement was signed between the EC and GCC in 1989 and the first meeting of the Joint Cooperation Council was held in March 1990. It was agreed to focus on industry, energy, agriculture, trade, services, and science and technology (*Bulletin of the European Communities* 1990, 3, p. 57). By October 1991 a free trade agreement had been drawn up by the two organizations.

The EC also involved itself in the Israel-Palestine question, quite apart from the statements made by EPC (see Chapter 12, p. 174). The declaration of the Madrid European Council in June 1989 had supported elections in the Occupied Territories (the West Bank and Gaza) as a step towards a dialogue between the parties, that is the Israelis and the Palestinians. The Council was concerned about human rights in the Occupied Territories and considered that the occupying power — Israel — should observe the Fourth Geneva Convention on the treatment of civilians. The EC gave aid to the inhabitants of the Occupied Territories through UNRWA, the UN agency in the area, to the extent of 388 million ECU from 1973 to 1989 and from 1981 to 1989 had given direct aid of some 23 million ECU. In March 1991 an additional 250 million ECU was approved for the Occupied Territories and Israel in order to reduce the impact of the Gulf conflict on the population there.

ASEAN

The Association of South East Asian Nations (ASEAN) is an international organization devoted to economic, social and cultural development and was established in August 1967 by Indonesia, Malaysia, the Philippines, Singapore and Thailand. Brunei Darussalam joined in 1984 and Vietnam is a candidate for membership. In January 1992 the members decided to form the ASEAN

Free Trade Area (AFTA). These states, with their population nearing 300 million, represent a resource-rich area which is by no means underdeveloped. ASEAN has attempted to liberalize trade between its members and has a Preferential Trading Agreement, established in 1977, aimed at expanding intra-regional trade.

Consideration had to be given to trade links with the EC when the United Kingdom joined the Communities in 1973, thereby ending its preferential Commonwealth agreements with Malaysia and Singapore. In 1974 a joint ASEAN-EC Study Group was established to examine mutual problems, especially those of trade, but little came of it until the first ASEAN-EC Ministerial Meeting (AEMM) in Brussels in 1978. The results were limited: further meetings were to be held every eighteen months and the EC was to have more involvement in ASEAN development projects. An ASEAN-EC Cooperation Agreement was signed in Kuala Lumpur in 1980 which committed the two sides to closer co-operation in trade, industry, investment and technology transfer (Drummond 1982, p. 313). As a result a network of governmental and non-governmental links have been established between the two groups, including a Business Council, set up in 1983, and industrial conferences. In 1980 a Joint Cooperative Committee was created to oversee collaborative activities and a first meeting of the two sides' economic ministers took place in Bangkok in 1985.

The main outstanding issue between the EC and ASEAN is that of market access, particularly in the case of textile exports from the ASEAN members. Increasingly, these countries are developing their own industrial processes and have been accused by the EC of dumping. The EC accounts for about 14 per cent of ASEAN's total trade and foreign investment but has been over-shadowed by the Japanese presence in the area (Atarashi 1985, pp. 109–27). The fear of the EC is that ASEAN states may follow Japan, Korea and Taiwan in breaking into the European consumer market to the detriment of EC industries.

India and China

It is ironic that the countries with the two largest populations in the world are ones that have perhaps some of the weakest links with the EC. This is partly a result of the economic systems of the two countries: China is a state-trading nation with a comparatively small external trade sector, and the Indian government strictly regulates aspects of its foreign trade. It is also the case that many Chinese and Indian exports are of the type that the EC wishes to restrict, such as clothing and textiles, and that their low per capita incomes make them unattractive markets for EC exporters.

A general trade agreement was signed with China in 1978 and renewed in 1985 and a textile settlement was reached in 1978 with renewal in 1984

(Redmond and Zou Lan 1986, pp. 133–55). However, the events in Beijing in June 1989, when student demonstrators were killed, led the EC to hold back the development of economic links with China to show their displeasure at the government's repressive action. In October 1991 members of the EC Commission visited China and had their first joint meeting since 1987. A memorandum on technical arrangements for co-operation in information technology and in telecommunications was signed and a meeting of trade exports to examine trade barriers was arranged. EC-Chinese relations are being normalized, but still the level of contact with this potential economic giant is low. The same can be said of EC contacts with India: these seem to be mainly about the textiles question and that of intellectual property with the Commission attempting to prevent pirating of books and patented material (*Bulletin of the European Communities*, 1991, 10, pp. 73–4).

Japan

The EC's relations with Japan have not always been easy. It was only in the early 1970s that the Communities attempted trade negotiations with Japan. By then, the Japanese economy had experienced an annual 10 per cent real growth in its GNP for the previous 20 years. However, Japan restricted imports and gave financial assistance to exports (Spero 1990, p. 79), and EC demands for a 'safeguard clause' against a sudden expansion of Japanese imports led to the breakdown of trade treaty negotiations in 1971. However, a mutual exchange of permanent delegations was agreed in 1975. By 1980 the EC had turned its attention from criticism of Japanese exports to opening up the Japanese market for EC products. Japan responded by liberalizing some of its markets, restraining its export growth and agreeing a number of Voluntary Restraint Agreements with EC countries, and stimulating its home demand (Daniels 1989, p. 282; Spero 1990, p. 82).

Attempts by the Japanese to establish car assembly plants within the EC have received a varied response. The French have opposed such activities on the grounds that they undermine the indigenous European industry, while Britain has welcomed such plants because of their employment potential. This difference in tone by EC members has been noted by Japanese commentators (Murata, 1987/88, p. 8). The EC has attempted to regulate such assembly plants to make sure that they do not become a funnel for almost complete Japanese imports and Commission comment on Japanese trading practices has often been harsh. Delors said of Japan in January 1990 that 'they cannot expect the West to apply the principles of openness and free trade indefinitely while these are denied to Western companies in Japan' (*Bulletin of the European Communities*, Supplement 1/90, p. 10). This was in response to the visit of the Japanese prime minister to the Commission and his remarks supportive of the G24 action in Eastern Europe.

The EC must find ways of co-existing with the world's most vibrant economy. In the view of one commentator: 'In the future as in the past Europe will find competition with Japan arduous and daunting. To meet this challenge a single currency, a single foreign policy and educational strategy are no more than essential beginnings' (Daniels 1989, p. 284).

Australasia

Both Australia and New Zealand had close trade ties with the United Kingdom under the Commonwealth preference scheme that existed before Britain joined the EC. This meant in the years immediately before British accession that 13 per cent of Australia's farm exports went to the United Kingdom, despite the distance, and that this figure fell to 3 per cent in the three years after 1973 (Miller 1983, p. 203). Australian products, such as food and fibres, found themselves up against the CAP and other EC restrictions and their other world markets have been adversely affected by the EC's agricultural export policy.

Since British membership Australia has reoriented itself away from its former European market and towards the Pacific Basin. It has looked more to Japan for its markets and to the United States on security matters. In trade matters Australia has been active in the Cairns Group in the GATT Uruguay Round, demanding the elimination of agricultural subsidies. This Group — which also includes Argentina, Brazil, Canada, Chile, Colombia, Hungary, Indonesia, Malaysia, New Zealand, Thailand and Uruguay — has often been supported by the United States, especially in its attacks on the CAP (Woolcock 1991, p. 19).

New Zealand was granted special continued access to its traditional British market after the United Kingdom joined the EC. The Luxembourg agreement of 1971 that decided this led to Protocol 18 of the Treaty of Brussels in 1972 which decided on the pricing arrangement for New Zealand butter exports to Britain for the 1973/77 period. These years were spent by the New Zealanders trying to maintain these prices and on the question of the quota system that would follow in 1977. They managed to obtain a 25 per cent share of the British butter market for after 1977, though there has been a constant battle to reduce that share (Lodge 1983, pp. 212–14). New Zealand attention was turned to protecting their lamb exports after the EC introduced a sheepmeat regime in 1980. A deal was struck that allowed continued access to the British market, and this was eventually replaced by a 205,000 tonne quota for the whole of the EC at a zero tariff, a figure to be renegotiated by the end of 1992. New Zealand has tried to diversify both the range of export products and their market but, having more limited resources, has not been so successful as Australia: in 1991 59 per cent of New Zealand's sheepmeat export went to the EC and 42 per cent of their butter to the United Kingdom.

New Zealand have been active in the Cairns Group in GATT as they would clearly benefit from a general lowering of agricultural subsidies, especially those that are part of the CAP.

Conclusions

The EC's commercial relations with the non-European world have a layered pattern. Like other developed states, EC countries offer tariff preferences for the manufacturing exports of less developed countries (LDCs) and have operated a Generalized System of Preferences for these LDCs. However, the EC provides a more generous network of preferences for the Lome ACP states and for the countries of the southern Mediterranean. A patchwork of trade and co-operation agreements have been signed with other parts of the world, though these often reflect historic interests rather than the importance of the area involved.

Trade relations with non-European developed states have not been problem-free. Dealings with the United States must be uppermost in the EC's plans, as these can affect the shape of the world trade framework. Relations with Japan will start to take on increased importance in that context.

The EC is part of a world market and its economy is competing on the global stage. The task for the future is for the institutions of the EC and the European Union, in their commercial policy, to contribute to a world economic structure that will provide the context for orderly competition. If they fail, the questions will be whether EC enterprises can survive and under what conditions.

References

Aliboni, R., 1990, 'The Mediterranean dimension', in Wallace, W. (ed.), *The dynamics of European integration*, Pinter, London.

Atarashi, K., 1985, 'Japan's economic cooperation policy towards ASEAN', *International Affairs*, 61 (1), 109–27.

Bulletin of the European Communities, 3/90, 10/91; Supplements 1/90, 1/91, Commission of the EC, Brussels.

Daniels, G., 1989, 'EC-Japan: past, present and future', in Lodge, J. (ed.), *The European Community and the challenge of the future*, Pinter, London, 279–84.

Drummond, S., 1982, 'Fifteen years of Asean', *Journal of Common Market Studies*, 20 (4), 301–19.

Ginsberg, R.H., 1983, 'The European Community and the Mediterranean', in Lodge, J. (ed.), *Institutions and policies of the European Community*, Pinter, London, 154–67.

Ginsberg, R.H., 1989, *Foreign policy actions of the European Community*, Lynne Rienner Publishers, Boulder, Colorado.

Krenzler, H. and Kaiser, W., 1991, 'The transatlantic declaration: a new basis for relations between the EC and the USA', *Aussenpolitik*, 42 (2), 363–72.

Lodge, J., 1983, 'The European Community and New Zealand', in Lodge, J. (ed.), *Institutions and polices of the European Community*, 209–16.

Miller, J.D.B., 1983, 'The European Community and Australia', in Lodge, J. (ed.), *Institutions and policies of the European Community*, 203–8.

Muniz, B., 1980, 'EEC-Latin America: a relationship to be defined', *Journal of Common Market Studies*, 19 (1), 55–64.

Murata, R., 1987/88, 'Political relations between the United States and Western Europe: their implications for Japan', *International Affairs*, 64 (1), 1–9.

Redmond, J., and Zou Lan, 1986, 'The European Community and China: new horizons', *Journal of Common Market Studies*, 25 (2), 133–55.

Spero, J.E., 1990, *The politics of international economic relations* (4th ed.), Unwin Hyman, London.

Woolcock, S., 1991, *Market access issues in EC-US relations*, Pinter, London.

12
European political co-operation

From the beginning, the European Communities have had a strong political element tied in to their essentially economic nature. This was true of the European Coal and Steel Community; it held for the European Economic Community and Euratom; it can be seen in the development of the unified European Communities; and it is an important aspect in the emerging European Union. Yet EC member states have shown a reluctance to extend the competence of the Communities' institutions to a central part of their political activities — foreign and security policy. They have instead preferred to separate these elements and to limit their activity to co-ordination of their individual policies. Most of all there has been a reluctance to use the Community method for defence. This chapter will trace the institutional development of the EC's political role, will emphasize the evolving involvement of the EC in foreign and security matters, and will deal with the question of the European Union and defence issues.

Early days

The European Coal and Steel Community had political as well as economic foundations. One of the aims of Robert Schuman was to make 'any war between France and Germany . . . not only unthinkable but materially imposs- ible' (Hallstein 1962, p. 10). A further security consideration was the outbreak of the Korean War in June 1950 and the fear that this could just be a feint for a Soviet attack on Western Europe (see Chapter 1, pp. 12–13). In August 1950 the idea of a European army was put forward in the Council of Europe's Assembly and gained the backing of Winston Churchill, then leader of the Opposition in Britain. The idea was taken up by the same team that had produced the Schuman Plan and which was led by Jean Monnet, and by

October 1950 the Pleven Plan (named after the then French Prime Minister) proposed a European Defence Community (EDC). This would have meant 'the creation, for our common defence, of a European Army tied to political institutions of a united Europe' (Pleven, cited in Vaughan 1976, p. 56) and thus demanded a political authority — the European Political Community — that would give political guidance to the EDC as well as the ECSC.

Though the treaty was signed by the six Community states — France, West Germany, Italy, Belgium, Netherlands and Luxembourg — in May 1952, it began to unravel in the following two years. The treaty could not endure the death of Stalin, the end of the Korean War, British and American involvement and internal French politics (Fursdon 1980). Its replacement — the Western European Union (WEU) — was not a Community institution and represented the move towards co-operation on defence issues rather than the creation of a common policy with common institutions.

The beginning of the functioning of the European Economic Community in 1958 was followed shortly by the coming to power in France of General de Gaulle. De Gaulle, who soon became French president, was opposed to the development of supranational institutions for any of the Communities and placed emphasis on national decisions, in particular in vital areas such as foreign and security policy. He built up a strong Franco-German relationship and, through this, he tried to advance the idea of regular meetings of the heads of state and government to co-ordinate the foreign policies and deal with other political problems of the six Community countries. This idea — and the plan for a small secretariat in Paris to service the meetings — was rejected by the Dutch who considered that it would pre-empt the creation of a common political union with its own foreign policy.

The Fouchet Commission was established in 1961 by the six EEC members to examine these sensitive political questions but its report demonstrated the disagreement between France and the other five governments. Fouchet proposed a European political union which would consist of a Council of the heads of state or government or of foreign ministers, a European Parliament and a European Political Commission made up of senior officials of the foreign ministries of the Six. The aim was to bring about a common foreign policy; to ensure close co-operation in the scientific and cultural field; to contribute to the defence of human rights, fundamental freedoms and democracy; and to adopt a common defence policy (Vaughan 1976, pp. 173–8). These proposals, though they seemed to be far-reaching, placed power in the hands of the governmental representatives, with even the proposed European Parliament a shadow of that agreed for the ECSC, the EEC and Euratom. They were rejected by the Benelux states in particular.

Extension and EPC

At the Hague Summit of December 1969, at which the broadening of membership of the Communities was agreed, it was also decided to deepen the activities of the organization. Political and foreign affairs were touched on in three parts of the final communiqué. The ministers confirmed that the work of the Communities 'also means paving the way for a united Europe capable of assuming its responsibilities . . . and of making a contribution' (para. 3, cited in Vaughan 1976, p. 181). They reaffirmed 'their belief in the political objectives which gave the Community its meaning and purport' (ibid., para. 4) and they instructed their foreign ministers to study how best to make progress 'in the matter of political unification, within the context of enlargement' (ibid., para. 15).

In response to the Hague request, the foreign ministers produced the Luxembourg Report in 1970. It was agreed that member states should consult each other on foreign policy matters, but should use an intergovernmental approach rather than EC institutions. In what became known as the Davignon Procedure, it was proposed that the foreign ministers should meet twice yearly and that a Political Committee of senior foreign ministry officials should meet at least four times a year with a fairly general mandate to undertake work on tasks delegated to them by ministers. The Commission of the EC could make its views known over matters of overlapping competence, for example when foreign trade matters were involved (*Bulletin of the European Communities*, 1971, 6, p. 52).

The foreign ministers' Copenhagen Report of 1973 refined the process of foreign policy co-ordination. A system of 'correspondents' from each country's foreign ministry who would keep in contact with each other and would meet together to follow up the implementation of decisions was formalized; meetings of the foreign ministers and the Political Committee were to be more regular and a telegram system between the ministries — called COREU — was set up. This co-operation was to remain intergovernmental and was not to be part of the Communities' institutions, though the Commission was to be invited to political co-operation meetings and it was emphasized that both the EC and political co-operation was directed towards European unification. As a result of the Copenhagen Report, the Political Committee established working groups on subjects such as the Conference on Security and Cooperation in Europe (CSCE), the Middle East and Asia (Ginsberg 1989, p. 49).

The Paris Summit of 1974 tidied up the emerging institutional network. The meetings of EC heads of state and government were to take place three times a year and designated the European Council (not to be confused with the Council of Europe sitting in Strasbourg). It was to deal with EC and political co-operation matters and co-ordination of these would be facilitated by the presence of foreign ministers and EC Commission members. Meetings of the Conference of Foreign Ministers under the heading of European Political Cooperation (EPC), as it was to be known, would be collocated with those of the same ministers meeting as the Council of Ministers of the European Communities, though the institutional framework of EPC and the EC would still be separate.

The Tindemans Report on European Union in 1976 recommended that the EPC process be fully integrated into the EC institutions, but this was not accepted by member states. The Genscher-Colombo Proposals of 1983 proved more influential, coming as they did from the foreign ministers of the Federal Republic of Germany and Italy. The two wished for the EPC to be confirmed in a treaty and for the European Council to be seen as the highest formal decision-making body of the EC. They also wanted more majority voting in the Council of Ministers and security issues to be considered by the EPC.

The 1981 London Report suggested a more nuts-and-bolts reform of EPC. It suggested buttressing the Council Presidency of the EC (and thus that of EPC which is held by the foreign minister of the same country) with the officials — and, in the case of the EPC presidency, the foreign ministers — of the state holding the presidency immediately before and after. Thus Portugal would be assisted (in the EC/EPC of twelve members) by the Netherlands and the United Kingdom. The report emphasized the need for consultation between members before any international initiative, before and during international conferences and in dealings with Third World countries. It also proposed a crisis management package with a Conference of Foreign Ministers being convened at forty-eight hours' notice, and stressed the value of the annual informal gathering of foreign ministers under what was known as the Gymnich Formula. In 1983 the heads of state and government agreed on a Solemn Declaration on European Union which committed them to 'joint action' on major foreign policy issues, prior consultation in the field of foreign affairs and co-ordination in the economic and political aspects of security.

The Single European Act

The 1986 Single European Act (SEA) brought together a number of the strands mentioned above. Title II amended the treaties establishing the EC; Title III provided treaty provisions for the EPC; and Title I included common provisions and linked the EC and EPC together in the common aim of progressing towards European unity.

The SEA set out the institutions of EPC: the European Council of the heads of state or government of the member states; meetings — at least four times a year — of the foreign ministers and a member of the European Commission; the Presidency of the EPC, being the same country as that presiding over the EC and being responsible for initiating action and representing EPC positions to third countries; the Political Committee consisting of the Political Directors — senior civil servants of the member countries —

with the task of maintaining EPC's continuity and preparing ministerial discussions; the European Correspondents Group consisting of civil servants responsible for monitoring the implementation of EPC; and Working Groups, as established by the Political Committee (SEA, Title III, Article 30.10). Finally, a Secretariat based in Brussels was created to assist the Presidency and carry out administrative matters (ibid.).

The Single European Act also clarified the intended content of EPC. There was to be information and consultation on 'any foreign policy matters of general interest' before members took their final position (Article 30.2). The external policies of the EC and EPC policies 'must be consistent' (Article 30.5). A readiness was expressed to co-ordinate more closely positions 'on the political and economic aspects of security', and to maintain the technological and industrial conditions for security, though this was not to impede security co-operation of members within the WEU or NATO (Article 30.6). Members would endeavour to adopt common positions at international conferences and towards Third World countries and would intensify co-operation between their diplomatic representation in such countries (Article 30.7, 30.8 and 30.9).

The aim of EPC was to try 'jointly to formulate and implement a European foreign policy' (Article 30.1). It was not to create a *common* foreign policy. Instead the idea was effectively to exercise the combined influence of the member states, to draw together their positions and implement joint action. This allows for national foreign policies to be pursued, though it does try to establish a framework for them.

Clearly the EPC, as set out in the Single European Act, was still separate from the EC and its institutions. The role of the European Parliament and the Commission were limited and the European Court was excluded altogether. Institutions different from those of the EC were established and their inter-governmental nature preserved. However, by placing EPC together with the reform of the EC in the Single European Act, the parallel nature of these institutions was stressed.

EPC's record

It took until 1973 for the basis of EPC to be established and the 1986 SEA for it to be formalized. Even then the objectives of EPC were more concerned about *how* foreign policy should be conducted — by consultation, co-ordination and common actions — than *what* that policy should be. Evaluations of EPC have thus tended to stress the ability of the members of the European Communities to remain united in the field of foreign affairs rather than the content of any joint policy or its effectiveness in terms of outcome. A report on EPC in 1988 claimed that 'in measuring progress in EPC, what matters is the degree of cooperation on substance and cohesion in action' (EPC Statements 1988, 1989, p. I.25). Indeed, by the mid–1980s it also was possible to detect the EC members moving forward from using EPC just for consultation towards more co-ordination and common action. There even seemed to be the emergence of an 'EC interest', apart from the sum of the various member interets (Ginsberg 1989, p. 89).

However, it is possible to identify certain themes that have arisen in EPC. One of the first areas for discussion was that of the Middle East as the Arab-Israeli Yom Kippur War of October 1973 forced the issue on to the agenda of the emerging political co-operation of the then nine EC members.

Western Europe was particularly vulnerable to the use of oil supplies by the Arab members of the Organization of Petroleum Exporting Countries (OPEC) to achieve their diplomatic ends in the question of Israel and Palestine. Indeed the EC's Cophenhagen Summit in December 1973 was disrupted with the arrival of an Arab delegation with which EC foreign ministers, having just promised to 'construct Europe' and 'play an active role in world affairs', then proceeded to broker with on an individual national basis (Wallace 1983, p. 385).

By the following year an EC-Arab dialogue on a wide front had developed using a number of forums such as the Washington Energy Conference and the UN. The main partner in these talks was the Arab League. Basically the EC members wanted to secure their petroleum supplies at what they regarded as a reasonable price, while the Arab countries wanted European diplomatic support in their campaign against Israel and for Palestinian rights. There were some areas of overlap, such as cultural co-operation and aid to the poorest countries, but these matters were peripheral in the minds of the interlocutors. However, a deal was not so easy to reach. For the West Europeans to have taken a strong pro-Arab line on Middle Eastern affairs would have caused a split with the United States, as well as leading to an adverse response by sectors of European public opinion. The Europeans also had another string to their bow: all the EC states, except France, became members of the newly created International Energy Authority in 1974. This body aimed at bringing a more unified response by the industrial consumers of petroleum to the adverse (for them) market conditions and had some limited success in that area.

By 1980 the EC member states finally decided on a diplomatic initiative on the Middle East. The Venice Declaration of that year was seen by them as being a balanced approach, advocating international guarantees for mutually recognized borders and the creation of a Palestinian homeland. It was virtually ignored by the Arab states and rejected by Israel. Furthermore, it was seen by the United States as unwarranted interference in the region. It did, however, represent an EPC initiative in a very sensitive security area and was followed up by the EPC Council President visiting the Middle East in following years (Ginsberg 1989, pp. 77–80; EPC Statements 1988, 1989, p. I.52). Again the success of the EPC's action over the Arab-Israeli dispute is more in the development of an agreed line rather than in an effective policy outcome.

A second area of importance for the development of EPC has been that of relations with the USA. The West European-America relationship is a complex one and its intricacies endure regardless of the existence of the EPC. What the EPC provided was an opportunity for the core West European states to organize their relationships with the United States on a more one-to-one basis. This effort got off to a bad start in the 1970s when the reaction of the EC to events in the Middle East, especially the Yom Kippur War and its aftermath, made the US suspicious of the emerging EPC, particularly if it was to have consequences for the solidarity of the NATO alliance (Ginsberg 1989, p. 67).

Deteriorating US-West European relations in the late 1970s and early 1980s — the period of the arrival of the New Cold War — were reflected in EPC. The cause of the rift can be found in the different understanding of détente by the two and in their varied interests. On the whole, the EPC countries had regional European interests, while the United States had global concerns (Bowker and Williams 1988, pp. 251–3). In the case of diplomatic and economic sanctions on Muslim fundamentalist Iran (from 1979 to 1980), sanctions against the Soviet Union in 1980 because of their invasion of Afghanistan in December 1979 and then against Poland in 1982 after the imposition of martial law there from December 1981, European action through the EPC was seen as too circumspect (Bowker and Williams 1988, p. 253).

The New Cold War turned into renewed détente between the superpowers with the coming to power of Mr Gorbachev in the Soviet Union in 1985 and his meeting with President Reagan in Reykjavik in 1986, from which arose a number of arms control agreements. The West Europeans no longer felt American displeasure for not being supportive against the Soviet 'evil empire' and indeed EC experience was sought in helping along the process, first of Soviet disengagement from Eastern Europe in the late 1980s and then of managing the disintegration of the Soviet Union from 1991 to 1992.

The EPC's involvement in the Conference on Security and Cooperation in Europe (CSCE) proved to be useful in this case. The EC states had used EPC to co-ordinate their action within the CSCE from the beginning. All the EC states were represented in the negotiations from 1973 that led to the signing of the Helsinki Final Act by all the countries of Europe (including the Soviet Union, but excluding isolationist Albania) and by the United States and Canada (by virtue of their military presence in Europe). However, on economic and trade issues, the EC members were represented by the EC Commission. Also on other questions — such as human rights and security matters — the emerging institutions of EPC were used. The EC, remarked an American diplomat present at the negotiations, regarded this as 'a particularly successful example of foreign policy coordination' (Maresca 1987, p. 19).

By the end of the 1980s, the EC members were expressing their views on a wide range of issues through EPC. They took up human rights issues at CSCE meetings and supported the INF treaty that was to remove intermediate-range nuclear weapons from Europe. Their twelve ministers met in March

1988 exclusively to discuss the progress of the Vienna CSCE discussions and noted that 'on most issues in Vienna, the Twelve speak with one voice and are represented in the various negotiating sub-bodies by the Presidency' (EPC Statements 1988, 1989, p. I.32).

At the start of the 1990s, EC members had to face three major foreign and security challenges and EPC was one of the instruments — but not the only one — used by them.

A challenge to the world security order came in August 1990 when Saddam Hussein of Iraq invaded and annexed the neighbouring state of Kuwait. The immediate EPC response was to condemn the action and to call for Iraqi withdrawal. The EC also supported and imposed UN sanctions against Iraq. However, the EC members could not always agree on the mix of diplomacy and the threat of force that should be employed against the Iraqi leadership. On the whole the British pressed for full support of the US-led effort to build up a sizeable force capable of evicting Iraq from Kuwait, while France and Germany showed greater willingness to search for a diplomatic settlement (Cooley 1991, pp. 137–8). One American commentator noted that the discord among the Twelve shown during this crisis could 'only perpetuate the conditions of unhealthy reliance on the United States' (Brenner 1991, p. 676) and the President of the EC Commission, Jacques Delors, stated that the Gulf War, during which Kuwait was prized back from the Iraqis, 'provided an object lesson — if one were needed — on the limitations of the European Community' (Delors 1991, p. 99).

A further example was given in the EC-EPC treatment of the Yugoslav crisis which erupted in the summer of 1991. At a time when the states of Slovenia and Croatia (then republics within the Yugoslav federation) were attempting to break away from what they regarded as the Serbian-dominated Yugoslavia, EC members seemed to be trying their best to keep the federation together. Indeed, the day before the two breakaway republics declared independence in June 1991, the EC signed a loan agreement with the Yugoslav government (Cviic 1992, p. 88). Once civil conflict broke out, the EC-EPC involved itself in four ways. First, the EPC found itself delegated by the CSCE to resolve the conflict and it convened a number of conferences to this end, latterly chaired by Lord Carrington, the former Secretary-General of NATO. Secondly, it attempted to arrange ceasefires between the warring factions and sent unarmed monitors to observe these. Thirdly, in November 1991 EC ministers invoked sanctions against those elements that it considered to be responsible for the continued fighting — mainly the Serbian government and the Yugoslav federal army (Cviic 1992, pp. 88–90). Finally, when all else had failed, the EPC meeting in December 1991 — prodded by the Germans — decided to recognize in January 1992 those separate Yugoslav republics that wished international recognition. At that stage the Security Council of the UN took a more active role.

The third major challenge facing EPC-EC at the start of the 1990s was that of the collapse of the Soviet Union which was formally disbanded on 25 December 1991. Scared that economic and social deprivation in the new republics would cause security problems to the east of the Communities, EC ministers took action on two levels. The first was economic and had a number of aspects. The longer-run treatment of economic problems was a task for the newly established — by an EC initiative — European Bank for Reconstruction and Development and the G24, the group of Western industrial countries (Pinder 1991, pp. 86–103). The EC also provided the Soviet successor states with food and medical aid to help them survive the 1991/92 winter. EC officials were even dispatched to St Petersburg to make sure that the EC food was received in the shops, sold at the proper price and that the proceeds went to the needy.

The other response was by the EPC and it was the decision to recognize the successor republics of the Soviet Union and to support their membership of the CSCE and the UN. In doing this, the EPC ministers set down guidelines of expected behaviour for the governments of the new states and the Republic of Georgia — where there was a civil war at the end of 1991 — did not receive immediate recognition because of its failure to reach the EPC's standards.

The successes and failures of EPC have been used both by those who oppose further EC integration and by federalists as support for their case. The opponents point to the different commercial, strategic and geographical perspectives of members such as the United Kingdom, Ireland, Germany and Greece, and argue that these can only be represented in an essentially intergovernmental structure as the EPC, where each state has a voice and, if need be, a veto. They point to the shortcomings of EPC policy in the Gulf War and in Yugoslavia as demonstrating the difficulty of trying to force unity from diversity (Gasteyger 1992, p. 75). The federalists argue that the failing of EPC has been its lack of a Community nature and that foreign and security policy should keep pace with the growing interdependence in economic policy. This supports the 'argument for moving towards a form of political union embracing a common foreign and security policy' (Delors 1991, p. 99).

A note on defence

Since the rejection of the EDC in 1954, the European Communities have had minimal involvement in the defence policies of their members. As seen above, EPC has dealt increasingly with the security aspects of its members' external relations, albeit in an intergovernmentalist way. The EC itself has also been involved when there are commercial and economic factors involved, such as trade and financial sanctions. Until the late 1980s, neither the EPC nor the EC concerned itself with the military instrumentalities of security policy that represent defence policy. This was partly because of the wide variation in defence policies and capabilities of the member states, but mainly because other institutions existed — such as NATO and the WEU — for defence co-operation and co-ordination. Basically as long as the main perceived military threat to Western Europe was that of the possibility (however small) of a massive Soviet attack, then NATO and WEU, which tied, respectively, the United States and the United Kingdom to the defence of continental Europe, seemed the best defence options for most of the West European states.

At the end of the 1980s and beginning of the 1990s, the security situation changed radically as outlined in Chapter 1 (pp. 20–21). The drawing back of the superpower overlay — to use Buzan's word — from the continent of Europe, offered the EC states a new set of challenges — ranging from the threat of mass migration to nationalist wars in Eastern Europe — and the possibility that a different match of institutions could be used to meet these challenges.

Even though the Single European Act formalized EPC's involvement in security matters, it specifically ruled out any competition with NATO and WEU (Article 30.6c) and led the head of the EPC secretariat to remark that 'the "security dimenesion" is still on the drawing board in EPC' (Januzzi 1988, p. 104). With the end of the Cold War and collapse of the Soviet Union, not only was the security dimension taken up by the EPC with greater vigour, so was the possibility of defence co-operation. Academic works suggested that the EC might take its place in the panoply of defence and security forums available for Europe — the CSCE, NATO, WEU (Gambles 1991; Gnesotto 1991; Joffe 1992, pp. 53–68). Jacques Delors, President of the EC Commission, made it clear that he expected the EC to develop a defence competence (Delors 1991, pp. 106–9).

The Maastricht treaty

At the Maastricht European Council on 10 December 1991, the heads of state and government of the twelve EC countries adopted the contents of the treaty of political union, with the final document being signed on 7 February 1992. This established a European Union that would envelop the European Communities and supplement it 'by the policies and forms of co-operation established by this Treaty' (Treaty on European Union, Title I, Common Provisions, Article A). One of the objectives of the Union is 'to assert its identity on the international scene, in particular through the implementation of a common foreign and security policy which shall include the eventual framing of a common defence policy' (ibid., Article B).

It is important to note that the objective is a *common* foreign and security policy, rather than greater co-ordination and co-operation of national policies. Also the way is cleared for the Union to have a defence competence. How are these objectives — a common foreign and security policy and a defence policy component — to be achieved?

The Provisions on a Common Foreign and Security Policy (Title V) set out the objectives and the mechanisms. The five objectives (Article J.1.2) are:

- to safeguard the values, interests and independence of the union;
- to strengthen the security of the Union and its member states;
- to preserve peace and strengthen international security in accordance with the UN Charter and the CSCE's Paris Charter;
- to promote international co-operation;
- to develop and consolidate democracy and the rule of law, and respect for human rights and fundamental freedoms.

These are scarcely controversial aims but this level of generality has to be transformed into policy. Their implementation is to be pursued by two routes.

First, according to Article J.2, the member states shall inform and consult with one another on foreign and security matters to ensure 'their combined influence is exerted as effectively as possible' (as in SEA, Article 30.2a), but 'by means of concerted and convergent action.' This is the co-operation route and is only a minor development of the process seen in the SEA. In paragraph J.2, however, the council of the European Union is allowed to define a common position, when it deems it necessary, and member states are to ensure that their 'national policies conform to the common positions.' These positions are to be upheld in international forums and conferences. This is an advance on the SEA where the common position was to be 'a point of reference' which members would 'endeavour to adopt' in international forums (SEA, Articles 30.2c and 30.7a).

Article J.3 contains the procedure for adopting joint action in foreign and security policy. The Council of the European Union (consisting normally of the foreign ministers) is to decide — on the basis of guidelines from the European Council (normally a meeting of heads of state and government) — that a matter should be a subject of joint action. The Council will then lay down the principle, scope, objectives, duration and means of the joint action. The Council (acting unanimously) will define those matters of the joint action on which decisions may be taken by a qualified majority. Member states declared that, where a qualified majority existed, they would try to avoid preventing a unanimous decision. Joint actions commit the member states 'in the positions they adopt and in the conduct of their activity' and therefore represent a step down the road of a common policy. Member states can still take their own action in the case of 'imperative need arising from changes in the situation and failing a Council decision', though such measures should have regard to the general objectives of joint action and must be reported to the Council (Article J.3.6).

Article J.4 declares that the common foreign and security policy 'shall include all questions related to the security of the European Union, including the eventual framing of a common defence policy, which might in time lead to a common defence' (Article J.4.1). The Union is to request the WEU 'which is an integral part of the development of the European Union, to elaborate and implement' decisions with defence implications, and then the Council, in agreement with the WEU, is to adopt the practical arrangements (Article J.4.2). However, issues with defence implications are not subject to the 'joint action' procedure set out in Article J.3.

Paragraphs 4 and 5 of Article J.4 demonstrated the desire not to have policy incompatible with that established within the NATO framework (J.4.4) and not to prevent co-operation within NATO and WEU (J.4.5). As the 1948 Brussels Treaty which forms the basis for the WEU runs out in 1998, the provisions of Article J.4 may be revised in 1996.

Of the twelve members party to the 1992 Maastricht Treaty, three — Denmark, Greece and Ireland — are not members of the WEU. The rest made a declaration which is Annex II.29 of the Treaty and in this they express their willingness to develop the WEU as the defence component of the European Union 'as a means to strengthen the European pillar of the Atlantic Alliance.' To this end, they proposed to formulate concrete European defence policy and advance its implementation. They promoted ideas on how to develop closer relations with the European Union and NATO, as well as on the advancement of their operational role.

Article J.4 also covers the role of the Union's institutions in foreign and security policy. The Presidency is responsible for implementing common measures and representing the Union in foreign and security matters and is assisted by the previous and following state in that office. The Commission is to be associated with this work and the Presidency is to consult and inform the European Parliament. The Council is to define the principles of and the guidelines for the common policy, and is to take decisions for the defining and implementing of that policy. An extraordinary meeting can convene within forty-eight hours, or in a shorter period in an emergency. A Political Committee of Political Directors of the member states (as under EPC) is to monitor the international situation and the implementation of agreed policies. The Court of Justice seems to be excluded by Article J.11 from the provisions relating to foreign and security matters.

These provisions mean an end to some of the duality between EPC and the EC, though they still allow the member states to hold up the adoption of common policies and they keep out the Commission, the European Parliament and the Court from any decisive role in the process. However, it is a further step towards a common policy for the external affairs of the European Union, and opens up the possibility of common defence for the Union. The non-WEU members of the EC will clearly have some reservations about this, though Greece and Denmark can easily be accommodated within WEU. Whether this will be a stumbling block for the neutral candidates for EC-Union membership — such as Austria, Finland and Sweden — will depend not only on the

internal politics of those countries but more on the development of international events and the alacrity with which the European Union adopts truly
common foreign, security and defence policies.

References

Bowker, M. and Williams, P., 1988, *Superpower detente: a reappraisal*, SAGE,
London.
Brenner, M., 1991, 'The alliance: a Gulf post-mortem', *International Affairs*,
67 (4), 665–78.
Bulletin of the European Communities, 6/1971, Commission of the EC,
Brussels.
Cooley, J.K., 1991, 'Pre-war Gulf diplomacy', *Survival*, 33 (2), 125–39.
Cviic, C., 1992, 'Implications of the crisis in south-eastern Europe', *Adelphi
Papers 265*, International Institute for Strategic Studies, London.
Delors, D., 1991, 'European integration and security', *Survival*, 33 (2), 99–109.
EPC statements 1988, 1989, Ministerio de Asuntos Exteriores, Madrid.
Fursdon, E., 1980, *The European defence community: a history*, Macmillan,
London.
Gambles, I., 1991, *European security integration in the 1990s*, Institute for Secur-
ity Studies, Chaillot Papers 3, Paris.
Gasteyger, C., 1992, 'European security and the new arc of crisis: paper II',
Adelphi Paper 265, International Institute for Strategic Studies, London.
Ginsberg, R.H., 1989, *Foreign policy actions of the European Community*, Lynne
Rienner Publishers, Boulder, Colorado.
Gnesotto, N., 1991, *European defence: why not the twelve?*, Institute for Security
Studies, Chaillot Papers 1, Paris.
Hallstein, W., 1962, *United Europe*, OUP, London.
Januzzi, G., 1988, 'European political cooperation and the Single European
Act', in Tsakaloyannis, P. (ed.), *Western European security in a changing world*,
European Institute of Public Administration, Maastricht.
Joffe, G., 1992, 'European security and the new arc of crisis: paper I', *Adelphi
Papers 265*, International Institute for Strategic Studies, London, 53–68.
Maresca, J.J., 1987, *To Helsinki*, Duke University Press, Durham and London.
Pinder, J., 1991, *The European Community and Eastern Europe*, Pinter, London.
Vaughan, R., 1976, *Post-war integration in Europe*, Edward Arnold, London.
Wallace, W., 1983, 'Political cooperation: integration through intergovern-
mentalism', in Wallace, H., Wallace, W. and Webb, C. (eds), *Policy-making
in the European Community*, John Wiley & Sons, Chichester, 373–402.

13

Future prospects

This chapter hopes to provide a backdrop to the previous chapters, by attempting to summarize the notion of 'union' and the development of the European Community as it proceeds into the 1990s and beyond.

This introductory text has covered the historical evolution of Europe, the twentieth-century developments which led to the creation of the EC, its institutions and major policy areas, and the Community's external identity and relationships.

Therefore it can be useful to review the notion or concept of 'Union', of which the EC itself was seen by many as constituting the first stage, and the defining characteristics of the present Community, as it exists prior to assuming the mantle of 'Union'.

Maastricht and the heritage of 'Union'

As Chapter 1 showed, there was no deficit in visions, aspirations and plans for the political unification of Europe particularly by the mid-twentieth century: the Churchillian plan for Anglo-French union and the work carried out by Resistance movements and post-war federalist organizations in helping to establish the Council of Europe, are but two examples.

Ultimately, the more successful method — successful in the context of the EC's aims and methods, and its unique blend of conventional and 'unconventional' characteristics — has been evidenced by the creation and adaptation of the European Community, as it has both sponsored and epitomized the process of integrating sovereign European nation states.

In other words, the construction of European unity, through a process of economic and political integration, has been as much a characteristic or tactic underlying the foundation of the EEC in 1957, as it was of the ECSC in

1951. As Robert Schuman stated, upon presenting his plan for the ECSC in May 1950:

> Europe will not be made at once or according to a single overall plan. It will be built through concrete achievements which first create a de facto solidarity' (Pryce 1987, p. 46).

Both the ECSC and the EEC were these 'concrete achievements', and since 1957 when the EEC and EURATOM emerged in the Treaties of Rome, the integration process has been characterized by an incremental or step by step approach to fulfilling 'the foundations of an ever closer union among the peoples of Europe' (Treaties of Rome, Preamble).

The Treaty on European Union, constructed during the Inter-Governmental Conferences on economic and monetary union and political union during 1990/91, and which was signed at the Maastricht Council in February 1992, represents another of these steps.

It is worthwhile reviewing the major changes made to the nature, structure and processes of the Community in the new Treaty, prior to examining the concept of 'Union'.

First of all, the institutional changes effected by the Treaty:

(1) Primarily, it is the European Parliament which is the beneficiary of reforms. There are two dimensions to the EPs 'new and improved' position in the Union Treaty;

    (a) the revised Article 228.3 states that '... agreements referred to in Article 238, other agreements establishing a specific institutional framework by organizing co-operation procedures, agreements having important budgetary implications for the Community and agreements entailing amendment of an act adopted under the procedure referred to in Article 189b shall be concluded after the assent of the European Parliament has been obtained'. Previously, Article 228 had endowed the Commission with the power to conclude external relations agreements, with the role of the EP relegated to one of consultation. For some time it had been felt that the Community's powers in the field of international economic affairs — of which Article 228 was one aspect — was hampered by the lack of parallel power over international political and diplomatic interests. Within this argument was also dissatisfaction with the miniscule role of the EP in relation to external agreements.

    The EP's Draft Treaty on European Union of 1984 attempted to correct this deficiency, by stating that the EP as well as the Council should have the final right of approval over any international agreements involving the EC (Lodge 1986, pp. 116–23).

Under the new Article 228, the EP's role has been extended in order that its power of assent is in practice a meaningful exercise, and although its power of assent is not without restriction, under the new Treaty, the EP's assent will be required if certain major agreements are to take place — notably using Article 238 which covers Association or other agreements 'involving reciprocal rights and obligations; between the Community and non-EC states, and Article O (Final Provisions) where Parliamentary assent is required for accession agreements.

(b) The second formal revision of the Parliament's powers and functions is contained in the new Article 189b (see Chapter 2) which will introduce a conciliation procedure to draft proposals on subjects other than budgetary legislation, where the EP and the Council of Ministers have enjoyed co-decision-making responsibility since 1975.

The new Article 189b essentially extends the power of 'co-decision' for the Parliament in the areas of social and environmental policy although this phrase is not used in the Treaty, and the review clause in the Union Treaty which will enable the new provisions to be looked at anew by 1996, may well result in an extension of the power of co-decision to other policy areas — given that this possibilty was supported by both the EP during the 1980s and certain member states, such as Germany, Belgium and Italy, during the IGCs, whose Parliaments threatened non-ratification if the extension of EP powers was insufficient.

(2) There is one other important point to note in relation to the new Treaty's provisions affecting institutional matters. The principle of subsidiarity is now incorporated into the text — subsidiarity being a characteristic of many federal systems, where the powers and functions of the different levels of government or administration are clearly specified. In EC terms the notion of subsidiarity, directly or indirectly, has shaped the nature of debate over the future development of the Community — with specific political disagreement over issues such as a Social Charter, being linked to a wider discrepancy of opinion over whether the EC held a legal competency to act in the policy area.

Again, the inclusion of such definitions of power, authority and responsibility owe much to the earlier draft European Union Treaty, proposed by the EP in 1984.

The new Union Treaty first touches upon the concept of subsidiarity in Article A (Common Provisions) where 'this Treaty marks a new stage in the process creating an ever closer union among the peoples of Europe, where decisions are taken as closely as possible to the citizens'. The new Article 3b defines subsidiarity more precisely — 'the Community shall act within the limits of the powers conferred upon it by this Treaty and of the objectives assigned to it therein.

In areas which do not fall within its exclusive jurisdiction, the Community shall take action, in accordance with the principle of subsidiarity, only if and in so far as the objectives of the proposed action cannot be sufficiently achieved by the member states and can therefore, by reason of the scale or effects of proposed action, be better achieved by the Community.

Any action by the Community shall not go beyond what is necessary to achieve the objectives of this Treaty'.

This is a significant development, perhaps less so in terms of avoiding political disagreement over the EC's capability to act in policy areas, and perhaps more important for its 'signpost' function, in terms of the future development of 'Union' institutions. In other words, subsidiarity as defined by the Union Treaty appears to clarify the potential for the Community to act in relation to its member states, as opposed to clarifying the dispersal of power among all constituent levels of government or administration.

(3) Another change in direction arising from the Union Treaty concerns a number of Community policy areas.

(a) Not only was the EP's influence over certain policy areas extended, the principle of cohesion was reinforced. The new Article 130d creates a 'Cohesion Fund', to be set up before 31 December 1993, particularly in relation to environmental aspects of social and economic 'cohesion', and to 'trans-European networks' for transport infrastructure. The fifteenth Protocol attached to the Treaty also reaffirms the political commitment of member states and the Community to the goal of promoting social and economic cohesion, especially in the context of financial constraints imposed by convergence policies toward EMU.

(b) Another significant development concerns the new Title VI of the Treaty concerning co-operation over justice and home affairs. There has been no immediate transfer of competency from national governments to Community institutions, but this new Title stresses the 'common concern' of such matters as asylum, border controls on the movement of people, immigration policy, judicial co-operation over civil and criminal matters and police co-operation to prevent terrorism and drug trafficking (Article K1).

Therefore this policy area is one conducted through governmental — Council of Ministers — channels, although a Co-ordinating Committee is envisaged in order to provide the Council of Ministers with any necessary information. Thus this is one new area of policy-making which has been brought closer to the Community forum which, if the Council feels it necessary, may be employed to take joint action and to draw up conventions (Article K3). It may be that in future years this new form of co-operation, over policies previously guarded closely by governments, may be revised and extended, if events prove necessary.

(4) In addition, the Union Treaty has formally incorporated the notion of a common foreign and security policy for the EC (see pp. 179–81).

The new Title V of the Treaty (Articles J1–J11) lays out the objectives of such a policy, including the safeguarding of the 'common values, fundamental interests and independence of the European Union', along with the promotion of international co-operation and the consolidation of democracy and the rule of law.

In Article J3, the Council of Ministers is to decide whether a particular matter should be the subject of joint action, and if this is to be the case, define any subsequent decisions on the basis of qualified majority voting (54 votes to be cast by at least eight members). Article J4 also notes that the common foreign and security policy 'shall include all questions related to the security of the European Union, including the eventual framing of a common defence policy, which might in time lead to a common defence'. The Western European Union is thus asked to 'elaborate and implement decisions and actions of the Union which have defence implications' (Article J4.2).

It is perhaps this area of change in the Union Treaty that has a wealth of earlier initiatives, arising from attempts to promote political unification. The Fouchet Plan of the early 1960s, although very clearly an attempt to keep foreign policy away from supranational 'interference', was none the less an attempt to weld together the political interests and activities of the original six member states in an intergovernmental context. Precisely because of its deficiencies and failure to materialize, the search for political unification, via a co-ordinated European foreign policy, was continued in the early 1970s. The Tindemans Report (1976) stressed, amongst other issues, that EPC should no longer operate outside the framework of the Treaty of Rome, in order that the Council of Ministers could assume responsibility for foreign policy within the EC. This suggestion was largely backed by the Genscher-Colombo inspired Solemn Declaration on European Union (1983) and the EP's Draft Treaty on European Union (1984), although this did not necessarily seek the 'overnight' creation of a common foreign policy. The common foreign and security provisions in the new Treaty thus reflect much earlier work and aspirations for a Community, or Union, to act in external political and economic affairs (see pp. 171–173).

The phrase 'European Union' has been a popular one, much employed in the Community's history, and prior to its introduction at the Hague Summit of 1969, other related terms such as European unity, political unification and a 'United States of Europe' were in vogue.

Jean Monnet, undoubtedly one of the most significant European statesmen in the post–1945 era, noted that:

> Europe has never existed. It is not the addition of sovereign nations met together in councils that makes an entity of them. We must genuinely create Europe: it must become manifest to itself . . . and it must have confidence in its own future (Vaughan 1976, p. 55).

Not only was the Monnet-Schuman inspired process of integration a novel one in creating a truly European 'Community', but efforts taken since 1957 under the banner of fostering 'Union' have also been equally important although ambiguous.

Whether these were individually-motivated efforts, such as the Pleven Plan for the EDC or the Fouchet Plan for a political Community; or whether these have been collective governmentally-inspired initiatives such as the Hague Summit's creation of EPC and the formal goal of economic and monetary union; or whether they have been institutionally-sponsored designs, such as the EP's Draft Treaty on European Union — taken together, their common characteristic has been that of transforming the integration process by seeking methods or processes by which further, invariably deeper as well as wider, integration could occur.

So European 'Union' has, right from the outset, never been defined or laid down as a conceptual or pragmatic 'blueprint' for the future development of the integration process — at different periods and for a variety of purposes, 'Union' has meant varied objectives according to different aspirations and constraining conditions. For example, during the later stages of the 1990/91 Inter-Governmental Conference on political union, British party political debate revolved around the uses and abuses of the so-called 'F-word', denoting the perceived federal aspirations of the negotiations. For largely domestic political purposes, the British Government could not agree to an overtly federalist Treaty and the F-word was subsequently removed from the text. Whether the Treaty provisions represent a rhetorical or genuine federal development, the essential point remains that the concept of 'union' is often sufficiently muddy or flexible in order for all parties to feel that they have gained an acceptable agreement.

In many ways, the Europe of the 1990s is continuing along a variety of paths to its eventual destination, just as Monnet, Schuman and others emphasized in the 1950s. In summary, it is an imprecise science to attempt to define 'Union' — in EC terms, this is an 'essentially contested concept'.

However if 'Union' can best be described by a search to transform relations between member states of the Community in order to strengthen joint and supranational levels of authority, this has been perceived by some as a creeping form of centralization or federalism.

In order to discover whether in fact 'Union' can be automatically associated with a federal Europe, it is necessary to examine further the fundamental characteristics of the present EC.

Towards a European Union

What sort of creation is the planned European Union that should emerge from the European Communities by the late 1990s and beyond? There is no neat answer to this question because, as can be seen from Chapter 1, the genesis of the European Communities lies in the uneven and fractured history of a divided continent. However, it is possible to examine the nature of the beast to see which of the existing species it most closely resembles.

First, it should be established that the EC is at least an international organization. This is clear from an examination of a definition of an international organization as

> a formal, continuous structure established by agreement between members (governmental and/or non-governmental) from two or more sovereign states with the aim of pursuing the common interest of the membership (Archer 1983, p. 35).

The EC was established by a number of formal agreements — including the Treaty of Paris, 1951 and the two Treaties of Rome in 1957 — and these documents set out the common interests to be pursued by the original six sovereign states. The structure of the EC has been formally established and has not only endured but has developed.

Has it become something more than just an international organization? At least, it is certainly a very advanced international organization in institutional terms. Not only does it have a Council of Ministers and more regular meetings of civil servants, which are common aspects of international organizations, it has a Commission and a Court of Justice that are more sophisticated than equivalent institutions in other organizations. Furthermore, fairly advanced international organizations such as the UN and the Council of Europe so far do not have a parliamentary assembly with representatives directly elected by the citizens of the members, as is the case of the European Parliament.

A further point is that the EC's institutions have supranational elements, which means that they have legal powers that can override those of the member states. If this is the case, the distinction can be made that the EC is above the sovereign state members whereas almost all other international governmental organizations operate between their member states. While it can be argued that the EC members are merely delegating responsibility to its institutions, the Court of Justice has claimed that the EC treaties have established an entirely new legal order which has two important features. The first is that EC law has primacy over the law of member states; the second is that EC law is directly applicable to the citizens of the member states without, necessarily, the intervention of their governments. Thus in the case of *Costa* v. *ENEL* the Court ruled that

> The transfer by the States [of the EC] from their domestic legal system to the Community legal system of the rights and obligations arising under the Treaty carries with it a permanent limitation on their sovereign rights (Court of Justice, *Costa* v. *ENEL*, 1964).

Another point about the European Communities, and especially about the emerging European Union, is that they both aspire to be much more than an international organization – they aspire to some form of European unity. The Treaty of Paris, which set up the Coal and Steel Community, aimed 'to create . . . the basis for a broader and deeper community among peoples long divided by bloody conflicts' (Preamble). The Treaty of Rome, in establishing the European Economic Community 'determined to lay the foundations of an ever closer union among the peoples of Europe' (Preamble). The creation of a European Union is a stated goal in the preamble of the 1986 Single European Act, whereas the Treaty on Political Union, agreed in Maastricht in 1991, aimed at the establishment of a European Union and marked 'a new stage in the process creating an ever closer Union among the peoples of Europe' (Article A, Common Provisions, Treaty on Political Union).

There seems to exist the aspiration for the EC, and the European Union, to be something grander than a mere international organization, however institutionally well-developed. But what might this 'something' be?

One answer – and it was the one given by the majority of the heads of government negotiating in December 1991 at Maastricht – is that it should become a federation. The negotiating draft of the Treaty of Political Union included the sentence that 'this Treaty marks a new stage in the process leading gradually to a Union with a federal goal.' This vocation was challenged by the United Kingdom government and was expunged. Many of those involved in building the EC – Monnet, Hallstein, Spinelli and Delors – were federalists, and it is most likely that there will be other attempts to give the European Union federal aspirations.

How might it work out in practice that the European Union would become a proto-federation? There is some guidance in Spinelli's Draft Treaty on European Union, adopted by the European Parliament in 1984 (see above pp. 34–5). A 'neo-federalist' view has been advanced by John Pinder who tries to deal with the intermediary steps between inter-state relations and a fully fledged federation. Eschewing Spinelli's notion of creating a federation mainly by changing the constitutional framework, Pinder suggests a process with 'both a federal aim and steps towards it' (Pinder 1991, p. 216). He considers that both European Union and federation are solutions to the problems that will face Europe in the next century, but that the former will require a single market, economic and monetary union, a common external policy with co-operation on security; while federation also needs control of armed forces. Both would involve federal institutions, with majority voting in the Council, co-legislation by the Council and the European Parliament and 'full executive competence'; for the Commission (ibid.). Member states would keep control over domestic policies. The Union could be built up step by step, with the institutions being 'entrusted with new tasks' (ibid., p. 217).

This more gradualist approach has resonances of the neo-functionalist perspective, originally advanced by Etzioni (1965), Haas (1968) and Lindberg and Scheingold (1970). The original contention was that political groups in several national settings would 'shift their loyalties, expectations and political activities towards a new centre, whose institutions possess or demand jurisdiction over the pre-existing national states' (Haas 1968, p. 16). This view saw the elites of the EC states — politicians, trade union and business leaders, civil servants — eventually moving their operations away from the sovereign state and instead spending more time and trouble on the institutions of the EC, especially the Commission, the specialist committees and the European Parliament. As their activity became 'communitized' in one functional area (for example, the steel industry) so they would find it necessary to seek Community solutions in adjacent policy areas (such as transport or the coal industry). This 'spillover' view of the development of the Communities suggested a relentless growth of their competences to the detriment of the power and authority of the member states so that the latter would eventually become drained of many of their political activities. The result would be a structure 'closer to the archetype of federation than any past international organization' (ibid., p. 59) but by use of the neo-functionalist approach to integration.

The weaknesses of the neo-functionalist approach towards the EC's development — its automaticity, its optimism and the emphasis on elite politics — has been recognized (Archer 1992, pp. 94–101; Harrison 1990, pp. 144–9). Keohane and Hoffmann placed ideas of spillover and assumptions about the EC's inexorable advance through interest group activity in context. They viewed the EC as 'an experiment in pooling sovereignty, not in transferring it from states to supranational institutions'. The expansion of the EC's activities has taken place as a 'result of linkages among sectors, as envisaged in the [neo-functionalist] theory', but this is by no means automatic and 'depends ultimately on the bargains between major governments' (Keohane and Hoffmann 1990, p. 277). This mixture of neo-functionalist method and inter-governmentalist deals led them, writing in 1989, to conclude that

barring a major slump in the world economy, or catastrophic events in Eastern Europe and the Soviet Union whose international fall-out cannot be predicted, there are reasons to be at least moderately optimistic about the Community's future prospects (Keohane and Hoffman 1990, p. 296).

Since this was written, there has been a notable slump in the world economy and seismic events in Eastern Europe and the Soviet Union (which has now disappeared from the map). This has presented the EC with three new challenges: a stagnant or declining economy; the prospect of political and economic chaos on its eastern frontier; and an increase in the number of states wishing to join the EC. The response, in terms of going ahead with the Single European Market and Economic and Monetary Union, in its absorption of East Germany and aid to the other parts of central and eastern Europe, and in negotiating the EEA, can again be seen in terms of a mixture of neo-functionalist spillover (the SEM and EEA) and governmental initiative (East Germany and the aid packages). The Treaty on Political Union agreed at Maastricht likewise shows signs of such a compromise. The difference from the EC response to similar periods of crisis in 1973/74 and 1980/81 is that this time the EC has been seen to be more the starting-point, even of much governmental activity. The main threat remains that of a loss of legitimacy of EC institutions (as noted by Keohane and Hoffmann 1990, p. 294), especially in the face of increased domestic nationalism and failing economies.

If the EC is not yet federalist, more than intergovernmentalist and only partially responding to neo-functionalist theories, is there another label that fits it? One answer could be that of 'confederal', whereby many of the attributes of a federal structure exist, except that the individual sovereign states maintain a final veto right in crucial areas (for example, foreign and defence matters) and they can leave the union. Certainly the EC member states have kept a veto right in areas they consider to be important and although the EC treaties do not allow for a member state to leave, neither do they prevent this. Indeed, Greenland — part of one member state, Denmark — withdrew from the EC in 1985.

A refinement would be to describe the EC and the European Union as a consociation, after Lijphart (1969). This would portray it as a grouping of separate blocs (nation states, in this case) more inward-looking than concerned with links between themselves. Relations between the blocs would be undertaken by the elites and decisions would be the result of agreements and coalitions, with dissenting elites having the right of veto. Finally, the smaller blocs (in this case Luxembourg, Ireland, Greece) would have representation in the major institutions and their interests safeguarded (Taylor 1990, pp. 173–4).

In contrast to a neo-functionalist view of the EC, this would not require there to be a 'socio-psychological community' in the EC (ibid., p. 173) — a feeling that the EC was 'us'. It has in common with federalism the ability 'to accommodate sharp cleavages in society as long as they are clearly geographically demarcated' (ibid.). The main difference lies in the weight given to the agents of centralized government: in a federation these are strong, in a consociation the common interest is weak (ibid., p. 181).

The term consociation may be more fairly applied to the EC of the late 1960s and 1970s, but the element of common interest and cross-border activity is strengthening, and the veto rights of the member states' representatives weakening.

In the end, what the EC-European Union is or becomes will depend — as suggested by Keohan and Hoffmann's glance to the future — on a combination of internal politics and external events. These events will to a great extent determine the opportunities open for the polity of the European Union into the next century. The internal politics and economic development in the area of the existing EC — or of a wider membership — will fashion the willingness of the political elites (and the wider mass public) to use those opportunities. Especially with the levels of instability existing in the Europe of the 1990s, there is no guarantee that the future development of the European Union will be one of maturing to a federation on an almost linear projection. It is more likely to be a history of set-backs and disappointments among the triumphs and advances. It is up to the peoples of Europe — and their representatives — to overcome the adversities and seize the opportunities that are offered them.

References

Archer, C., 1992, (2nd ed.) *International organizations*, Routledge, London.

Burgess, M., 1989, *Federalism and European Union*, Routledge, London.

Etzioni, E., 1965, *Political unification*, Holt Rinehart & Winston, New York.

Haas, E.B., 1968, *The uniting of Europe* (2nd ed.), Stanford University Press, Stanford, Calif.

Harrison, R.J., 1990, 'Neo-functionalism', in Groom, A.J.R. and Taylor, P. (eds), 1990, *Frameworks for international co-operation*, Pinter, London, 139–50.

IEA Readings 33, 1990, *Europe's constitutional future*, Institute for Economic Affairs, London.

Keohane, R.O. and Hoffmann, S., 1990, 'Conclusions: Community politics and institutional change', in Wallace, W. (ed.), *The dynamics of European integration*, Pinter, London, 276–300.

Lijphart, A., 1969, 'Consociational democracy', *World Politics*, 21 (2), 207.

Lindberg, L.N. and Scheingold, S.A., 1970, *Europe's would-be polity*, Prentice-Hall, Englewood Cliffs, New Jersey.

Lodge, J. (ed.), 1986, *European Union: the EC in search of a future*, Macmillan, London.

Pinder, J., 1991, *European Community. The building of a union*, Oxford University Press, Oxford.

Pryce, R. (ed.), 1987, *The dynamics of European Union*, Croom Helm, London.

Taylor, P., 1990, 'Consociationalism and federalism as approaches to international integration', in Groom and Taylor, *Frameworks for international cooperation*, 172–84.

Vaughan, R., 1976, *Post-war integration in Europe*, Edward Arnold, London.

Index

Soviet Union, 17
and Cold War, 4, 7–8, 18–19, 175
collapse of, 5, 20, 155, 177
and Comecon, 149
and EC, 21, 146, 155–6, 177
Spaak Committee, 14, 46
Spain, 18, 68, 84, 96, 98, 99, 103, 162
STABEX procedure, 125, 127, 129
Stalin, Josef, 6, 7, 8
STAR programme, 97–8
steel industry, 10–12, 98
Stockholm Conference (1983), 19
Stockholm Treaty (1960), 16
subsidiarity principle, 115, 184–5
Sugar Protocol, 124–5
surpluses, agricultural, 63, 65, 67
Sweden, 15, 83, 134, 135, 143
Switzerland, 15, 134, 135, 139, 140, 143
Syria, 162
SYSMIN scheme, 128–9

tariffs, 46, 48
taxation, 53–5, 75
technical barriers to trade, 51–4, 57
telecommunications industry, 52, 97–8
TEMPUS programme, 151
Thailand, 163
Thatcher, Margaret, 18, 19, 24, 46, 71
Thomson, Commissioner, 94
Three Wise Men, Report of, (1979), 49
Tindemans Report (1976), 49, 172, 186
Tito, Josip, 154
trade policy, 46, 48, 50–55, 56–8, 121
and Common Agricultural Policy, 64–5
and Lome Conventions, 124–5, 127, 129
and Yaounde Conventions, 122–3
see also individual countries and blocs
training programmes, 111, 112
Transatlantic Declaration (1990), 161
transport policy, 47, 51, 52, 140
tripartism, 109
Truman, Harry S., 8
Tunisia, 162
Turkey, 146–7, 148, 162

Ukraine, 155
unemployment, 99, 108, 111
United Arab Emirates, 163
United Europe Movement, 9
United Kingdom, 3, 6, 7, 152, 176
accession to EC of, 16–18, 80, 135
agriculture in, 63, 68
banking and finance sector in, 53

and EC budget, 49, 71, 76
and EC environmental policy, 117
and EC regional policy, 94, 95, 101, 104
and EC social policy, 53, 99, 110, 111, 112, 113
and Economic and Monetary Union, 86, 87, 89
and European Free Trade Area, 15–16, 134, 135
and exchange rate systems, 80, 81, 82, 84
and former colonies, 123
public procurement policies in, 52
and Single Internal Market programme, 50
taxation in, 54
and Union Treaty, 187, 189
United Nations, 6, 7, 114, 118, 123
United States of America, 3, 4, 6, 9, 12
and Cold War, 4, 7–8, 18–19, 175
EC relations with, 57, 64, 159–61, 175
and international exchange rate system, 79–80, 85, 159
Uruguay, 161

VALOREN programme, 97
value added tax (VAT), 54–5
levy for EC budget on, 70–71
Venezuela, 161
Venice Declaration (1980), 174
Versailles Treaty, 3
Vienna, Congress of, (1815), 2–3
Vienna Convention (1985), 116
Vietnam, 163
Voluntary Restraint Agreements, 165
voting procedure in Council, 39, 40, 50, 186

Walesa, Lech, 20
Warsaw Treaty Organization, 19, 20, 149
Washington Convention (1973), 117
waste management, 117
water pollution, 117
water supply industry, 52
Werner Report (1971), 79–81
Western European Union (WEU), 5, 13, 53, 170, 178, 180, 186
Westphalia, Peace of, (1648), 1, 2
White Paper on Single Internal Market (1985), 49, 50–58, 73–4, 109
Wilson, Woodrow, 3
women, equal pay for, 108, 111
World Bank, 128, 129

Yaounde Conventions (1963, 1969), 122–3
Yugoslavia, 20, 21, 154–5, 176